HELPING

COUPLES

HEAL

FROM INFIDELITY

AND FIND LOVE AGAIN

CAROL JUERGENSEN SHEETS

aka *Carol the Coach*

LCSW, CSAT-S, CCPS-S, CPC-S, PCC

Praise for *Helping Couples Heal*

"This is a must-read for couples recovering from betrayal, PSB, and infidelity! Carol Sheet's deep empathy and compassion shines through and her inclusive examples and language make it accessible to all. Her chapters gently but directly guide couples through deepening recovery work and strengthening their connection to themselves and others. She breaks the process down into easy-to-follow steps, simplifying the complex recovery journey and making it more possible for relationships to walk through the process. The depth of her model and the power of her tools are an incredibly valuable contribution to our field and to the individuals and relationships working to find healing."

— **Dr. Laney Knowlton**, CST, CSAT-S, CCPS, CPTT-S, CCBRT, CCRDS-S, RAE
President of *Society for the Advancement of Sexual Health* (SASH)

"Carol Juergensen-Sheets brings many years of experience, along with clarity and compassion to the complex process of couples healing from addiction and betrayal. Her book offers grounded, practical tools for couples navigating the painful aftermath of broken trust. With clinical insight and a steady therapeutic voice, along with creative exercises, she provides guidance that respects the challenges of relational trauma while encouraging hope and repair."

— **Mari A. Lee**, LMFT, CSAT-S, CPTT-S, MBATT-S
Author of *Facing Heartbreak, Healing from Betrayal,*
and *The Mindful Way to Wellness*

"Carol Juergensen Sheets has created a compassionate guide for couples experiencing infidelity and betrayal trauma. With *Helping Couples Heal From Infidelity to Find Love Again*, she has provided a resource for both the betrayed partner and the betrayer that emphasizes empathy, mindfulness, and constructive compassion. For those navigating recent betrayal, I cannot recommend this workbook enough. It is written in Carol's signature conversational style, containing clear step-by-step instructions on how to use mindfulness-based tools as well as case studies from Carol's diverse professional career. She also emphasizes The Early Recovery Couples Empathy Model which is woven skillfully throughout the workbook. Lastly, the workbook is written with gender neutrality, which allows readers from all backgrounds to be able to access this wonderful resource."

—**Darrin Ford**, LMFT, CSAT-S, MBATT-CS, CPTT-S
Author of *Awakening from the Sexually Addicted Mind*, and founder of *The Mindfulness Academy for Addiction & Trauma Training* (TMAATT) and *Mindful Centers for Addiction & Trauma Therapy* (MCATT)

SANO PRESS, LLC
CLAREMONT, CA

Designed by Chris Bordey.

1st Edition

DISCLAIMER

The information provided in this book is for educational purposes only and should NOT be considered a substitute for professional medical, health, or legal advice. It is not intended to replace professional diagnosis treatment or guidance. The content is based on general knowledge, the author's personal and professional experiences, and the author's research, but may not be applicable to individual circumstances. The author and publisher are not liable for any actions taken based on the information presented. Consult a qualified healthcare professional for personalized medical advice and treatment. Consult a qualified attorney for legal advice.

ISBN-13: 978-1-956620-08-5

TABLE *of* CONTENTS

CHAPTER 14: MOVING INTO CONFLICT—USING THE 7 PRINCIPLES OF CONFLICT TOGETHER TO DECREASE SHAME 286-295

CHAPTER 15: YOUR NEEDS INDIVIDUALLY AND AS A COUPLE...... 286-295

Author's Note

I have always had a heart for couples who have been through the heartbreak of infidelity and desperately want to put their world back together but don't know how. To the partner, it is inconceivable that the betrayer could have done this. You are devastated, and it feels like you have been run over by a Mack truck. For the betrayer, you are examining what came over you and how you could have hurt the person you loved the most. You knew that your behaviors were wrong but had rationalizations for everything you did. Now that the affair is over, you question everything that motivated you from the start.

My work in problematic sexual behavioral disorder was the primer for working with couples who had experienced betrayal.

Some couples choose to end the relationship once sexual or emotional betrayal occurs, but most couples have so much invested in their relationship that they entertain what it might take to process the affair(s)and move on.

This book takes you step by step through what you will likely need to do to work through it, learn from it, and grow stronger from it. Unfortunately, all my books until now have been written for heterosexual couples that I have primarily worked with and knew so well.

As I began to work with more male partners who had been betrayed by their partners, they would unequivocally share their frustration that there weren't more resources for them. As I write this book on infidelity, I have a colleague who is writing one exclusively for gay men and a colleague who is writing for male betrayed partners, so I am thankful that we are continuing to meet the needs of our community no matter who you are! It was my colleagues who thought I was doing a disservice by writing to one type of couple because it seemed so exclusive.

I did not want to marginalize anyone, so I committed to writing in inclusive, gender-neutral language. However, I must admit it feels like I have depersonalized the process by not talking directly to you because that is what I do best.

My experience is that ALL couples benefit from these exercises and this work! So, of course, I would want to help everyone, and although I have written it for all types of couples—heterosexual, gay, lesbian, and transgender—I realize there are special nuances to each community, just as there are for African American, interracial, Asian, and Hispanic couples. So, I will try to go into the nuances as I tell the stories of each couple.

Most importantly, I want to help you with the process of restoration, and together, we can work as a team to move toward post-traumatic growth.

In post-traumatic growth, you cultivate inner strength as a couple to help others heal. If you decide to stay together, this book will show you how to learn to love again. The key ingredient is *empathy*!

—*Carol, aka "Carol the Coach"*

Introduction
A Beacon of Hope

This is a guidebook to help you both navigate the ordeal of sexual infidelity. Other than a child's death, it is likely the worst thing you will ever have to go through as a couple. Despite this pain and trauma, there is very little offered to get you through this crisis. At the beginning of the book, I will designate the person who committed infidelity as the **Betrayer (BT)** and the partner who has been betrayed as the **Betrayed Partner (BP)**. I do not mean to be harsh to the BT because if you are both reading this book, you are working on restoring the relationship and building a whole new union. I admire the work the BT is willing to do to make a living amends and work hard to rebuild trust. The truth is that the BT is initially doing 80% of the work! So, as we progress through the Three Stages of Partner Betrayal, as we move into the anger, grief, mourning, and loss phase, I will soften my language because of all the great work you will have done as a couple. I will begin to reference you, the BT, as the "Betrayer in Recovery" and later as the "Spouse." As we move into Chapter 15, I believe it will be *time to recognize that the betraying occurred in the past.*

Chapter 15 is pivotal to post-traumatic growth because as you do these grief and anger exercises, you will release much of the pain that keeps you tethered to the past, which will allow you to stay in the present. These processes will be the catalyst for you to ceremoniously let go of the betrayal. You will always have your intuition to guide you, and grief and anger work will organically move you into an acceptance state that leaves space to create more of a new life together. These grief and anger exercises promote a surrendering to "what was" with resignation that you might be stronger because of the trauma, betrayal, and pain. And that is why I felt it was time to shift the "languaging" to promote the work that you are each doing.

If you are together but not married, "spouse" may not be the right fit, but I did not want to confuse you further by calling you both "partners." I want to acknowledge that you have created a new marriage and no longer need to be defined by the "Betrayer" or the "Betrayed Partner." I commend you both for working hard to stay the course and create a whole new relationship!

For the Betrayer (**BT**): Your infidelity has impacted your identity and robbed you of your values. As a result, you have lied, choosing to go outside your marriage or partnership and secretly have a dual life, which has compromised everything you wanted for yourself, your partner, and your family. You hurt the one whom you loved the most. Now since discovery, you are watching your partner get sucked into the darkest despair one can ever encounter! You are waking up from the world of entitlement and witnessing the consequences of your behaviors, and you are truly sickened by the devastation you have caused. You are trying to do damage control, knowing you are the perpetrator of the rubble, all while questioning every fiber of your soul, including your values and perhaps your existence.

For the Betrayed Partner (**BP**): As the partner, your whole life as you knew it has changed dramatically. Maybe you sensed something was off, but like most people in a marriage or partnership, you attributed it to the rigors of life, the stress a couple can endure, and the development of the life stage you were in. You could not have, nor would you ever have been able to, imagine something like this occurring without your knowledge. It has changed your entire sense of knowing, safety, and uncertainty about the future. It has made you doubt yourself! How could the person that you loved do this to you? Who is this person that you thought you knew so well? How could this have happened to you, and why would God have allowed this into your lives? Now, you question everything and wonder if you will ever recover from such a breach of trust.

CINDY & ROGER—BAD ADVICE FROM THE CHURCH?

During our first session together as a couple, Cindy said, "I question who I married. How did I not know he was so good at lying? What was wrong with me not to see the clues?" She sat in a pool of pain and shame and wondered what was wrong with her that this could have gone on so long. Roger sat beside her but said nothing. He, too, was in tremendous pain, but he couldn't speak because of all the self-hatred he was feeling. His emotions were reeling, and they immobilized him. If an observer had been in the room, they would have tapped me on the shoulder and said, "Carol, Roger has lost all of his feelings for his wife. He is speechless, and he has lost all hope!" But what I knew was that they were both in great pain. She could never have imagined that this God-fearing, kind father of three could ever have a three-year affair with someone in the church.

Cindy was shell-shocked and humiliated. She questioned what was wrong with her, what the signs were, and what was wrong with their relationship that would have caused him to stoop to this level. And then the shame kept coming, and she wondered who else in the congregation knew about the affair and what they must think about her. Her mind started to race, and she started questioning everything about her relationship with her community.

When Roger admitted that he had gone to a religious leader for advice, Cindy felt betrayed again because the deacon had told Roger that they would handle it and that he should "protect" her from the betrayal. This left her questioning the judgment of the deacons and the church in general. Again, her mind started ruminating, and this resulted in her questioning who in their church community might know about the affair. She was so depressed that she didn't want to go to church again.

Infidelity can cause total havoc in your life, and it can leave you feeling hopeless. Yet, you have purchased this book, and you are secretly hoping the relationship can be repaired. As the spouse, you are afraid to admit you are hoping for a reconciliation because what person in their right mind would want to seek, repair, and accept what happened to them? But you understand that you have put everything into this marriage. You believe in the sanctity of your vows, and a part of you does not want to give up.

I explain to partners that this is not a person who purposely wanted to betray you. This is a person who got involved in unhealthy, unexplainable behavior and appears to have "lost their mind" and "sense of conscience." Now that the discovery has occurred, the BT wonders if the damage can ever be repaired. The BT is out of the fog of lust and deception and is experiencing the pain and devastation that has been caused and questions if it is possible to live with the destruction that has occurred from having caused you so much pain.

As you read this book together, know that my style is to write as if you are in my office and I am talking to both of you. If I want to write directly to either of you, I will delineate this by stating "For the Betrayer or BT" or "For the Betrayed Partner or BP."

Also, please read this knowing I am going back and forth to help both of you through the next steps. I trust you will begin to understand my style and how I merge the work you are both doing to move you both through this trauma dance you have been doing.

It is imperative you read all the material so that you know what I have said to both of you. You have survived the discovery, and now I will be sharing with both of you what you need to do to stay safe and decide on your future as a couple. You are likely both questioning your judgment, and your greatest fear is that this relationship is unsalvageable and you are both wasting your time. But you have hung in there and searched for the right resources, programs, or professionals to help you both find the essential values of safety and trust to find happiness again.

Well, I want to be the **beacon of hope** for both of you individually and as a couple. It requires a lot of hard work on both of your parts, but if the **willingness** is there and the BT is in good recovery, you can restore the relationship. I hesitate to say that so early in this book, but you can recover together and deepen your relationship. This is because the BT will have learned very important relationship skills. The book is a guide to work you through the grief that has occurred because of the infidelity, and that grief, anger, and mourning will actually help you both rebuild trust. Couples who get to post-traumatic growth and restore their relationship can find ways to give back and enhance the lives of others once they have healed. There is hope for you as a couple, but it will take time and following the steps in this book for restoration. Most importantly, it will take the BT to do the majority of the work to break down your defenses and show you how sorry he or she is for desecrating the relationship.

Religious institutions do not necessarily have mandates or protocols when infidelity occurs in the church. Many organizations that work with adultery, pornography, and lust are setting up procedures that will make you both feel safe. Religious Leader Training can be made available if your church affiliation wants to know best practices. See the Resources in the back of the book for more information.

Chapter 1

Willingness Is the Key to Restoring Your Relationship

IS THE BETRAYER WILLING TO DO 80% OF THE WORK TO RESTORE THE RELATIONSHIP?

You understandably want to know what you can do to get through this ordeal. You both have many questions about whether that is possible and whether you can ever restore the relationship and live a loving, meaningful life. I have worked with many couples who have been able to get through this, but it requires you both to be willing to do the hard work to get through it together.

For the Betrayer (BT): This means stepping up and doing 80% of the work to help the BP heal. It requires that you learn how to contain the pain and help your partner get through it, and you must do this over and over again, even when it seems like it is not working and even when it is met with pushback—and it will be met with pushback (because the BP is unsure of every part of you). Your spouse is going to be testing you at every turn because your partner cannot believe that your efforts are genuine...After all, look at what you have done to the person that you were supposed to have loved.

When people make choices to cheat, whether it be emotionally or sexually, they go into a state of denial and justify their behavior. Secretly, you probably never even entertained that you might be caught, and even if there were a couple of "close calls," you quickly forgot them and continued on your quest for the dopamine hit. When one makes the choice to have an emotional or sexual affair, they go into a state of denial and lose all empathy for how it would feel if they were ever found out. Your needs became all-important, and your brain chemistry went into overdrive. This caused you to be self-absorbed and self-interested, so you pursued your affair full force, thinking it was all about how it made you feel.

Then, one day, you realized that this affair felt very different from the initial "hit" you got from the fantasy, and you began to wonder what you were doing to have been so delusional and self-absorbed. You may have told yourself a million times that you were going to get out of the relationship before anyone found out, but you then had to deal with the aftermath of breaking off the relationship and the collateral damages it would cause. It became a vicious circle of chasing something you wanted and not wanting it anymore. You asked yourself, *How did I ever get myself so entangled in an unhealthy relationship, and more importantly, how can I get out of it without getting caught?*

Life continued to get very complicated, and it was becoming more and more difficult to hide from your deception. Thirty years ago, it was easy to hide from your community and family and live a dual life, but now, there is really no way to hide from the collateral damage that your behavior and your affair or affairs have caused. The internet is the very thing that made meeting new people and acting out possible, and now it has also contributed to a much greater chance that someone will find out about it and report your activity.

To the Betrayer (BT): Now that you are reading or listening to the book, you are showing a true willingness to make it right with your partner. Your work is going to show your spouse that you are learning and practicing the skills it will take to understand how you could have made the choices you did and fooled yourself into believing that there were good reasons for your infidelity. There is no doubt that there were many contributors to your poor choices, including past trauma, entitlement, compulsivity, character deficiencies, and poor role modeling as you grew up.

Most of the betrayers I have worked with have not had the guidance, nurturance, or role modeling in their families to help them develop the relational skills needed to create a true and secure attachment. For many betrayers or chronic betrayers, there is a sense of entitlement from these woundings or stunted emotional development, which leads to overall characterological deficits that were hidden with a pseudo genuineness.

We will look at those issues further in the book, but it is important for you right now to commit to building your relationship. You will need to learn some basic principles that will allow you to live in integrity, and you will have to show your partner over and over that you are willing to do whatever it takes to live a life of authenticity, transparency, and honesty. You will need to put your partner's needs first, practice empathy, and begin to do the hard things to understand the trauma that your partner is experiencing.

At times, it will look as if your partner is pushing back on all your attempts to be genuine and forthcoming with your new life. You may even doubt whether your partner is capable of ever trusting you again. I know that can be very tough for you, especially since the discovery of the betrayal was such a shock to you, especially considering who your partner thought you were.

Now, you are out of the fog, want to do the right thing, have reorganized your life, and are in the process of developing a good support program for you and your partner. You wonder why your spouse can't feel more secure in all the work you're doing. But the truth is it takes a traumatized brain anywhere from one to three years to feel safe and stable. If you are in months three, nine, or perhaps even a year of good recovery, your partner will likely still seem activated and triggered, which is a signal that you need to be even stronger to contain the pain and do the right thing.

We will be talking about empathy in future chapters, but what I want you to realize and understand is that "brain trauma" is a trauma state caused by betrayal. It matters not how long it takes to help rebuild this relationship; it is something you should want to do regardless of the outcome or amount of time it takes. I know it can feel very discouraging when it seems like your partner is not getting better, but I want you to continue to work on the all-important skills necessary to help your partner heal.

Communication can be your greatest skill, so I will have you both work on this skill together. In the next few chapters, you will both learn about reflective listening. The BP will be given opportunities to vent about the emotional state this affair has created and your partner's concerns for the relationship.

To the Betrayed Partner (BP): You will be giving voice to how the betrayal has shattered the world as you knew it and how your entire world has been violated by the sexual transgression. Your entire reality is riddled with doubt, and you don't know what is real anymore and are questioning your sanity at every juncture.

Have you had any of these thoughts?

1. How could this have happened to me?

2. Did I miss the signs?

3. Is there something wrong with me that contributed to the infidelity?

4. Is there something wrong with me for staying and seeing if there is a healing process?

5. Can the BT really change?

6. Will the BT get bored with our *less-than-sexy* life and return to old behaviors?

7. Should I cut my losses?

Then, do you ask yourself:

1. Why am I staying?

2. What is wrong with me?

3. What will people think of me if they find out?

4. Who already knows about this?

5. Do they pity me or question my sanity?

(Then you spiral into the anger and sadness that you are even having to ask yourself these things. You are a nice person. You would never have done this to someone you loved!)

The self-doubt is overwhelming, and the rumination and racing thoughts have taken control. You fear that you are going crazy, and you are scared...You are really scared!

As a couple, you will need to decide if you want to invest in the time it will take to move through the recovery from sexual infidelity. It will be a long journey. Many couples do make the choice to work through it together.

This book is going to show you how to do it, and then you can decide if your relationship is worth the work it is going to take to heal. I always tell BPs that they are in the driver's seat now because they get to choose whether to try the recovery road. Many choose it because they do not want to break up their families, finances, and their life more than it is already broken. The heartbreak may be that you didn't even know there was deception, and you thought that life was less connected because of the rigors of your routine as a family. It can be difficult to manage an exhausting job or the responsibilities of a home or family life without both of you going your own separate ways to get things done for the sake of your household.

SANDY & TOM: *STRONG VALUES THAT CRUMBLED UNDER LIFE'S PRESSURES*

Sandy and Tom were both climbing the corporate ladder at their prospective jobs. They were college sweethearts, and when they first married, they talked about the things they would share once they got to a financial place of security. They always envisioned children but knew that raising them in a private Catholic school would require funding that equated to the equivalent of college tuition. They had their first son four years after they got married, giving themselves enough time to be together, take some trips, and create a vision for the future. It was tough to juggle their careers and their little one, but they tag-teamed well together. Two years later, they planned for their second child, which proved to be a much more difficult undertaking.

Then, an unplanned third pregnancy occurred, resulting in twin daughters. Sandy experienced some postpartum depression and took a year's leave of absence as the cost of a nanny was prohibitive. Sandy began to notice that Tom relied on her for the majority of the childcare. She was thankful to be feeling better but was gaining resentment because she didn't particularly sign up for the job of being a full-time mother of four, all within a five-year time frame.

Tom also felt the stress of being the sole breadwinner. His job required longer hours at work, and he began to steal time from the family to go to the neighborhood bar with coworkers. Within several months, he became friendly with a coworker and longed to spend time with her as a respite from the rigors of his family. As he and Sarah admitted a serious attraction to one another, they denied the emotional affair they were having and tricked themselves into believing they were keeping it in check because it had not become sexual. Although it was becoming more and more time-consuming and physical, it hadn't yet evolved into a sexual affair.

Sandy wasn't happy with the extra hours Tom was spending away and began to press for more details, which meant Tom had to become more elaborate with his lies. They started fighting more and felt the disconnection from each other. One night, after several drinks and connection, Sarah and Tom decided to go back to her home. They had sex, and Tom felt both exhilaration and guilt at the same time. The affair went on for another 14 months, but Sarah became more discontented with Tom's attempts to juggle two lives. Tom found himself in the middle of a triangle, and no one was happy. He eventually confessed his affair to Sandy, and Sandy suggested that they get couple's therapy.

They decided on ERCEM because they both liked the premise that *he* would need to do most of the work to begin to build trust. Once they addressed their intention for what they wanted to accomplish and Tom was able to share what he was willing to do, it shifted something inside of Sandy that gave her a small sense of hope for the relationship. This work did not happen overnight and actually took about three years of hard work. Tom had become so depressed about what he had done that we got him to a medication prescriber to help with the depression. Together, they established the safety and boundaries they needed to begin to work on their relational skills and create a whole new relationship with themselves and their family. Three years into the work, Tom reported there was something comforting to being the person who did most of the emotional repair. "I had caused it, and I needed to fix it. Plus, it was a way to prove to Sandy that I was willing to make a living amends."

If you are both reading this book, you are both motivated to see what is out there to help heal the relationship. It can be done, and—believe it or not—it can be strengthened to a whole new level. This story about Tom and Sandy highlights the radical change the betrayer needs to make, but Sandy and Tom did want to repair their relationship and rebuild a new one. Since Tom had not been an active part of raising their four kids, it was gratifying to help them grow up in a different way.

To the BP: I know you may not feel up to the challenge, so move slowly and take lots of breaks for self-care. The Betrayer is going to help you by getting better and proving to you that the betrayal was an impulsive, misdirected way of seeking something that was unrealistic. If the BT cannot reprioritize values and be the person you have always wanted in your life, you can decide how to proceed, but for now, keep reading together and look at the steps to heal. You may be ambivalent about how to proceed, and you are reading this book to see if you both possess the stamina it may take to help each other heal.

When I wrote a book on compulsive problematic sexual behavior (sexual addiction) called *Help.Her.Heal.*, I explained to addicts that if the sex addict could help the partner heal, it would expedite the partner's healing. The same is true with infidelity. I believe strongly that if the betrayer can help you heal, it will help the BT grow exponentially while helping the relationship repair the severe attachment rupture that has occurred. And when you, the BP, begin to see the intense work the BT is doing to be a person of integrity and the BT's dedication to the recovery process, you will be able to begin to build trust in your spouse.

This book is going to ask you to take risks, so there will be times when I recommend you try some exercises and activities you may not be ready to explore. Take your time and go slow, but know that therapeutically, it can be helpful to try each exercise to see if it fits both your desire and hope for the future. If you absolutely don't feel comfortable, skip the exercise and go on to the next exercise. However, when it seems impossible, I would ask you both to use the "Fake It Until You Make It" approach. Although it may sound like a disingenuous request, betrayers and the betrayed have found that if they can push themselves to do the hard work until they make it, they follow the principle of "Act as If."

"Act as If" suggests that you decide what you would like for your life and act as if you had the power to make it happen. You cannot control the behaviors of others, but you can, however, control how you let their behaviors affect you both now and in the future. You can't erase the pain of infidelity, but you can evaluate if the BT is doing the hard work to reassess how the betrayal could have happened. You can also make a choice to wait and see how sincere the BT is in their actions, which will slowly build up your faith in your spouse's convictions to do things that will help you heal and begin to trust the BT again.

When people want a particular relationship, specific job, or desired outcome, they should absolutely act as if they are experiencing the outcome of their desires. If you want this relationship to not only survive but thrive, you should look for ways to heal so you can create a connection that is honest, open, and filled with integrity. If you can clearly name and claim what you want, you can look for opportunities to respond accordingly. In Chapter 18, we will go into more detail about this very important concept, but right now, we want to focus on what can make you feel safe.

These next two exercises exemplify the concept of "Act as If." I would like for you both to practice some vulnerability as you start this book by agreeing to declare an intention for the relationship. If there were no obstacles and you could trust the BT to maintain a strong recovery program, what kind of relationship would you like to be in, and how could you contribute to it to make it loving and fulfilling?

To the BP: I would suspect you are too hurt to trust your partner to deliver the relationship you had mutually agreed upon and built your whole marriage or partnership from. That is totally understandable. The BT has destroyed your sense of reality, and you are questioning everything about your life right now. I actually want you both to create an intention for your relationship.

You may be asking me how I could expect you to make a declaration for the relationship when you are not even sure you can continue it. However, you are reading this book together and are wondering if you have a chance to rebuild your life together. So, for the possibility of the relationship, just put it out there and ask for what you would like. When you write it down, you are more likely to make it happen. Intention starts with hope. Let's start small and write out a statement that expresses what you would like to get out of reading or listening to this book. We will use this as a foundation for your intention statement.

WHAT I HOPE TO GAIN FROM THIS BOOK

Exercise: Both of you need to write out a statement (even though it may change) that "owns" why you want to get through this book and grow stronger—post-traumatic growth. Now, I realize you both may have doubts, but part of the intention of this book is to help you navigate through this betrayal and grow stronger so you can lead the life you deserve! This requires vulnerability for how you both like to see yourself heal.

> **To the BT:** Please answer the following statement: Our relationship has been through so much, but what I hope to accomplish as a couple as I finish this book is to:

To the BP: Our relationship has been through so much, but what I hope to accomplish as a couple as I finish this book is to:

Now that you have decided what you want to achieve by reading this book, it is time for you to become even more vulnerable and create an Intention Statement for your relationship. Even though there is much uncertainty, spend some quiet time and complete the following statement:

To the BP: As we work through recovery together, what I want most for my relationship is:

To the BT: As I work on gaining more and more sexual and emotional integrity and as I continue to improve my relational skills, what I want most for my relationship is:

I would like you both to find a space where you can move to chairs face-to-face and look at each other as you slowly read the Intention Statement to each other. I know it will be difficult to share this level of vulnerability with each other, but it is necessary because it simultaneously plants a seed of hope for the relational recovery that is possible.

This is the first time since the betrayal that either one of you had the courage to dare to hope for more. I applaud you for writing the intention statement down and sharing it with your partner. Hopefully, you both took it well and now feel more grounded to proceed both with caution and the expectation that if you do the work, it works. You will not only repair the relationship, but you will both get stronger!

Note: This small exercise will evoke lots of feelings, so make sure to find some time tonight to journal your thoughts and feelings about it. To help you journal the following questions:

- What feelings came up for you?

- What level of vulnerability occurred?

- Are you fearful that you will not be able to forgive your partner?

- Is there guilt that you may have contributed to the marital problems?

- Did you believe your partner can change and sustain the changes?

- What defense mechanisms showed up, and how did you handle them?

- Did you recognize a seed of hope as you shared your intention? (It is normal to feel sad when opening up to this type of vulnerability.)

It hurts to remind yourself of what you thought you had that was contaminated by the BT's poor choices, impulsivity, and deceit.

As a coach and therapist with over 40 years of experience, I know that setting an intention and making a declaration for what you want in a relationship is very important. If your discovery has occurred in the past 18 to 24 months, it can feel daunting for you, the betrayed, to "put it out there" and even admit that you might want to invest in the relationship. But, if you are reading this book, at least a small part of you is willing to consider the possibility. If you are the betrayer, you probably feel unsure whether you have the right to set an intention or make a declaration, but I promise it will help you stay strong.

Now that you have created an intention for what you hope to get out of this book and what you hope for your relationship as you do the hard work of rebuilding it, I would like for you to take a deep look into what you personally are both willing to do individually to work together on the restoration of your marriage or partnership. This assignment is a bit harder, so I am going to share some intentions and declarations from the couples I have worked with.

That way, you will have some idea of what they look like. Later in the book, as your relationship gets stronger, I will show you how to further use them to embed the changes you are seeing.

INTENTIONS FOR THE BP:

- I am willing to watch the BT work diligently on restoring our marital values and learn the skills to repair our relationship.

- I want us to build a strong, faith-filled, honest relationship, so I will be open to the changes the BT is making.

- I will watch my partner's progress and assess whether I can be safe in this relationship.

INTENTIONS FOR THE BT:

- I will do whatever it takes to help my partner heal and validate the anger as the BP works through this process.

- I will learn the skills to rebuild the relationship I destroyed and be patient when my partner pushes back and does not believe in my changes.

- I will develop my empathy skills so I can begin to be worthy of my partner's trust.

Now, it is your turn. I would like both of you to write out your own declaration of what you are willing to do based on the recovery work you have started since discovery day. This declaration will acknowledge the effort and intention you have for this relationship by acknowledging your own work that you may have done or will need to do.

<u>My Intention (BT Example)</u>

"Now that I have been in good affair recovery for 13 months, I am able to see that I can be the person my spouse wants me to be, and I will continue to work on developing authenticity and transparency in all we do."

<u>My Intention (BP Example)</u>

"Now that my spouse has maintained good affair recovery, I am ready to slowly work on trusting that we can work through this together, one day at a time."

INTENTION STATEMENT FOR OUR MARRIAGE/PARTNERSHIP

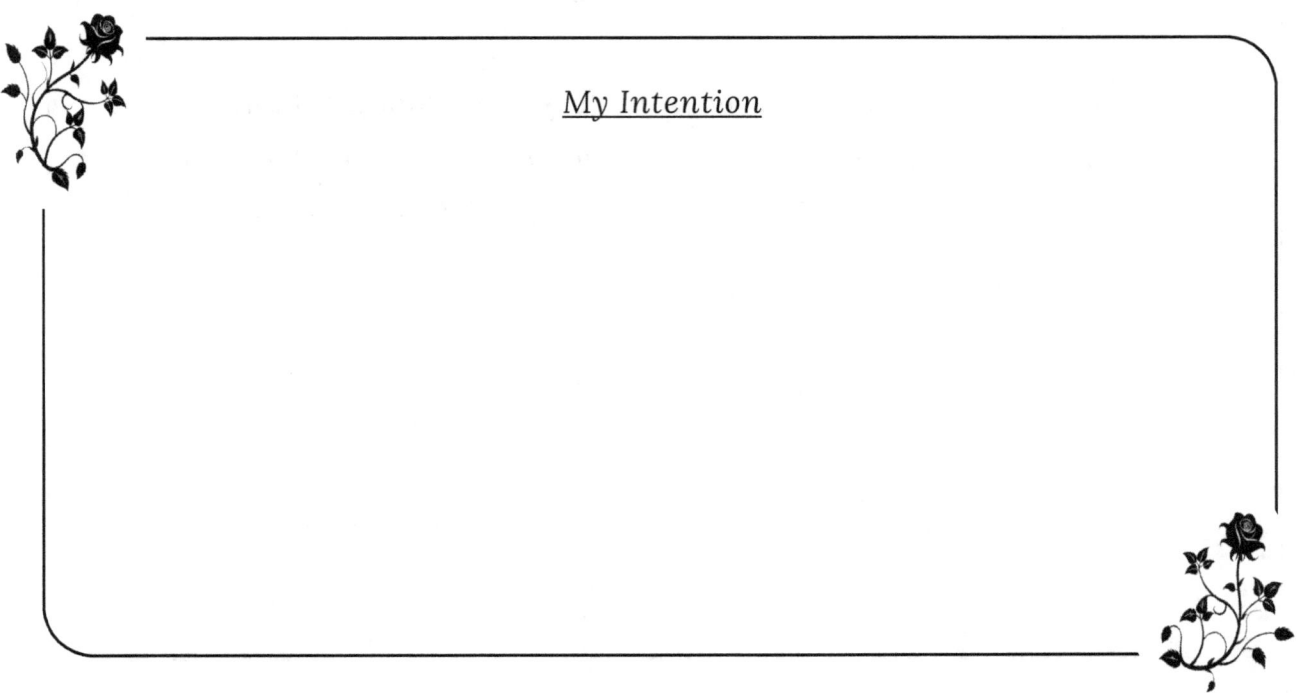

My Intention

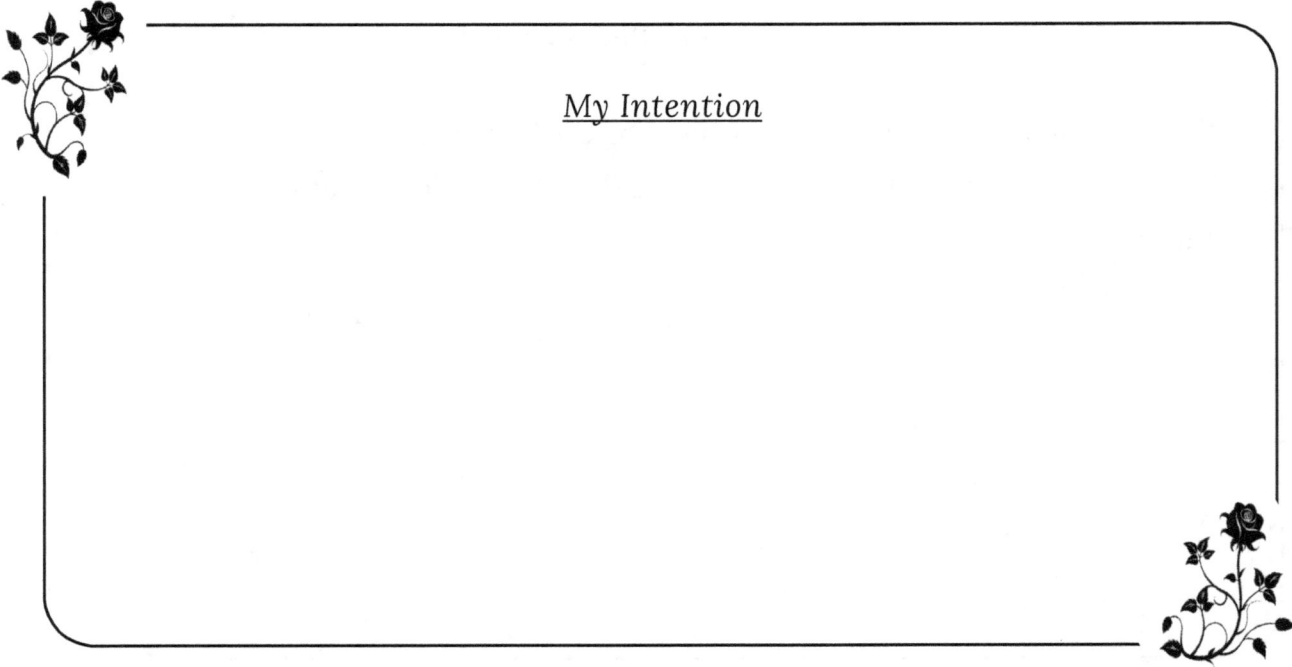

My Intention

I want to commend you both for your vulnerability and hope. In the book *Daring Greatly*, Brené Brown, who is the leading expert on vulnerability, says that the definition of vulnerability is uncertainty, risk, and emotional exposure. She describes it as "that unstable feeling we get when we step out of our comfort zone or do something that forces us to loosen control." Further, she says, "Vulnerability is not weakness; it's our most accurate measure of courage."

This journey to explore the creation of a new marriage or partnership is the epitome of acknowledging your own vulnerability. It is risky to take this book's steps for you both to heal. Just by your decision to read this book together, the BP has accepted the willingness to slowly move toward repairing this relationship.

> *The BP is going to wait and see if you do what it will take to work through sexual betrayal.*

And for you, the betrayer, you must acknowledge that you are willing to do everything possible to create safety for your partner! I know there is fear and trepidation that you will not always do everything perfectly; however, if you follow the steps in this book, you will have a guide to helping your partner heal from the devastation of emotional and sexual betrayal. You both can do this, but do it slowly and methodically—it is not an easy process.

> *"Just remember that vulnerability is uncertainty, risk, and emotional exposure." ~Brené Brown*

Chapter 2:

From the Beginning:

You Must Come into the First Session Together—

No More Secrets!

There are many reasons that people cheat, although if you are in a monogamous relationship where there is a contract to be faithful, there are no excuses. Yes, there are couples who subscribe to all types of relationships with other people, but that is not why you are reading this book today. You are here because there has been a serious violation of your covenants, and you both want to repair the relationship, grow stronger as a couple, and be examples of what a loving, honest, caring relationship can look like.

WHY WOULD YOUR PARTNER CHEAT?

It is hard to conceive why the person you love would ever want to betray you. It is not just the act of being with someone or something else, but it also is about the secrecy, lying, and deceit that prevents a true closeness or, as biblical scripture states: "Treasure marital fidelity and remain faithful to one another. So then, they are no longer two but one flesh. Therefore, what God has joined together, let no one separate."

And yet, research suggests that there are justifications and rationalizations for people to be unfaithful. "There's a multitude of reasons why people cheat," says Kenneth Paul Rosenburg, M.D., a psychiatrist and author of *Why Men and Women Cheat*. According to a 2017 article published based on research in the *Journal of Sex Research*, explanations for infidelity often fall under three main categories:

1. Personal problems, beliefs, or characteristics

2. Issues with your relationship in general

3. Situational factors like accessibility via the internet, long business trips, or substance abuse

Dr. Rosenberg says it is important not to underrate emotional affairs, which can be just as devastating. Emotional affairs are the precursor to most physical intimacy. It starts out innocent enough with communication and close environmental proximity and morphs into taking the next step.

Other reasons include:

1. Lack of stimulation in the relationship. Your relationship has moved into a transactional state, and it lacks the endorphins to provide satisfaction.

2. Low self-esteem of the BT. Suddenly, the BT is in a situation where someone makes them feel good, and it becomes an insatiable need to feel worthy or special about themselves. The dopamine becomes so strong that it interferes with the brain's executive functioning, and the attraction becomes a temporary drug. Once the drug wears off and reality sets in, the BT begins to regret their involvement, and now the BT is trying to juggle two relationships at once.

3. This can also happen when people cheat for the "high." Although a mid-life crisis or a dopamine deficiency can play into a gnawing desire for a hit to interrupt the rigors of life, it is never a reason to cheat. When a person shows good emotional maturity, the partner will look for ways to spice up the relationship and create new excitement. However, some BTs choose the easy route, and I call it easy because there will always be people out there who want a relationship bad enough that they will settle for being second in hopes of becoming first.

4. The compulsive use of the internet makes cheating available, accessible, and anonymous initially until it isn't. If the infidel has an addictive tendency to abuse money, drugs, alcohol, or work, the propensity for infidelity becomes greater because once the spouse becomes sexually or emotionally aroused, they are likely to go after that feeling again. If infidelity becomes compulsive, it can be characterized as problematic sexual behavior. Unfortunately, in today's society, with the internet making cheating more accessible, men and women alike are searching

out a quick transaction, which eventually turns into something more. When sexual acting-out behaviors occur more frequently, there are many more opportunities for the acting-out relationship to go wrong. Many BTs have been extorted for money when a simple affair turns into full-blown extortion.

5. Our society has become so transactional that there are websites dedicated to men and women who are looking for someone who is married to allegedly avoid the complications that can occur in having an extramarital affair.

To the BP: I know you have spent a lot of time researching who can help you both work through this process, and more than likely, your focus has been finding someone who has the specialty of working with couples within the context of infidelity. It is most frequently the BP that does the work, although this is gradually changing because the Betrayer wants to show up and do the hard work of restoration.

To the BT: Your partner is in a state of shock and goes into automatic, figuring out the best option for the two of you. The BP has done the research and has looked for a specialist who has training in repairing the relationship The partner wants to believe that this deception is out of character for you and needs to find someone who can help you be the person you were meant to be. The BP is in survival mode for the relationship!

THE ERCEM APPROACH IS DIFFERENT

I want to see you both because I want to explain how the model works and explain the impact of the trauma on your relationship. This is a couple's issue that has impacted both of you, and I believe that each of you needs to understand how the BT could have lost control of the marital values and commitment to the relationship. How did the BT lead this double life and lie to you and do this to you and the family? This has left you shell-shocked and wondering if there was anything about your life that was real. Worse than that, it has left you wondering if you will ever be able to trust again and if you will ever be able to trust yourself!

All relationships have problems, conflict, and dissatisfaction among the meaningful moments and the life you created as a couple. When infidelity occurs, you both need to know what prompted the infidelity, and if there was dissatisfaction, why didn't the BT share what was missing in your relationship? That is what is necessary for any relationship. It is never okay to make solo decisions that originate in deceit and secrecy.

Now that discovery has occurred, it is important for you both to understand how the BP is in a traumatized state, which leaves the brain in a compromised position, and the BP's brain is probably in survival mode and is acting from a flight, fight, or freeze mode. The BP's brain has been greatly impacted, and the executive functioning has been compromised. The BP is not able to think or make decisions as well, and they are very emotional.

To watch a short video on partner betrayal, go to:

- www.sexhelpwithcarolthecoach.com/about

  o Scroll down to the first video:
    The Brain Science of Partner Betrayal.

This video depicts a woman who discovered that her husband was involved in all sorts of acting out. The infidelity caused some brain dysfunction that naturally occurs when traumatized. But more importantly, it causes the partner to doubt him or herself. Is there anything that resonates with you about this video?

The BP will need a specialist who works with the couple and understands this traumatized state as well as the need for extreme partner sensitivity. An ERCEM specialist will have the tools and resources available to help you both.

I originally developed the Early Recovery Couples Empathy Model (ERCEM), which helps couples simultaneously heal from compulsive sexual acting out and sex addiction. Hopefully, you do not need ERCEM for chronic acting out that has morphed into compulsive, problematic sexual acting out. But infidelity can escalate into other types of behaviors, so it may be important for you to seek a specialist who knows how couples can get the facts in a safe way that allows them to start over. This will be discussed further in Chapter 3.

What I discovered was that with some modification, ERCEM had the tools and resources to help create a new marriage or partnership that is built on the foundation of honesty and truth. When you combine these two very important values with transparency and integrity, you have the building blocks to create a whole new relationship that is better than the first and can support the relationship you deserve.

ERCEM is extremely partner-sensitive, and that is why it is imperative that the BP agrees to work together to find healing. If the betrayed partner is not interested, the decision has been made, and ERCEM is not the appropriate intervention for you as a couple. However, if the BP is willing, I would like you to come in as a couple. That way, I can share with both of you the protocol that will help you work through this crisis.

To the BP: If you are willing, I see you both for the intake. Remember, it is your decision when and how you decide to work on this relationship, so I always leave the option open. If you choose not to come to that first session, an ERCEM specialist will be happy to work with the betrayer because they know how this ordeal has impacted everyone involved. I know that you did not ask for this, nor did you sign up for it, and therefore, you get to decide when and how you will participate in ERCEM.

Most couples follow the ERCEM protocol and come in together for the first time. It is important for BP's own sense of security that BP gets to meet me and hear what we are going to recommend from the very start. That is how ERCEM specialists work. They are partner-sensitive and want to help the couple work through the crisis of betrayal. Their desire is to disseminate information as quickly as possible to create a treatment plan that promotes safety and recovery from the time of intake.

To the BT: You are both in shock! The discovery of your infidelity has put you in a traumatized state. You never thought you would get caught, and now you are in an extreme state of distress. You have watched your spouse experience a deep sense of trauma, and you cannot believe that you did that to the person you loved! Your partner is so traumatized by the discovery that it is quite possible they haven't eaten or slept for days.

It is crucial to have both of you in the office at the first session to get valuable information from each of you and share resources so you both get some direction from the start. Historically, you as a couple were seen together and infidelity was discussed, but there was no emphasis on partner sensitivity or trauma. This resulted in the couple being thrown into a situation they were not ready for, which kept them in a state of confusion, chaos, and uncertainty.

Counselors started to delve into the problem without seeing it from a partner-sensitive trauma approach. Hence, the partner could not find the needed safety. You were both thrown into couples therapy without knowing the important steps to help couples heal. You were supposed to share your feelings and thoughts without learning how to use reflective listening and other relational skills that promoted safety and stabilization. The couple was guided into talking about the reasons for the infidelity before they had the skills, and it became a free-for-all in the session.

ERCEM believes you must learn specialized communication skills and exercises to build in safety, which may take one or two years to see real relationship repair. There has never been a model like ERCEM until now, and ERCEM will help you navigate this crisis together.

This is a relational trauma, and you both need assistance immediately. ERCEM is going to keep you safe in the process!

This book is going to customize a treatment plan for you both that will undoubtedly increase the success of your individual treatments and the relationship simultaneously.

For the BT: I recommend ten recovery tools to help you get the needed support so you can build a strong support plan to decrease urges and cravings for the affair partner or the potential for future affair partners. I know that today you stand strong and that you would never do this again, nor would you want to hurt BP, but the cravings can come back when you are angry, bored, or have had your self-esteem shaken. While you are following these tools, I suggest that you become educated on what supports you can access day or night to ensure your behaviors are safe for your partner.

For BP: You also need to create a support plan that will help you when you feel triggered or when insecurity or jealousy sets in. Pay attention to what is happening to your body as a result of the trauma and stress you are feeling due to the sexual acting out. Notice how infidelity impacts your mind, body, and spirit. Not every betrayed partner feels trauma, but research shows that the discovery of partners acting out generally produces a trauma response. This can leave you feeling dazed and confused about what is happening to you. You will have a better outcome if you seek immediate counsel with a partner-sensitive treatment specialist who understands the brain science of trauma. This is because you have someone normalizing all the reactions you are having. It keeps you from being with a professional who implies that you need to get over it and move on. Although marital problems are NEVER just one person's issue, "the person who acted out outside of the marriage" should do the initial restoration work. Once safety and stabilization have been restored, then both parties are invited to look at how they contributed to the marital issues and work from that place.

Your marriage can be restored, and you can have a better marriage than you could ever imagine. It may even assist you both in rejuvenating your sex life and the physical closeness that looks today like it is lost forever.

This model requires that you both understand the brain science of trauma so you can begin to set yourselves up for healthy expectations. It teaches you a typical timeline as a general guideline for brain science recovery. It takes the brain a certain amount of time to recover from trauma, and research suggests that if you have had other betrayals in your life or your partner is not willing to show you empathy and compassion, you will heal slower as a result.

When you both come in together for the first session, you are both learning about the brain science of partner betrayal, and the BT is beginning to get the education needed to help you heal. BPs will need safety, which means you will need the immediate tools to get yourself healthy while simultaneously supporting your partner through this pain.

You both may be asking, what are the tools and treatments that promote good recovery? We will go into greater explanation in Chapters 3 and 4. Typically, the formula is that after discovery of the affair, you discuss with a specialist what you both will need for safety. Sometimes, the partner needs the BT to find other employment. At other times, the couple needed to block all numbers that pertained to the affair partner. Many couples decide who the pivotal people are whom they can share the information with to solidify what the couple needs from the outside world.

> *Sometimes, doing ERCEM does not result in reconciliation,*
> *but it does result in clarity.*

PATRICK & EMMY: FINDING SAFETY MEANT SEEKING SUPPORT AND CLARITY FROM THE TEAM

Patrick and Emmy looked like they had it all. Patrick taught at a major university, and Emmy had her own marketing firm for the largest hospital corporation in the state. They had done a fantastic job of raising four children and taught their children values following the doctrine of the Catholic church. From the outside looking in, they seemed to be living the life that everyone would envy. They were incredibly social and were invited to all the Gala Events in the city. They both volunteered their time extensively raising money for the American Cancer Society. But even with that kind of status and community reputation, the couple sat on the couch looking totally defeated.

Emmy shared with me that although she would never be opposed to therapy, she remained shell-shocked that she and Patrick were in my office, revealing her greatest nightmare. Patrick had been having a 14-year affair with a research scientist at work. The affair partner (AP), Betsy, had called Emmy and spent two gory hours telling Emmy about how happy she had made Patrick. During their two-hour conversation, Betsy would go back and forth between glamorizing the relationship (while you went on your two-week cruise with your dying mother, Patrick and I did a ten-day vacation in Bermuda) and sharing a more realistic perspective on how she had settled for this duality because Patrick had said that he could not under any circumstances divorce Emmy because of his standing in the Catholic Church. So, the AP put up with being the other woman to appease Patrick. She admitted to Emmy that although she often felt like she was playing second fiddle to Emmy, she appreciated the fact that Patrick supported her financially, bought her cars, and funded her vacations, reinforcing how special their relationship was and would continue to be. Then, the bubble burst as Betsy was contacted by another one of Patrick's affair partners who reported that she, too, was having an affair with Patrick, and she was tired of Patrick's "s**t" and ready to expose him. Together, both affair partners contacted Emmy to share the extent of their relationships with Emmy. Emmy was overwhelmed by the information, so they both sent her pictures of times they had been together with him. They were time-stamped, going back over 15 years.

Emmy questioned if there was anything in her life with Patrick that had ever been real. She doubted herself, her sanity, and her ability to know what would be in her family's best interest. Every time she felt like kicking him out, she wondered if there was a reason to stay and fight for the family she thought she had! Why would she even consider sharing space with a man she didn't know? A man who had kept such secrets from her, resulting in a lifetime of deception.

She wondered if she was just acquiescing to counseling so she could say they had done everything to repair the marriage they never had. Was she going through the motions so she could end their lives together once she got strong enough emotionally to leave? She told me, "I am not sure why I haven't left yet. It is like my brain has left my body, and I am unable to make decisions that would be, under normal circumstances, a *no-brainer*." But there was nothing normal about why they were in my office, and even I questioned what I was supposed to be assessing since Patrick's life was filled with such duplexity. It was difficult to discern whether I was dealing with a sociopathic personality or someone who had such a catastrophic need for emotional diversity that he was not capable of living an authentic life.

As I met with the couple, I explained that I could not possibly know what the reason was for the deep duality behind Patrick's motives, but I could ensure a safety protocol that would allow them both to decide what they were willing or capable of executing while we gained diagnostic information and helped both of them to decide what their next steps would be.

After I explained the concepts of ERCEM, I shared the three stages of partner betrayal with both. Since it was evident that Emmy was in great trauma, I helped them understand that the shock of the infidelity had compromised her executive functioning, and I suggested several scenarios that would allow her brain to rest and begin the healing process.

1. Patrick needed some significant testing to determine the potentiality of psychopathology. Was he a sociopath or a narcissist? Did he have a conscience, and if he did, where did it go as he continued his life of indulgence? Testing also helped to identify what kinds of relational skills he would be capable of delivering while they decided how to proceed.

2. After the testing, we would need to go over a plan that assured that Patrick would have no further contact with his affair partners and an accountability system to assist him in his due diligence and help Emmy feel more confident that he was a man who was begging to start a reparative process.

3. Patrick needed extensive healing and would benefit from an extended 6-, 9-, or 12-week program to begin to assist him in understanding why his deception was so entrenched in what appeared to be an insatiable need for "something else out there to meet his needs."

4. His residential stay would allow Emmy some time to let her brain reset, and she could determine if she wanted a formal therapeutic disclosure to find out the depths of his other lives. She could not move forward without the truth and all the truth to determine what kind of person she was dealing with, and we could begin to address what her options were in her next steps for her safety.

Of course, she was dazed and confused by what she had learned, and she was in no shape to begin relational repair. She needed a professional to help her navigate the beginnings of what were the next steps to increase safety. Later, she told me it was important to find someone who would not rule out the possibility of reconciliation, so, for the sake of her children and her family, she needed the professional to remain neutral in the situation.

Unfortunately, Patrick's testing did not come back with much hope for a healthy prognosis. The testing indicated that although he did not have a true antisocial personality disorder, he did have the features that included narcissism, entitlement, manipulation, impulsivity, disregard for others, and deception. This further complicated things because she questioned how he could have appeared to be a God-fearing man who did so much for her, their family, and the community. She felt so sickened by the extent he had gone to have full-fledged relationships that she did not feel that she could feel safe with him in the house. She felt that residential treatment was necessary to see what other professionals would find when they did the deep dive into his life. Patrick agreed to this recommendation only if she would not expose his affairs to their community.

I could see that he was not willing to do anything to help increase safety. Unfortunately, it was all about him. I told her that I could not do ERCEM with them because he showed no willingness to help her heal in the way that would support her. I did agree to do one or two sessions to help her discuss what she would need going forward. I wanted him to hear that Emmy's needs trumped his, and I felt it was in his best interest to allow Emmy to share what she needed and see why I validated her needs. Emmy decided that she could not abide by his stipulations as she would need support from her family, church, and circle of friends. Patrick was not willing to do anything to build in safety. Instead, it had to be his way. That showed both of us that he was incapable of empathy and putting Emmy's needs before his own for restoration purposes! Willingness is a foundational principle for ERCEM, and he just didn't have it to give to her. Some would argue that his antisocial features made it impossible for him to really have empathy for her pain.

She told me that she was so thankful that they had sought out ERCEM because it "cut to the chase" and showed her that if Patrick wasn't willing to do the hard work for her safety, it helped her reposition herself to keep her own self safe. Emmy needed to begin to develop lifelines as she went through the reparation process. Patrick wanted to prevent this for her because of his fear of exposure. We could not get him to see that ERCEM has a safety protocol in place to make relational repair possible.

The good news is that this is not a typical ERCEM case. More often than not, the couple reaps great benefits from learning relationship skills after infidelity recovery and the establishment of truth.

As a couple, you will need to find ways of creating support to help you refocus on your relationship. It is crucial to relational repair. We will talk later about how important it is to find the "right" people whom you can trust to build in the support infrastructure as you follow the recommendations for success. Safety can't occur until a minimum of 90 days of abstinence from all acting out behaviors occurs. That means you both put in safeguards so that the affair partner can't contact you, and if they do show up at work or other places, there is a contract that you will tell the BP of the encounter within a certain time frame that the partner feels is necessary for safety. Together, you have to think about likely scenarios that could occur so you have a preparedness for the inevitable. It emphasizes that you are working on this together!

You both begin the therapeutic process of assessing needs. It is not unusual for betrayed partners to need a therapeutic formal disclosure so they will have access to the truth. I always tell partners that you will likely need more information to make a good, informed decision about how you are feeling and what you are going to need moving forward. A formal therapeutic disclosure entails going through the process of hearing all the information about your acting out. This should be done with a specialist who can navigate this process and keep you both safe. This also reduces the multiple questions that the spouse may ask until safety has been established. I mandate that the BT take a polygraph afterward (unless the partner does not want a polygraph) to make sure that truth was established and to encourage a second reassessment of the facts. More about formal therapeutic disclosure and its counterparts will be discussed in Chapter 6. Regardless of the choices, I encourage my couples to consider this process for relational repair.

FORMULA FOR INCREASED SUCCESS OF RECOVERY:
THINGS TO ASSIST IN RECOVERY REPAIR

1. Come in together so that your ERCEM therapist can inform you about these 10 requirements for a successful first phase of recovery. (Your ERCEM therapist will help you both decide when it would be helpful to meet individually with an additional professional during your early recovery couples work.)

2. Oftentimes, the ERCEM specialist works with your individual therapists and coaches to maximize the benefits.

3. Discuss the psychodynamics of infidelity to ensure that you both understand, if possible, the cause of acting out.

4. Create a strong recovery program that supports the start of the betrayer's recovery for a minimum of 90 days, as I believe it takes 90 days to establish healthy habits as the foundation for a life of integrity, honesty, and truth.

5. The BT has to agree to do 80% of the work to restore safety and healing.

6. Practice the 10 recovery tools for recovery from infidelity.

7. Advocate for a full therapeutic disclosure (if desired by the partner) followed by a polygraph examination. Reminder: This is not necessary for all couples, and the decision should be made by the betrayed. If it is requested by the betrayed, it needs to be done by a *therapeutic disclosure specialist.* That information is discussed in Chapter 6, and a link to trained specialists is provided.

8. The partner participates in an emotional impact letter to release feelings while simultaneously helping the process of empathy development for the betrayer. This gives voice to the pain experienced and sets up a safe structure to begin the empathy process.

9. The betrayer will write a restitution letter acknowledging the damage that has been caused.

10. The couple will start early recovery couples work if the partner decides to continue with the marriage and the BT maintains good recovery.

11. If either party chooses not to commit to the principles cited above, they may decide to separate in integrity.

It is imperative that the couple understands the limitations that can occur in a coupleship if either person is not invested in working together to heal. When trauma or infidelity goes untreated, it will impede the couple's ability to heal and keep the couple vacillating in Stages 1 or 2 of partner betrayal. Please re-read the principles above and then answer the questions to the best of your ability.

- Can each one of you agree as a couple to commit to supporting each other with the ten principles above? *Circle one:* Yes / No

- Do you have reservations about any of them? *Circle one:* Yes / No

- If yes, please answer the following: The principle I worry about the most is: _____

    _____

    because _____

    _____

Each of you needs to be honest so you can work together or leave in integrity. Share with your partner what your fears are in proceeding further.

- My greatest fear is that: _____

    _____

    _____

Share your fears and trepidation with your ERCEM therapist so that the specialist can work with you to make them less frightening and more realistic.

Chapter 3

Safety and Stabilization Requires "Extreme Partner Sensitivity"

WORKING THROUGH INFIDELITY REQUIRES CO-CREATION AS A COUPLE

Couples have many questions about how to navigate the treatment they both may require to get through partner betrayal and infidelity. Many professionals assumed that the partner needed to assess what was wrong between them, and they needed to decide what the betrayer was not getting or what was missing in the relational bond so that the therapist could assist the couple in implementing that into the relationship to begin the process of restoration. Although problems in the coupleship are never one person's issue or fault, it is important to understand that although both parties may have had unmet needs, it was never permissible to go outside of the relationship to meet those needs.

Infidelity is a relational problem and needs to be addressed as such. However, safety for the BP is of the utmost importance, and it will be important for the BT to take on 80% of the work for the first year to increase safety and to reassure the partner that restoration and reconciliation will be possible due to the good works of the BT. The infidelity has shifted the autonomy of the BT, and the betrayer will need to operate from a very transparent position. This will automatically show the BP that there is real effort. The partner will see the BT's effort, which will provide great reassurance to the partner. This kind of effort provides safety and stabilization, which promotes the couple's recovery. ERCEM acknowledges the need for crisis management and builds in that safety.

As we learn more about the trauma that occurs with infidelity, we realize that a partner may not be able to navigate the consequences of unfaithfulness. It is key for both of you to understand what happens to a partner once discovery of partner betrayal occurs. When you both understand how trauma is affecting the brain, it will be easier for the BT to speak softly, be less defensive, and validate the BP's feelings and thoughts.

It is so important that we use a model that ensures safety for the partner and a way to work together to heal the damage of infidelity. Many betrayed partners have said to me, "Carol, I so appreciate this ERCEM model because I can tell my spouse is working hard to help me heal. I just wish you could hypnotize me to 'not remember' because I cannot get the thoughts, feelings, or images out of my head, and it is working against my desire to give one-hundred percent to our relationship again. It is working against trust building."

I, of course, understand the frustration, and, having been trained in hypnosis, I know that it would be contraindicated to hypnotize someone to forget. The memories are there to keep you safe and remain alert to the signs of both recovery and relapse. This video shows you both how the brain goes into survival mode, and it will take great time and effort to work through the pain. ERCEM will help you go through the three very important stages of affair recovery, and hopefully, with BT working equally hard, the two of you can get to the other side and grow from the tragedy. But what are some reasons that people cheat? There are some very specific nuances to types of infidelity.

10 THINGS THAT I COULD DO TO INCREASE/STRENGTHEN/FORTIFY PARTNER SAFETY

1. I could increase _____

2. I could add _____

3. I could learn _____

4. I could participate in _____

5. I could start/could stop _____

6. _____

7. _____

8. _____

9. _____

10. _____

To the BP: When you think about the BT's recovery, what could be added, altered, or changed to make you feel more safe, secure, and confident that your partner is taking their recovery seriously? What do you wish your partner would do to upgrade their program? Although we know that the work is theirs to do, we also know that you can be incredibly helpful in helping the BT determine what you need to heal. Part of your healing is dependent on the energy the BT puts into affair recovery management, but the other part comes from your willingness to see the progress and acknowledge the work that is being done. Let's look at what you need to feel more secure as you watch the BT work the program and witness the progress being made.

It is not uncommon for you to want to remain silent about the BT's progress, but please know that the relationship requires that you notice the effort and respond accordingly. And you will be surprised at how much more healing occurs when you work together. To get to the point where you can acknowledge the changes, you must assess what the BT can do to provide more safety. Ask yourself, what might you need to feel better about the BT's individual recovery?

I WOULD FEEL MORE CONFIDENT ABOUT THE BETRAYER'S RECOVERY IF:

1. _____

2. _____

3. _____

4. _____

5. _____

6. _____

7. _____

8. _____

9. _____

10. _____

These fears or issues are great check-in material that helps the betrayer identify what you need to feel safe. In Chapter 10, you will find out more about check-ins and how they improve both your communication and awareness of how recovery is going for both of you. It also provides an opportunity to assess what would help you move forward in your healing. With ERCEM, the Connection-Shares focus on struggles and the appreciations that each of you is doing together.

As the BT, *what do you believe your partner needs for increased safety?* This is your top priority. To develop your empathy muscle, I would like for you to list ten additional things you could do for your recovery that would help fortify your partner's belief in your recovery that was not identified.

LIST 10 ADDITIONAL THINGS YOU COULD DO TO STRENGTHEN YOUR AFFAIR RECOVERY.

1. _____

2. _____

3. _____

4. _____

5. _____

6. _____

7. _____

8. _____

9. _____

10. _____

AS THE BETRAYER CONTINUES TO STRENGTHEN RECOVERY

To the Betrayer: You may have experienced your partner doing some ferocious reading, listening to podcasts, and searching online for the best treatment therapists and coaches in the country. It is not uncommon for BT to allow the partner to take on that role as the BT continues to do the needed work to get healthy. After 9 months, 12 months, or even a year and a half of good recovery, it can feel laborious for the betrayer to have to follow the requests of their partner. This experience may have occurred in therapy when you told your counselor, "I'm working a good recovery program and making lots of headway into making my partner feel loved again, and yet it doesn't seem enough. Why is my partner expecting me to continue to work so hard when my recovery is solid?"

A partner-sensitive therapist will help you as a couple decide what is realistic in terms of treatment. Because the partner has so much at stake in the relationship and wants you to participate with 150% of your energy, the BP may be afraid to let go of the reigns and trust that the process has worked. If all this investment worked to "put you back together again," it may feel very scary to trust that the relationship is going to sustain the love and trust that you have rebuilt. This fear can leave the BP thinking the worst: that your affair recovery will not be enough to keep the relationship together forever! For the betrayer who is working good recovery, it is common and normal for you to feel like you are getting messages from your partner that you are just not working hard enough or doing it well enough. These concerns come from the amygdala—the part of the brain searching for safety. If your intentions are pure and you are 100% stable in your own recovery, you will need to figure out a way to pay attention to your betrayed partner's need for ongoing security.

For the first 12 to 18 months, your focal point will solely be on your partner. You will be learning relational skills that include focused listening, direct communication, reflective listening, and empathy strategies to make the BP feel heard and understood. This must be your primary focus so you can build the safety and security needed for the betrayed partner to trust you again. Initially, it can feel overwhelming and one-sided to put your partner's needs first and keep your partner at the center of your attention, but it is a necessary step to rebuilding the trust that your infidelity has destroyed. Practicing the all-important empathy skills immediately will demonstrate that you recognize the damage your infidelity has caused and that you are willing to do anything to earn back your partner's confidence.

It will take many months before the BP can let their guard down and join you in a more mutual relationship because your partner is reeling from what has happened. As they begin to trust you and let their guard be taken down, you will have opportunities to share more of your needs and wants. However, for the first year, it will be your responsibility to put your partner first. Your choices have resulted in harmful behaviors and have impacted your partner's emotional, physical, and spiritual sense of self. The work that you do will work toward a living amends to increase trust. When you have two individuals who want to work toward reconciliation and restoration, there are many things you both can do to get through partner betrayal.

The partner-sensitive approach to couple's work is that BP should also have a say in what would provide safety within the coupleship and as the BT finds the support to work through the disloyalty to the marriage. There may be times the BP can make suggestions that might benefit the relationship, ensuring that the BT's main focus is to increase the BP's sense of safety. There is no doubt that betrayers want very much to help their partners heal, yet from time to time, it can be frustrating when their partners are much more ambitious in their readiness to heal the relationship. They may make suggestions that include programs that require two to three hours of work per week with accountability partners for the BT and meetings or groups that provide a sacred space for the BT to heal. Other times, couples will go to intensives that require that they both spend three, five, or seven days working with a team of professionals who have made it their mission to help couples work through the betrayal. Working together keeps the betrayer forward thinking to keep the brain recalibrated, and it allows the partner to heal from the betrayal at a more consistent rate.

Chapter 4

Is Female Betrayal Different?

I want to speak briefly about the dynamics behind female betrayers and betrayed male partners. If this does not apply to your situation, you may still be interested in the differences, or you can skip the information altogether and resume reading Chapter 5.

FEMALE BETRAYERS

Interestingly, female betrayers usually betray for different reasons than their male counterparts. According to Robert Weiss, research shows that nearly as many women cheat as men, which makes sense because it takes two to tango, so to speak. That said, men and women often cheat for different reasons, with the motivations typically (though not always) falling in line with our general understanding of male versus female sexuality. Basically, men tend to be comfortable with a purely sexual experience devoid of emotional connection, while women tend to be more interested in sexuality that includes (or at least promises) a degree of emotional intimacy. So, both men and women engage in infidelity, but they often do so for different reasons.

Generally, a woman's decision to cheat is driven by one or more of the following factors:

- A woman may have an issue with sex, porn, or love addiction. In such cases, a woman with unresolved childhood trauma, especially sexual trauma, will attempt to self-soothe her emotional pain, anxiety, and depression with romantic and sexual fantasies and activity. For this woman, sexual behavior is not about having fun; it's about numbing out.

- A woman may feel unappreciated, ignored, and neglected in her primary relationship. If a woman feels more like a housekeeper, nanny, or financial provider than a loved and respected wife or girlfriend, she may seek external validation through hookups and affairs.

- A woman may have an issue with alcohol or drugs—substances that affect her decision-making, possibly resulting in regrettable sexual decisions (including infidelity).

- Some women cheat because they have unrealistic (and therefore unfulfilled) expectations about what their partner and their relationship should provide. A woman may think her partner should fulfill her every whim and desire twenty-four-seven, failing to see that this is an impossible standard. And when her expectations are not met, she may seek external fulfillment.

- A woman may cheat because she lacks self-esteem. She may feel unattractive, old, disempowered, or whatever and seek extramarital romance and sex to bolster her view of herself. She may reason, "If someone wants to be with me, I must be worthwhile."

- Some women cheat because they are reenacting or latently responding to childhood trauma—everything from abandonment to overt sexual abuse. Often, this is a way of trying to control or master abuse they couldn't control or master as a child.

- Some women just don't understand what love really feels like. They think the rush of first romance (technically referred to as limerence) is what true love feels like. These women fail to understand that in healthy long-term relationships, the neurochemical rush of limerence is replaced over time with less intense but ultimately more meaningful forms of intimacy and connection.

- A woman might cheat because she craves intimacy but isn't getting it from her primary romantic partner. More so than men, women feel valued and connected through emotional interaction and communication. If a woman is not getting this need met at home, she may seek fulfillment elsewhere.

- Some women cheat to alleviate boredom or loneliness. This is especially likely with women who find themselves at home for long periods of time (perhaps caring for young kids or even after the kids are grown and gone). These women feel a lack of importance and meaning, so they use hookups and affairs to fill the void.

- Sadly, women who cheat usually don't realize how profoundly their secretive sexual and romantic behaviors can affect the long-term emotional life of a trusting spouse or partner. Infidelity hurts betrayed men just as much as it hurts betrayed women. The keeping of secrets, especially sexual secrets, damages relationship trust and is painful regardless of gender.

In his book, A *Man's Guide to Partner Betrayal*, Adam Nisenson identifies 7 stages of what he calls *Masculine Betrayal Trauma*. He explains that these stages don't follow any particular path; they simply represent a range of psychological states that men tend to encounter. From shock and pain to nurturing strength and personal growth, each stage offers unique insights and practical guidance.

THE SEVEN STAGES OF MBT RECOVERY™

1. *Initial shock and ego injury*: The first stage is marked by a profound shock to your ego, leading to feelings of humiliation and inadequacy.

2. *Questioning self-worth*: At this stage, intense self-reflection and doubt surface, leading to questions about your desirability and value as a partner.

3. *Anger and projection*: A common response is projection, where anger is directed outwardly as a defense mechanism, often accompanied by blaming your partner or the person with whom they were unfaithful.

4. *Competitiveness and jealousy*: You may experience a heightened sense of rivalry, driven by a need to restore your pride and counteract feelings of inadequacy.

5. *Withdrawal and isolation*: You may have a tendency to withdraw socially to avoid discussing the betrayal for fear of being judged or seen as a failure.

6. *Rebuilding and transformation*: This stage involves significantly reevaluating your personal values and beliefs about relationships, leading to making changes about how you feel about your actions and behaviors and how you see others.

7. *Positive growth and resilience*: The final stage is characterized by developing a more resilient ego. You are informed by lessons learned and have a deeper understanding of your emotional needs and boundaries. You are learning to steer your ego, not the other way around, and you know what you need to recover from setbacks and new challenges.

NAVIGATING BETRAYAL WITH THE MBT RECOVERY MODEL

"Navigating through the stages of Masculine Betrayal Trauma is unique to each of us. It's important to explore each stage to process all your emotions and foster a greater sense of self. As you progress, you will start healing from

From Nisenson's *A Man's Guide to Partner Betrayal*, reprinted with permission © 2024.

the immediate pain caused by the betrayal and gain clarity about what direction you want to take in your life and who you want to become. The journey has its challenges, but you will be flexing your emotional resilience muscles during this time."[2]

Here is an incredible diagram[3] that depicts The Seven Stages of MBT Recovery as described above. It is the journey a male betrayed partner experiences due to his childhood of origin issues, societal expectations, and the lack of validation that men in general have not been given to express their true feelings and emotions.

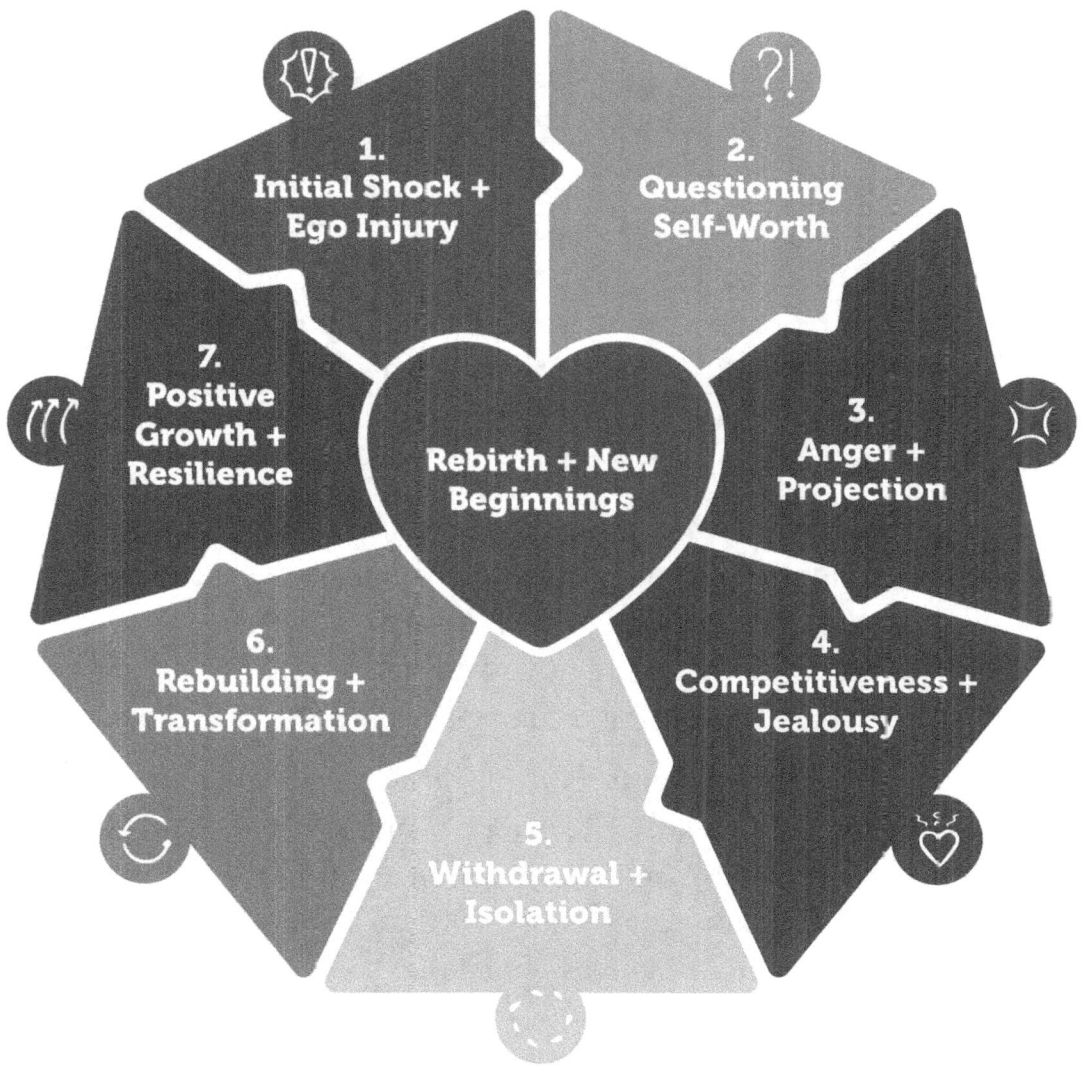

Nisenson explains:

"The MBT Recovery™ Model (Masculine Betrayal Trauma) helps you navigate the aftermath of your partner's infidelity. It provides a framework to understand and process your emotions and reactions triggered by betrayal. Recognizing where you stand in this journey is essential for several reasons.

- *Validates feelings*: Understanding the stages of MBT Recovery™ helps you realize that your emotional responses are normal and expected. In a world where men are often discouraged from openly expressing vulnerability or hurt, knowing that your feelings are real, valid, and worthy of acknowledgment—regardless of what society wants you to believe—can be both freeing and healing.

- *Guides emotional processing*: By identifying which stage of MBT Recovery™ you're experiencing, you can better focus on relevant coping strategies and emotional work. Each stage requires a different approach to healing. Understanding this helps you adapt the recovery process to your specific needs.

- *Brings self-awareness and insight*: The MBT Recovery™ model encourages you to develop deeper self-awareness. With this insight, you will understand your responses to betrayal, including how your ego and self-worth are impacted, leading to more clarity and acceptance.

- *Helps with navigating your healing journey*: Knowing your stage in the MBT Recovery™ model means you can follow a roadmap on your healing journey. It helps you set realistic expectations and recognize that healing from betrayal is a process that evolves over time.

From Nisenson's *A Man's Guide to Partner Betrayal*, reprinted with permission © 2024.

- *Empowers through knowledge*: Understanding the MBT Recovery™ model empowers you with knowledge. This understanding allows you to take active steps in your healing rather than feeling helpless in the face of your emotions.

- *Facilitates support and communication*: Recognizing your stage in the MBT Recovery™ model can also help you communicate your needs and challenges more easily to therapists, counselors, and support networks. It becomes a language to articulate your experiences more clearly."[4]

As you can see, betrayed male partners may have different experiences than female partners and yet, much of the work they may need to restore the relationship involves restoring one's self. I would highly recommend that you read *A Man's Guide to Partner Betrayal* as it validates the male perspective, and yet I believe Nisenson has a lot to say that would resonate with female betrayed partners as well!

SAM & ANNETTE: *LOOKING FOR LOVE IN ALL THE WRONG PLACES— A GAME GONE WRONG*

Sam and Annette had been married six years when Annette decided to create more of a life for herself and pursue tennis lessons. After the birth of her second child, Annette felt she was no longer interesting to herself or her husband. She had put on 35 pounds and felt self-conscious in front of her friends and family. Although her husband never put her down, he did encourage her to run with him. Together, they pushed a stroller for two. Annette explained, "I just could not enjoy myself as running is not my thing, and pushing two children around and keeping up with my husband was exhausting."

Although Sam would offer to take the children, she decided that she would take up a healthier sport that would get her out of "Mommy Land" and afford her an opportunity to be with other adults. She had taken tennis in high school and college but never saw herself as a serious competitor. She called the racquet club and signed up for lessons, and that's when she met Tyler, the adorable 30-year-old tennis instructor with the winning smile and compliments galore.

Initially, she enjoyed being noticed and loved Tyler's genuine attention. He was shocked that she was such a natural, and she loved the fact that he seemed to appreciate everything about her skill and style. She joined a league to get better, and her performance exponentially improved. She initially resisted her schoolgirl giddiness but eventually rationalized that this was a normal reaction to feeling alive again. She couldn't get enough of Tyler and started making innuendos about wanting to get to know him better. She felt a renewed sense of self and even shared with her husband how Tyler felt she was a natural and was always noticing the positives. At times, he would vacillate from being a normal instructor to being extra interested in her progress. She told herself she was more fun to be around now that she "had a life."

When Tyler took summers off to work at another club in another state, she found herself being moody and told her best friend, "It is like I am addicted to him, and I am going through withdrawals." She actually shared her strong feelings for Tyler with three close friends, but met their reactions with intermittent caution. Her feelings went underground, as well as their communication. She stopped sharing her feelings with anyone, which seemed to increase her cravings for more "Tyler communication." And when communication was sparse, she would find herself in a foul mood and take it out on Sam or the children.

Her life seemed more boring, and she realized that she needed a stronger fix. She called Tyler and invited him to a US Open tournament in New York. She pleaded with him to let her repay him for his kindness and instruction. She assured him that they would have different hotel rooms. That is when the lying really started because she had to plan an elaborate scheme that her husband would believe and that would account for the four days out of town.

And scheme she did. She had a month to construct a story about her old college roommate who had terminal cancer and needed friends to care for her in rotation. She posed several fake telephone calls with friends who were part of the care and concern committee of friends. Sam later admitted that it all seemed so strange that Annette would feel so incredibly compelled to care for this friend, but Sam also knew what a big heart she had. For nine months, Annette planned trips away but was beginning to become more disappointed at Tyler's lack of responsiveness. Annette began to expect Tyler to reciprocate the elaborate visits, but after about nine months of rendezvous, Tyler began to avoid her phone calls altogether.

Annette became more demanding and hysterical, but that seemed to create more avoidance. Tyler texted Annette and explained that he had met someone else who was closer in age and had similar interests, and Annette fell into a rage. She threatened to expose him at the club, but Tyler explained that he had secured a new job and would be relocating. Annette had never felt so abandoned and tried to go back to the club to reinvest in her tennis regimen, but it no longer held the zest it once had when Tyler had been part of the regime. She sought out her friends to share her grief and yet felt their judgment and lack of understanding. Feeling abandoned and alone, she decided to take her own life. She left a suicide letter for Sam and acknowledged her lack of feelings for him. The attempt resulted in a four-day coma, and that is when her friends shared with Sam their fears that Annette was reacting to Tyler's rejection of her.

The couple went into couple's therapy, but the therapy did not last more than three months. Sam's fraternity brother had recommended me in hopes that I might be able to kickstart a marriage that looked lost in a vortex. That is when Sam and Annette showed up in my office. Sam was heartbroken but wanted to work on the relationship despite the fact that Annette did not. Annette was a broken woman who had no energy for revitalizing their marriage. She literally was in an identity crisis that left her feeling hopeless and resigned to an empty life.

This couple was not a candidate for ERCEM because there was no intention for Annette to show up and do the hard work of relational repair. She did not have a healthy sense of self or attachment. It would have been unconscionable for me to have expected Annette to give what she had never gotten, so I encouraged Annette to seek individual counseling with one of my colleagues and seek medical attention for a deep depression that she was experiencing.

As I read from her paperwork, she had experienced a difficult childhood with her mother having left her father when Annette was six years old. Her father could not care for his six children, so Annette lived in an orphanage-type setting, although they called it a boarding school, until she was ten. Her other siblings were placed in other settings, and Annette had no contact with them until young adulthood. Annette had had a lifetime of attachment ruptures, and her failed affair had left her no other option but to take her own life. Sam was receptive to waiting for Annette to seek treatment, so I referred him to an individual therapist as well. Not every affair can be recovered, but Annette needed an opportunity to assess whether she could trust her relationships and work toward secure attachments with her children.

As you both read this book, there has to be not only a willingness but an ability to do relational repair. Annette was clearly not able to do this work today. My hope was as she repaired the severe, complex post-traumatic stress from her past, she could begin to develop what she would need in a healthy relationship to move forward individually and perhaps with Sam.

ERCEM, the early recovery couple's empathy model, teaches the BT to work on the skills necessary to focus on what the couple needs after betrayal. Then, couples will need to work together and co-create what is in their best interest. Let me say it again to both of you so you can convey it to whoever you are working with: Infidelity is a relational problem, and it requires that the betrayer do most of the work. ERCEM specialists can help you determine if the BT can create safety and learn the relational skills to move forward. Annette was not able to work on the relationship because there was severe damage to her psyche and functioning. I will tell you that she did return to our sessions to work on her relationship with her children. Although Sam had moved on, he was able to provide a healthy co-parenting relationship that was affirming to both.

SPONSOR/ MENTOR/ GUIDE

ACCOUNTABILITY PARTNERS

READING

MEETINGS

PRAY, MEDITATE, JOURNAL

RCA AFFAIR RECOVERY 12-STEP

ACCOUNTABILITY TOOLS

INFORMATION

GROUP THERAPY

ERCEM

Chapter 5

The 10 Recovery Tools
to Increase Your Success

To the Partner: Understandably, you wonder what recovery tools could work for your betraying partner who has chosen to be deceitful and lie to you. I do not blame you for being skeptical and would expect nothing less. I have recommended these ten recovery tools because they are an incredible resource to assist a betrayer who wants good, solid recovery. These tools also act as ways for you to observe due diligence as the BT works through the harm that was caused.

So many partners ask, "How will I know that BT is really in recovery? Although the BT assures me that they have come to their senses, I am so afraid that they will be tempted or will deceive me again." These tools provide a measurement of their continued commitment to the recovery process and will help you gauge their efforts.

For the Betrayer: Utilizing these 10 tools is a tangible way for you to practice the skills you will need to learn to cope with urges and cravings, and it will keep you strong while you recircuit your brain and develop new neural pathways to replace the old neural pathways of desire. The tools are diverse and help a person integrate the step-by-step formula for promoting habits that reinforce the person you want to be. It will be a measurable tool to help your partner know you are being diligent in your recovery.

I tell partners, "You will know your betrayer is genuinely serious about the program if they have an excitement for the new person they are learning to be. If the desire starts to slack and begins to get lax, your partner is telling you indirectly that they do not think they need the assistance and support, which could not be further from the truth."

To the Partner: You have been overwhelmed by what has happened to you and did not know that you likely qualified as a trauma survivor. As you view the chart on the next page, you can see what ERCEM believes that you need to find more safety and truth. What you need now are tools to increase your sense of safety and stabilization and how you can get to the truth in the safest way possible. You no longer feel safe, nor do you feel stable, and you fear for your sanity.

ERCEM STAGES

1. Acknowledging the need for *safety*, *truth* through *acts of empathy*

Discovery: Managing the Trauma

Finding Sobriety:
The 10 Recovery Tools

Finding the Truth;
Disclosure; Polygraph

Giving Voice to the Pain:
Emotional Impact Letter,
Restitution Letter: Acknowledging
the Damage Caused with Empathy

Developing the Relational Skills
to Do Empathy Work

Empathy Work: Teaching Them
Co-regulation of Triggers
and Emotion Regulation

2. Working Through the *anger*, *grief* and *loss of sexual betrayal*

Identifying the Processes That the
Couple Can Do Together

Teaching the BT Shame Resiliency
Skills so that They Can Be Present
for the Work

Grief Work

Anger Work

Addressing the Fears

Externalizing, Surrendering,
and Acceptance

3. Choosing Post-Traumatic Growth

Acknowledging the Changes

Making the Choice to Trust Again

Identifying Their Strengths
As a Couple

Finding Purpose

Creating and Living Out
the Vision

Leaving a Legacy
in the Coupleship

As we work together as a couple to navigate this tsunami of pain, we discuss how both of you can work together and separately to ensure that you find, as Dr. Barbara Steffens says, "safety in an unsafe situation." This requires you to ask yourself, "Can I make these commitments for my own affair recovery and to make my partner feel safe?"

TYPES OF MEETINGS FOR INFIDELITY

Meetings are crucial to help you find a safe place to be with other people who are learning how to manage their fidelity. The first five recovery tools have to do with attending meetings. I highly recommend meetings that are either faith-based or Twelve-Step-based because I have seen them be the most effective. In a Twelve-Step program, you are expected to recognize that your life has become unmanageable and that a power greater than yourself can restore you to sanity. For many, a higher power is God. For others who do not believe in God, the higher power may be the collective support of the group you are in to build sobriety. Regardless of what group you are in, they can help you be the person that you have always wanted to be and restore you so that you maintain good sexual integrity.

The Twelve-Step program reinforces the need for connection. It has you do the hard work of looking at all your past feelings, failings, and wounds so you can acknowledge and process them and stop medicating yourself with dopamine and infidelity. Once you have gone through the steps, it is up to you to make amends to the people that you have hurt, recognize when you are falling back into old behaviors, and give back to your community because you are a changed man. Like all the spiritual practices, "It is out of great suffering one experiences the process of transformation, and once transformation occurs, you will want to give back to others with similar problems." Unfortunately, I work with so many people who go to meetings but never work the steps! When you do the Twelve Steps, you actively work on transforming your life! Don't shortchange the work that needs to be done.

Faith-based organizations like *Living Truth* also promote psychoeducation, support, and small groups to assist betrayers in creating sexual integrity. The cornerstones of *Living Truth* are the *Men in the Battle*® and *Women in the Battle*® networks. These video-curriculum-based recovery groups for men's sexual integrity and for women impacted by their partner's sexual betrayal take a multi-dimensional approach to recovery. Every aspect of the whole person is addressed to experience lasting change and healing. Spouses of BT's participate in empowerment opportunities to learn boundaries, find support within their communities, and go through coaching to find empowerment with hope and healing after sexual betrayal in *Women in the Battle*.

Living Truth also equips parents to prepare their kids for our over-sexualized culture and resources ministry leaders who want to guide those they serve. For more information, visit https://living-truth.org/men-in-the-battle.

To the Couple: There are additional faith-based groups to support the betrayed.

Pure Desire Ministries has been helping couples for over 30 years. Pure Desire's goal is for you to be sexually healthy. They have a *Seven Pillars of Freedom Model*, which is for men who struggle with infidelity, porn addiction, and other forms of compulsive sexual behaviors. Written from a biblically-based and clinically informed perspective, men will unpack their past pain and trauma, gain valuable tools for their recovery journey, and understand their whole story. In a safe group environment, men will break free, heal their relationships, and take back their lives. For more information, visit https://puredesire.org/shop/seven-pillars-of-freedom-kit.

To the BP: There are additional faith-based groups to support the betrayed.

Written from a biblically based and clinically informed perspective, *Betrayal & Beyond* is for women who have experienced the devastation of sexual betrayal. Intended for group use, this curriculum will walk women through the healing process: helping them establish safety and boundaries, gaining a greater understanding of how betrayal trauma is impacting their lives, establishing emotional awareness, and equipping them to make informed decisions about their future. For more information, visit https://puredesire.org/shop/betrayal-beyond-kit.

To the Betrayed: This is a valuable Twelve-Step group that provides an opportunity to learn self-care and boundaries and find valuable support to work through the trauma and find yourself again. https://www.isurvivors.org is a wonderful support system for anyone who has gone through the devastation of betrayal and infidelity.

Unraveled: Managing Love, Sex, and Relationships is for women who struggle with compulsive sexual behaviors. In a safe group—and through the use of weekly exercises, strategic tools, and self-care focus—women will learn to live in sexual health. Written from a biblically based and clinically informed perspective, breaking free from the pain and shame of sexual brokenness comes from a greater understanding of who God is and who He created us to be. For more information, visit https://puredesire.org/shop/unraveled-kit.

To do this, you need healing from the effects of unwanted sexual behavior and betrayal trauma. The problem is you are stuck in a pattern that makes you feel powerless. Pure Desires Ministries believes you were designed to live a life without sexual brokenness or betrayal trauma and the effects they can have on your future. Like you, they once felt powerless but have found freedom and healing. They now have shared this healing with hundreds of thousands of men and women around the world. https://puredesire.org.

Both of these faith-based programs work from a very similar process in that they want you to look at your life, see where the wounding and holes are, and determine what needs to occur spiritually to feel whole again. There is much connection with other people, and oftentimes, they offer opportunities for you to hear how other people have worked through this process and navigated to healing. It becomes an arena for you to understand your problem and get the fellowship you need through God and the connection with other group members. There are many other faith-based programs that promote sexual integrity. It is important for you to do the work to decide the best fit for you.

To the BT: Regardless of the type of group or support that you choose, it will promote the following goals that increase your success with sexual integrity.

The first five recovery tools include:

- *Going to Meetings*: As a person on this journey, I would ask you to rely on what the program requires of you.

- *Finding a Sponsor/Mentor/Guide*: Find someone who can hold you accountable but also help work you through the steps of your infidelity program so you are not doing it alone.

- *Reading*: Read the book that is predominant in the organization you are a part of to better understand the philosophy behind the work.

- *Doing the Hard Work That Is Required*: If you are in a Twelve-Step program, that means you must work through all Twelve Steps.

- *Having a List of the Accountability Partners in the Fellowship*: Have people you can call at any time of the day or night when you have urges or cravings, when you are doing well and want to celebrate, or when you are having a rough time with your partner or family member.

The next five steps have to do with ongoing work that will keep you present, focused, and moving forward in your recovery:

- *Seek a professional who has been trained in infidelity or ERCEM*. It is important that the professionals are trained in trauma. We recommend an ERCEM specialist who has been trained in early recovery couples work from an empathy model. To find ERCEM specialists, go to the directory on sexhelpwithcarolthecoach.com

- *Go to a therapy or support group.* You'll be able to crosstalk and really explore your struggles and challenges in your relationships and your sobriety.

- *Pray, meditate, or journal.* You need to become self-reflective. You do not have to do all three; you need to do at least one out of the three. Needless to say, if you do two or three, you are increasing your results.

- *Read information on affair recovery.* Do so to understand how you can get healthy and support others on their journey.

- *Use accountability tools.* Maybe you will seek a polygraph test once a year to help keep you accountable. It allows your partner to feel safe and allows you to think about the outcome of your behavior before you give in to a potentially unhealthy one. Even though it can feel like a restraint, it provides much liberation. Other sobriety tools include software filtering systems that report infidelity, like a GPS so your partner will be able to track your whereabouts for safety.

These tools are a guide for you and for your partner.

To Betrayed Partners: If betrayers are following these steps with rigorous focus and attention, they will likely demonstrate the work they are doing to promote faithfulness and monogamy. Some partners may resent the extra set of eyes and will complain that this keeps you "in their business," but for the first three to five years, your responsibility as partners who have experienced infidelity is to stay safe.

A betrayer in good recovery who has been exposed to the new perspective of Early Recovery Couples Work is pleased to use these tools because they help reassure their partner that they ARE doing the hard work for the relationship.

To get a copy of these tools, go to: sexhelpwithcarolthecoach.com/resources.

Chapter 6

Infidelity Restoration Requires Two Perspectives

It is a Recovery Issue, and It is a Relational Repair Problem

For the Betrayer: If you are like most of the people that I work with, you are now dealing with the aftermath of your infidelity and are experiencing your spouse in a very traumatized state. I am grateful you both have found a partner-sensitive therapist because we work differently than many therapists. Upon first contact, I make sure to let you both know I want to see you together for the first session. What I know for sure is that I can help you with your infidelity if you are motivated to change. Your treatment plan must deal with your own personal recovery from infidelity. But it will require more than infidelity recovery; it will require simultaneous relational recovery because you have fractured the most precious partnership that was ever bestowed upon a couple. Your poor choices robbed you of your sanity, and, as a result, you participated in horrendous behaviors that have left your partner shell-shocked and bleeding out.

It is difficult for your spouse, whose brain has been severely compromised due to the discovery of what you have been doing, to understand how you could have continued in this immorality and madness. You thought about stopping hundreds of times, but your fear of the repercussions was more powerful than your ability to discontinue the behavior. It was more than the sex. Your excitement more than likely included the pursuit, seduction, or fantasy that lit up your brain and produced an abundance of dopamine.

As might be expected, you were hoping to experience the same high that you initially got when you first started to see each other. What seemed so pleasurable initially quickly wore off. Your infatuation may have worn off week two or month two. Infatuation is a heightened state of arousal, but it doesn't last once the relationship becomes more realistic and you start dealing with the rigors of life. Managing two relationships is tough enough as you try to compartmentalize each relationship and keep your stories straight, but it becomes even more complicated once the affair partner becomes more dissatisfied with the lack of congruity in your relationship. This may be when you wished you could turn back time and get out of it.

You may have made the attempt and saw the affair partner (AP) heartbroken, and you recanted your desires. Or you may have made an attempt and found that the AP had different plans and threatened to expose or extort you, and you realized that your simple desire to have two lives was turning on you. Seeing more than one person is incredibly complicated and never results in the fantasy that was conjured up in the mind of the betrayer. Sometimes, betrayers juggle more than one affair.

There are many other types of cheating that cause trauma to the BP. Emotional affairs are often rationalized as not being as damaging as physical affairs because there was no touching or physical acting out. However, emotional affairs are incredibly destructive because they keep you from connecting with your partner, and it is a type of infidelity that is easily minimized or justified. Oftentimes, it is the emotional affair that is the feeder for a more physical affair.

THE SEXUAL BETRAYAL CYCLE STARTS WITH AROUSAL OR FRIENDSHIP

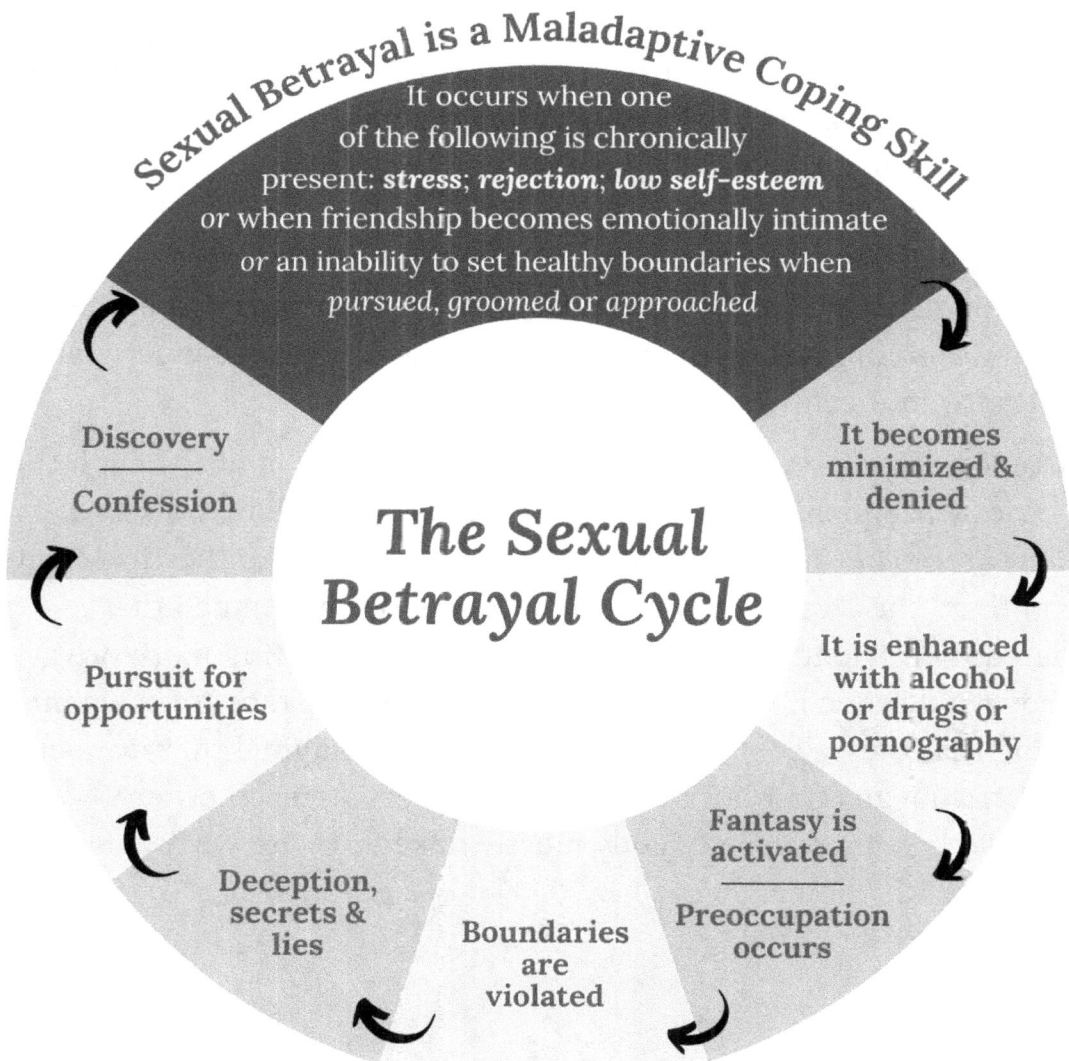

TEDDY & SONDA: *WE TOLD OURSELVES WE WERE JUST FRIENDS*

Teddy and Sonda had been high school sweethearts and married about five years after college. They both expressed having a solid relationship with each other and felt gratified that their lives were moving in the direction that they had always wanted. Teddy was a top executive for a utility company, and Sonda managed a boutique close to their home. Their children were in middle school and were involved in sports. Lindsay was in gymnastics, and Timmy was in traveling soccer. The family had a pretty good handle on managing the rigors of life, although there were times—many times—when they had to split up to assist the kids in their activities.

The soccer parents became close friends because they typically were out of town supporting their kids' soccer games and tournaments. Everyone was fairly close, and as the kids went to bed to rest up for the next game, it was not unusual for the parents to stay up at the hotel drinking and enjoying letting their hair down from their hectic week and stressful competition on the field. Although Teddy never intended to have emotional feelings for one of the soccer moms, he would check in regularly with Kate, who was going through a rough divorce and reeling from her own rejection within her relationship. His compassion for her led to feelings of care, concern, and interest that went beyond a casual friendship.

Both Teddy and Kate were really drawn to each other, and although they kept it strictly friendship, they would find themselves taking walks away from the other parents because they did not want it to seem like they had feelings for each other. They would remind each other about how much they appreciated their friendship and would look for ways to find more private time. They would then always end the evening, breakfast, or tournaments, reinforcing that they were "just friends." They both laughed that it was like they were having an affair because they started calling each other when privacy could be ensured, and Teddy mostly talked to Kate when he was at work or on the way home.

Kate's husband had filed for a divorce and was living in their lake home. Although this was devastating for Kate, she was thankful that she had Teddy to lean on. Teddy knew that his feelings were escalating because he had fantasies of holding and kissing her, especially when she felt sadness about her marriage. He shared his thoughts with her, and Kate responded by saying she, too, had had these preoccupations, especially as she slept alone at night, wrestling with her reality.

Meanwhile, Sonda told Teddy that she felt like they needed to take turns going out of town as she did not want Timmy to think she was not interested in his games. Teddy felt nauseous and froze at sharing his time with Kate. He knew he needed to agree with Sonda, but he spent hours thinking of ways to offset her plans. When Sonda spent time with the soccer parents, Teddy would look for ways to see Kate during the week when she returned. Again, he rationalized his behavior, telling himself that Kate needed him, they weren't sexual, and men and women could be good friends. What he minimized was the lies and deceit about hiding his time with Kate and the emotional energy he was giving another woman.

As Sonda started attending some soccer events, she was approached by another soccer mom who said that she was so glad that Sonda had returned to these events because she felt that Teddy was having an affair, and she had not known whether to contact Sonda. Sonda was shocked and totally taken aback by her friends' allegations, but when she heard about the late nights and Kate and Teddy leaving together, she felt sucker punched by her friend's suspicions. She wondered if she should call Teddy immediately or address it immediately with Kate. She joined the parents and noticed that Kate would not look at her. She immediately felt that Kate was hiding from her. That evening, she decided to look up their family phone records as she believed this would confirm or deny the allegations of the affair. She was nauseous as she got into their phone account and saw hundreds of phone calls during the weekend themselves or during Teddy's time at work. Her husband was truly cheating on her.

She didn't sleep at all and could not wait for their return home. It was exhausting to act as if nothing was wrong in front of her son. She also didn't say anything to Kate for fear that Kate and her husband would hide their tracks. She checked her credit card statements and saw some bills that looked abnormally large during the soccer games, but there were no hotel bills or purchases that made her suspect.

She wondered how this could be happening to them. They loved each other, they were operating like a well-oiled machine, and they had a good sex life. Perhaps it wasn't as frequent as in the past, but their lovemaking was just that...an expression of true love.

After the kids went to bed, Teddy was preparing to go to bed, and she asked him to step out in the garage. She wanted nothing to impact their kids. She told him to get in the car as she accused him of having an affair. He was shocked, vehemently denied it, and promised her that there was nothing going on. As he lied, he focused on her implications of a physical affair and said that he would never lie to her. He said that Kate was like all the other soccer moms, and he begged Sonda to believe him.

Sonda then pulled out several months of phone bills and showed him the proof that she had. He started to cry and confessed to their friendship and admitted that he had lied to her but maintained his innocence about a physical affair. He was shocked that she had been approached by a soccer mom, and he realized that he had been in his own real world. He begged her for forgiveness, and she asked him to go somewhere else for the night. She needed to think about her next steps. And she insisted on calling Kate together and telling her never to talk to her husband again. Together, they left her a message, and Sonda called her despicable. The next morning, Kate called and reaffirmed that she was despicable and that she hated herself for deceiving Sonda and overstepping her boundaries with Teddy.

Teddy and Sonda called for an emergency appointment in part because they were not sure how to navigate the remainder of their son's games and then, more importantly, to discuss whether they could stay together. Luckily for Teddy, Sonda had such good family values that she did not want the kids to be affected; therefore, she was not going to ask Teddy to leave their home.

We discussed the fact that it was understandable that Teddy should not go to any more games without Sonda, but how would they handle their daughters' gymnastics? Was there anyone who could take their daughter to her competitions?

Did Sonda have anyone in her family or amongst her friendships that could pitch hit for her until soccer season was over?

Was Sonda going to tell anyone who could be additional support to her and not judge them for their decisions?

As any betrayed spouse would do, Sonda wondered how they would handle this for the many years to come. We needed to keep Teddy and Sonda in the present and address issues that were most important now. Psychologically, Sonda was shell-shocked because there was no marital discord or problems. Teddy pleaded to do a deep dive into how he could have let this happen, so he went into an affair recovery group to understand what drove him to pursue something that was not within his values.

Sonda spent the next year in early recovery couples work, navigating how they were going to get through this and whether she could ever trust him again. She felt so betrayed and found herself wanting to minimize it because it had not escalated sexually, but her entire reality of what they had was shattered. They did the hard work of making her feel stable by putting into place an affair recovery plan that entailed a constant examination of reality.

Their work required that he put a plan in place that reassured her of his love, fidelity, and stability. He worked hard on his insight into his defense mechanisms, which kept him in denial, and he shared his insights regularly with Sonda. They did this with an ERCEM therapist who knew what Sonda needed for safety. They spent months working with the therapist, talking about her newly founded and understandable insecurity. He stood with her as she expressed her anger and grief for cheating her by trusting him and them as a couple. She did an exercise called the Vesuvius, where she spewed out her anger about the betrayal. He held space for that and acknowledged all the pain he had caused her.

She even shared her desire for a new location to stop the memory comparisons from before and after the discovery. Although a demographic change may not stop the bleeding, it helped them set up a new life that freed them up to start a new vision. Sonda had wanted to live out her life trusting him, but she feared that it may never occur.

One day, she made the **bold decision to trust him again because of all the hard work they (and he) had done, and something shifted in her as a result.** She explained to her coach on Zoom, "Post-traumatic growth is a choice, and one day, I realized if I wanted the life I desired with him, I would need to take that step and go all in." Teddy said he felt the shift and secretly thanked God every day for her grace. Together, the couple worked the exercises at the end of the book and felt stronger every day!

Today, they share their story in workshops and marital retreats with other couples in a church setting and describe what they needed to do to repair the relationship and get stronger. Sonda made the choice to actively seek forgiveness and move together with Teddy toward purpose.

After an affair has been discovered, people are secretly relieved that they have been discovered. They wanted something to stop the affair, but they weren't strong enough to stop it themselves. Or perhaps they tried, but the affair partner (AP) was resistant to the attempts. There was a good chance that the AP had created the fantasy that at some point they would end up being together and is now suffering a severe attachment wounding. The BT is immobilized and trying to do damage control without being discovered. After struggling with how to resume a normal life again, the BT is spending an inordinate amount of time doing collateral damage with the AP, which results in relief once the affair is discovered or confession has occurred. The BT is shell-shocked by what has been done and typically feels helpless to know how to proceed. The BT wants to restore the relationship and wants to "stop the bleeding" but is not sure how to do this without the partner falling into a traumatized state.

To the BT: You feel horrible that you have put your partner in this place, and you wonder how your self-absorbed needs could have put you both in this position and robbed you of your conscience, mental well-being, and sanity. Somehow, someway, you were able to do unthinkable things, and, in your stinking thinking, you believed that your partner would never find out. That is why it is so important to do whatever you can to create safety and find the proper support to show that you have every intention of being the partner that you should always have been in your marriage or partnership. This problem was created by you, and yet it has impacted every facet of your relationship. You are the crucial element in helping your spouse's healing.

If you can put BP first, contain the intense pain, and work a good support program, you are much more likely to find success and bring the relationship into a new state of being. This model will teach you how to do it, but it won't be quick. I am not sure if your BP is in the fetal position on the floor or if they are raging at you nonstop for the betrayal. Perhaps you have left your partner in such a traumatized state that they are in bed 24 hours a day, unable to find the strength to get up, go to the bathroom, eat, or shower. Shock, rage, and depression are three trauma responses betrayed partners frequently have when they have been betrayed.

ERCEM: THE NEW RECOVERY MODEL—FINDING SAFETY

Together, all three of us are going to work on strengthening your recovery tools and your relational skills. There are many therapists who believe the couple needs to immediately start couples therapy to get to the heart of why you acted out. ERCEM believes that the BT must work on finding a support system that promotes integrity while working on restoring the relationship by first working on safety and trust building. Your partner is doubting everything about your life together and questions if it is even possible to build trust again.

To the Partner: You have every right to know what the BT is doing and what the treatment plan consists of, and you will get to weigh in as to what you believe would strengthen your relationship. You are an active part in the process of recovery and will want to check in to determine the efficacy of the recovery program. I recently had a partner request that her husband find a partner-sensitive therapist to maximize his success. Her husband was comfortable with his therapist and did not want to change, but he agreed to interview other therapists who had a specialty in affair recovery and partner sensitivity. After he met with several professionals, he was able to see her point and added the ERCEM specialist to their team. ERCEM is the "Gold Seal" in helping couples because it incorporates empathy into the therapy from day one and works with the BT to continuously look at the infidelity and damage through BP's eyes.

A similar situation occurred with a gay couple I was working with, and the BT showed great empathy. The partner told me that he was very uncomfortable with his husband's relationship with his mentor. Billy shared with us that the relationship appeared to be "way too friendly" and, as Billy said, "intimate," so he asked Mark to switch mentors because he felt discomfort with the amount of personal sharing that was going on in the recovery process from the mentor. Mark was saddened that Billy was requesting that he get another mentor because he felt so comfortable with his mentor. He told us, "It is the last thing that I want to do, but if that is what would make Billy feel more comfortable, I feel like I owe it to Billy to display impeccable accountability and show him that I am one-hundred percent in this to build trust."

Mark's ability to show empathy and see it from Billy's point of view increased the healing, and the couple made great strides. He wanted to make a case for how his mentor was helping him, but his desire to help Billy feel safe came before his own needs. Once he started operating from the question, "What does Billy need to feel safe?" their relationship repair expedited toward healing.

We are looking at the different programming and treatments for all types of infidelity and finding that different professionals believe different things. If you do not have an ERCEM specialist in your area, check the directory at www.sexhelpwithcarolthecoach.com for a list. There are ERCEM coaches that can work with you virtually anywhere in the world.

If you can put your spouse first, contain the intense pain that you have caused, and work a good affair recovery program, you are much more likely to find success and bring the relationship into a new state of being. As a couple, you will need to engage in reconnecting together, but first, you need to develop the empathy, compassion, and resiliency needed to stand alongside the BP as you both deal with the pain. You will be learning a process to help your partner heal, and the coupleship will go through the stages of grief and recovery together. This will require that you learn about trauma and how it has affected your spouse as you both work on developing the skills and techniques necessary to work through the three stages of partner betrayal. This is done while the BT continues to strengthen the resources to refocus on the values required to have a healthy relationship. It is an arduous undertaking for both of you, but you can get through this and grow stronger!

That is why I need you both here for the first meeting. Together, you will need to know about the treatment recommendations I will be making for both of you and the resources that are available to supplement your work. Unlike the old school of treatment recovery, you will be working together to create more healing. The partner is an active part of BT's treatment, and you need to know what to expect and measure the determination and focus of BT's work. A trained specialist is always the best choice to help you on this journey. However, if you don't have the finances to seek a specialist, you can use this book, as well as other resources, as a guide to do the work. It is a roadmap to help you both work through the three stages of partner betrayal.

THE THREE STAGES OF PARTNER BETRAYAL:
SEEING PARTNER BETRAYAL THROUGH THE EYES OF TRAUMA

As you navigate through working together as a couple, it will be important to find a specialist who has been trained in partner sensitivity. I ascribe to the APSATS model, which seems to be the most partner-sensitive, and it was derived from trauma pioneer Judith Hermann. Hermann's trauma work was groundbreaking—she conceptually identified three phases of trauma treatment that a survivor would need to work through the trauma. You are a trauma victim. Although the BT never meant to hurt you and certainly never meant to cause extreme trauma, that kind of relational betrayal undoubtedly causes trauma, which is why you need a partner specialist!

Most partners need to know how this could have happened. They want an understanding of why it started, how it started, and all the questions in between. They want a timeline, and they want a witness. In this next chapter, we will talk about the safest way to get that information.

Chapter 7

Your Job is to Provide Safety:

Sharing the Truth is the First Gift of Empathy

THE FOUR REQUIREMENTS FOR BETRAYERS AFTER DISCOVERY

To the BT: Now that BP has discovered what you were really doing, you will need to do whatever it takes to redefine yourself in recovery. The four requirements for restoring the relationship after discovery are:

1. LASER-FOCUSED AFFAIR RECOVERY

A period where the BT has proven good recovery, so the BP has more assurance that you want to get healthy and are willing to do what it takes to find and maintain integrity. The betrayed needs to know that you have the right support in place to begin healing. Your recovery is dependent on a strong support system. You will need to build a strong "committee" to assist you through the transformation it takes to maintain good integrity. Very few people are strong enough to do it by themselves, and that is why support is crucial in the process of affair recovery. Attending a program with lots of accountability and support, which contains an abundance of longevity, hope, strength, and integrity, will be crucial to getting you through the tough times. As mentioned earlier, there are many support groups that can provide assistance as you gain recovery. AffairRecovery. com, BeyondAffairs.com, InfidelityHelpGroup.com, and Infidelity Survivors Anonymous (ISA) are just a few of the groups that are available to support you in this process. You cannot do this alone, and your partner will be watching to see how you navigate your affair recovery. You must treat this process as if your life depended on it. You cannot get lazy or complacent because that would set you up for other weak moments that will compromise your relationship and trustworthiness.

> As a betrayer in good recovery, your job is to provide safety.

2. THE FORMAL THERAPEUTIC DISCLOSURE

For the BT: Once you have established some good solid recovery, you may want to participate in a formal disclosure by a partner-sensitive trained therapist who will be able to provide your partner appropriate safety and stabilization while your spouse hears the entire truth of your infidelity for the first time. I also recommend that you have a therapist who has been trained in doing formal therapeutic disclosures.

My colleagues, Janice Caudill and Dan Drake, have written a series of books to help both of you understand why this is so important to the relationship and how it can provide safety and stabilization once the BP learns the truth. Not only does it help you both work through the process of finding out the truth, but it also helps the brain stop ruminating about what else might not be known. In my endorsement, I called their series of books "the Bible for helping couples utilize the disclosure in the safest way for the sake of the partner." The book series *Full Disclosure* is the gold standard for you both to know how to prepare and what to expect from the disclosure process.

We know how tough it is for you, the Partner, to try to put the pieces together and continue to wonder what really happened and, more importantly, how this could have happened to you. There is no way to right the wrong that has occurred when sexual infidelity robs you both of the integrity and trust needed in a healthy relationship. You have both been deeply affected. If trust is ever to be restored, it may require that you learn the truth so that you can make an informed decision about what you want or need to proceed.

My colleague Dr. Laney Knowlton recognized the traumatized partners and betrayers may need a simple instructional Booklet to help them with the process of disclosure so she developed *The Connected Recovery*® disclosure process. In this set of three booklets she gives guidelines that walk betrayers and partners through the process step-by-step. This model applies to any level of betrayal, ranging from a single affair to extended patterns of behavior. The process includes four letters: the What & How letter, the Why letter, the Impact letter, and the Amends letter. Letters one, two, and four are written and presented by the betrayer, while letter three is written and presented by the partner. Booklet A is for betrayers and Booklet B is for partners. The first section of each is almost identical and explains the disclosure process in general, including three handouts, one of which breaks the betrayer's part of the process down into bullet points, another breaks the partner's process down into bullet points, and a third that explains how to set up the presentation of each letter and what to do on the day of the disclosure. The booklets differ from that point forward.

Booklet A walks betrayers through how to write and present the first two letters, how to receive the third, and how to write and present the fourth. The appendix of Booklet A includes several timelines and exercises that may be helpful for betrayers. These exercises are also available separately in the Exercises Booklet (published primarily for clinicians who want to use the exercises separately). I recommend partners not read Booklet A or go through the Exercises Booklet as the questions and exercises may be unnecessarily triggering.

Partner-sensitive professionals recommend that you participate in a formal disclosure ***only if you feel the need to go through that process.*** Most partners feel it is necessary to know the truth to determine what has preempted their marriage and, more importantly, what has been going on with their cheating partner that they would have never in a million years imagined. Some BPs explain that they already have enough information to know how damaged the BT is, and they do not want to put any more thoughts or images into their brains. There are no wrong or right answers here—it is whatever you as the BP needs!

In a formal disclosure, a therapist works closely with the BT to create a timeline of all the indiscretions that occurred from the time the couple first met each other until the present. The partner may want to understand the history of how the pattern of infidelity began, so ask the partner where they want the disclosure to start. Although this process is gut-wrenching and raw, it helps the BT reveal all of the secrets, and it allows the partner to hear the truth.

This process of BT writing out the timeline usually takes three to six weeks.

- The BP is asked to list all questions that have to do with the "facts" of the acting out. Sometimes, a partner will have 20 questions that need to be answered in the disclosure and timeline. (I recently had a wife who had 139 questions that needed to be answered. It took us quite a bit of time to pare those down to the basic information that was needed. But ultimately, the BP determines the number of questions.) The BT is to answer all questions that are fact-based in the disclosure in conjunction with the acting out.

- After the disclosure, the BT is asked to bring the partner to the polygraph appointment to ensure that EVERYTHING was revealed by having two to four polygraph questions that suggest that BT was honest. The partner is not allowed to sit in on the examination but is available to review the results with the polygrapher. An examiner needs to be willing to include the partner as they report their findings. Sometimes, couples must travel hundreds of miles to seek out a good polygrapher who understands partner betrayal. The disclosure can affect partners in many ways, but in general, most partners reported that they felt the disclosure was helpful in "stopping the bleeding." They were tired of the staggered disclosures and wanted a safe way to hear it all. They were now able to understand the timeline for how the affair had started. The disclosure showed the couple how the compulsivity had ramped up. Although most betrayed partners feel devastated by the facts, they also express relief at finally knowing the truth.

There is a lot of controversy about the reliability of a polygraph. I know there are a lot of people who believe you can fool the polygraph examination. Also, there are some personality types that might be proficient at deception. If we are dealing with a person who has no conscience and is sociopathic or severely narcissistic, chances are that they may be able to skate through a polygraph. This is because the BT may have no feelings and is so well-defended and guarded that they can hide from their own feelings. Therefore, when asked the two to four questions an examiner would ask, the BT can lie without any perceptual change in heart rate or breathing and pass without suspicion. However, more than likely, the BT does not have a serious personality disorder, does have a conscience, and would not be able to fool the examination. Very few of my clients fall under the criteria of sociopath or narcissist.

A polygraph ensures honesty. Most betrayers may still want to minimize and lie to avoid causing you more pain and themselves more anguish, but taking the polygraph adds an extra dimension of pressure to be authentic, honest, and transparent. Some people question the authenticity of a polygraph, but if you have a good polygrapher and measurement tool, it is unlikely that the betrayer will be able to deceive a polygraph.

There are many different types of polygraphs, so you will need to educate yourself on what you feel is the most effective. It is important to seek an examiner trained in infidelity because you will need to work with the examiner for the next three to five years if you fear the BT has slipped back into old behaviors. The process of polygraph testing keeps you both safe. It helps BTs be accountable for their actions, and it helps partners feel protected and become more stabilized. Betrayers in good recovery tell me that regular polygraphs in the first two to three years helped them to "do the next right thing" as their brain calmed down and developed new neuropathways that reinforced healthy behaviors.

3. THE EMOTIONAL IMPACT LETTER: ALLOWING THE PARTNER TO GIVE VOICE TO THE PAIN

An extremely helpful tool in teaching BTs empathy is when the BP writes an emotional impact letter. This process originated out of the work of Schneider, Corley, and Irons (1998). This tool is an important adjunct to a formal disclosure because it helps you give voice to the atrocity you have undergone and for your spouse to know how profoundly you have been affected. It is an opportunity in a safe place to make sure you are heard. You are able to share your thoughts, feelings, and pain while BT quietly listens. It is a chance for the BT to hold BP's pain in an empathetic way while BT quietly listens. The emotional impact letter gives the BT an opportunity to accurately hear the pain. It also teaches the BT to metaphorically "hold the pain" while the partner emotes. I tell betrayers to imagine you are holding your hands together like you would if you were holding water in your hands, and every time your partner shares feelings with you, imagine that you are holding them.

This can be done after you have processed the formal disclosure. I have found that most partners feel compelled to share their feelings two to four weeks after the disclosure has occurred. Partners may need to take more time before they feel ready to write out their thoughts and feelings. The important thing is that you feel ready to write out your thoughts and give them a voice. It is also good to externalize your feelings so that these thoughts do not remain silent. There is no prescription for length of time needed after a disclosure. Only you will know how long it takes before you can write the Emotional Impact (EI) letter!

The Process:

- Once you have participated in the disclosure and heard the truth, you are to write about how the BT's actions have affected you.

This typically results in you highlighting times when the BT had deceived, manipulated, and gaslighted you. In the emotional impact letter, you may want to describe the anguish of being abandoned during the birth of your second child, being left at home during an appendicitis attack to fend for yourself, or not being able to locate the BT when your teenage daughter was in a near-fatal car accident. The impact may have included the pain of feeling increasing separation, never having sex anymore, and the many nights you would wake up to a gnawing feeling that something was wrong.

- This letter is a way to convey the pain and is a direct result of what you heard in the disclosure and what you experienced prior to and including the discovery of the affair. It is a formalized way to give your pain "voice," and it can be very cathartic. The betrayer's responsibility is to stay quiet and listen to your pain. The information in the emotional impact letter will be used as a template for the BT to write a restitution letter. Most partners report feeling like they have found a safe way to purge the pain in a contained place. It almost always provides a sense of relief, and it provides a profound opportunity for the BT to show empathy when the restitution letter is completed.

4. THE RESTITUTION LETTER WITH EMPATHY—ACKNOWLEDGING THE PAIN

The restitution letter is not an amends but an opportunity to share with your partner that you heard the pain and sadness your infidelity has caused. You are acknowledging what you did, yet you are not asking for forgiveness.

You start by receiving a copy of the emotional impact letter and use that to write your restitution letter. In this letter, you acknowledge that you heard the pain and the trauma the BP described. You are not explaining, defending, or apologizing for your behavior. You are repeating back verbatim what was described in the emotional impact letter. When you do this, you are validating the feelings, thoughts, and beliefs that were described. You are practicing empathy by recognizing BP's perspective on betrayal. The most important thing is to acknowledge the EI with empathy and let the BP know that you caused the excruciating pain.

You are expected to have your letter ready within two weeks of the emotional impact letter. Some BTs may need more time and should talk to their professional to assess what is the best course of action for the BT. Attending to it in a timely manner shows the BP the importance of responding with empathy to the pain that was caused. It creates an opportunity for your spouse to feel validated and reaffirmed. For many couples, it is a chance for you and your partner to get closure on the secrets and begin to rebuild your relationship. Many partners say that when the betrayer does the restitution letter and shows that the partner's feelings and thoughts were acknowledged, it shifts the BP's thinking and is a game changer in the relationship!

Note: Not all partners want a formal disclosure, and it is the partner's prerogative as to whether BP wants or needs one. This applies to the emotional impact and restitution letters as well. Remember that it is imperative to use a partner-sensitive therapist or coach to guide you in all three of these processes to ensure that "it occurs in a safe place" for both of you.

I have used Early Couples Recovery Work to do the emotional impact letter and restitution letter without the disclosure. It is an equally powerful empathy exercise! If you decide against the disclosure, we can still do these processes referencing the infidelity and the destruction it has caused you. It is an opportunity to get clear about the overwhelming feelings and then decide how to proceed. When the betrayer allows the partner uninterrupted time to share feelings and can address each point, the partner again feels heard and validated, making it a bit safer to communicate about other things.

Addendum: If the BP wants a formal therapeutic disclosure, it will be necessary to participate with specialists who can take you both through the process so the partner has the full truth and can determine how to proceed. I recommend that you work with two types of trained specialists. If you want a licensed clinician, you can go to the following directory to work with someone who is trained in this very specialized field:

https://kintsugirecoverypartners.com/find-a- clinician/#!directory/map.

If you desire to work with a professional but are unable to find someone in your area, you will want to work with a coach who has been trained in truth building. To find a coach who has expertise, go to:

https://kintsugirecoverypartners.com/find-a-coach/#!directory/map

Warning: Many ERCEM professionals have had formal therapeutic disclosure training and can be found on the ERCEM directory at www. sexhelpwithcarolthecoach.com. It is not uncommon for BT or BP to go to well-meaning professionals who have not been properly trained. I had one woman who had been through two disclosures that were botched from the start. The first time, her husband and his therapist asked her to come in and surprised her with a disclosure. She was not prepared to hear the truth and had no support before, during, or after to help her process the information.

In the second disclosure, she set it up but was not consulted, so she did not get to contribute by asking questions that were necessary to put the pieces together as to why her husband had multiple affairs. She had no input to get the information that she wanted! Be wary of well-meaning therapists who have not had training in this important process! The disclosure was incomplete, and she told me she felt more "in the dark" after the disclosure than before it.

The third time, she went to the disclosure during her lunch hour, and the well-meaning therapist booked a 50-minute session (when the average disclosure takes three hours). My client not only did not get a complete disclosure but also went back to work afterward and did not get the proper self-care. It is imperative that your professional receives the formal training so you have the proper preparation and aftercare to keep you safe. Again, I reiterate, since this is the most important part of the initial safety and stabilization phase, the professionals cited above have been through the gold standard of disclosure training and have the skills to help you follow up with processing the information necessary to work through disclosure and find the truth.

Chapter 8

You Both Need to Understand Your Feelings

As you start this journey, we will be talking about feelings and emotions. When identifying emotions, we have found it helpful to reduce them to five basic feelings:

- Anger
- Sadness
- Happiness
- Fear
- Loneliness

As a partner, you are flooded with feelings, and as the betrayer, you may be afraid to express your feelings—you believe you are not entitled to having them after the betrayal. Nothing could be further from the truth, and you both must express them to feel a sense of authenticity. To keep it simple, I ask you both to identify the primary feeling you are experiencing. All emotions can be condensed down to any of these five feelings.

The difficult task is to determine which feeling is predominant at the time. You may be aware that you feel several feelings at one time. Oftentimes, the feeling most uncomfortable for you is the one you avoid. Women typically feel and express sadness when the main feeling that they are experiencing (and avoiding) is anger. This frequently changes when partners are in the betrayal trauma state because their amygdala is activated, and as a result, they go into the fight part of the "flight, fight or freeze" stage and feel uncontrollable anger and rage. This is a survival mechanism because nothing in their life feels real! When this occurs, it can further compromise their sense of safety because they wonder what is happening to them. They have never felt so out of control with anger before, and they wonder if they are going crazy.

Using feeling self-regulation will allow you to recognize the feeling, describe it, identify where you feel it in your body, and then determine what helpful message it might be trying to send you so you can take better care of yourself. Partners who use the "Feeling Check-In Method" no longer feel controlled by their feelings. Instead, they use their feelings to guide them to better self-care.

This picture identifies the 5 Primary Feelings, and as you can see, all other feelings fall under these 5 Primary Feelings.

THE FIVE PRIMARY FEELINGS

As you look at this picture, you will notice how so many feelings fall under the primary feeling. Which feeling feels the most comfortable and which feels the most uncomfortable, and why?

The feeling I am most comfortable expressing is: _____

The feeling I avoid the most is: _____

Why? _____

_____

_____

_____

THE DAILY FEELINGS INVENTORY FORMAT—A GUIDE TO LEARNING ABOUT YOUR FEELINGS

1.	How am I feeling today? (Circle One) HAPPY SAD ANGRY FEARFUL LONELY
2.	Where am I feeling the emotions in the body?
3.	What might I need to learn from my feelings?
4.	What proactive step can I take today to honor what my feelings are telling me?

The Daily Feelings Inventory Format allows you to take some quiet time and assess what you want for the day. This simple tool empowers you to put yourself on the front burner—you get to decide how you want to live your day and what direction you want to take. It is a simple exercise of self-empowerment. The belief is that when you tune in to what you need, you are more likely to have enough energy for yourself and others. You can create any structure you need to set aside time for a feelings check-in. Most people find it helpful to find a quiet time and place to write a paragraph or two on what their primary feeling was throughout the day and where they felt it in the body. Each person is different and will store their feelings in their body differently, so this process teaches you to take an inventory of how your mind and body process feelings.

Journaling your feelings helps you honor them and decide how they can motivate you to make necessary changes for yourself. As illustrated in *Unleashing Your Power: Moving through the Trauma of Partner Betrayal*, the daily "Feelings Inventory" has many benefits, allowing you to:

- **B**—Be in the moment

- **A**—Attend to what is going on inside of you

- **N**—Nurture yourself

- **K**—Keep telling yourself distress is normal. Looking at ways to assess the things that you can control or recognize the things that are out of your control

We call this "BANK"ing your feelings and awareness so you can use them to guide you! Your feelings are your friends, so don't run from them. Instead, ask yourself, "What are they telling me so I can use them to grow stronger?"

Another technique I find grounding and calming for both the unfaithful and the betrayed partner originated from Tara Brach, who is a psychologist and Buddhist meditation teacher. She encourages us to be curious about what we see, feel, and need. I have elaborated on her technique to help couples through infidelity.

The acronym she uses is R.A.I.N.

- **R**—Recognize

  Recognize and notice the thoughts, feelings, and sensations that are present within. Life is so busy we tend to ignore what is happening to our bodies and what it might be trying to tell us. Infidelity can have such powerful emotions that it can be helpful to notice where we feel them in the body and write them down so you can begin to sit with them.

- **A**—Allow

  Allow the thoughts and feelings to be there without trying to alter them. This teaches us to sit in the feelings even if they are uncomfortable or cause distress. Allow yourself to breathe with them. It can be helpful in allowing them if you lean into them as being purposeful and there to reveal something you might want to do for your own self-care. I encourage you to give them a peaceful, gentle color as you take in the breath and breathe out a color that represents the uncomfortable feeling.

- **I**—Investigate With Kindness

  Be curious about your thoughts and feelings. Focus on where you feel the feelings and ask what they might be trying to tell you. You have both been through so much, and it is time to choose constructive compassion to investigate further if there is some part of you that you can attend to with self-care.

- **N**—Nurture

  How might you nurture yourself as you acknowledge your own pain and suffering? What might you need in the here and now to begin to make friends with the feelings? It makes sense that you might want to focus on what has been done to you, but you have the choice to care for and nurture yourself in the here and now, and when you do, you begin to take charge of your life again with a sense of mastery. So right now, what kind and gentle statement can you make that nurtures you?

Chapter 11 has all types of mindfulness exercises that will help you further regulate. This chapter helps you both recognize and manage your feelings.

For the Betrayed: Although you are trying to ascertain what you might have control over to keep yourself safe, it can be freeing to let go of the need to manage all the conceivable things that the betrayer could be doing. Now that you know what the betrayer did, they will never be able to fully deceive you again!

Banking Your Feelings, RAIN, and *The Feelings Inventory* are the vehicles that allow you the opportunity to let go of the need to control your feelings and your environment and stay focused on yourself. It is a gateway to trusting your intuition again. This seems elementary, but once you have been deceived, it is hard to know what is real, what is feared, and how your mind might be seeing and experiencing things that are not "really" there. This is perhaps the toughest thing to discern because your mind and body are on high alert, and you are watching for any sign that says you are not in danger. You know that you could not tolerate it if it were to occur again.

This is a reason that I say that you need a specialist who can help guide you both through this process and move towards restoration. You can do it the old way where both of you see a therapist who has you process the pain of betrayal, but you need a specialist who will help you help you access safety and stabilization while helping the betrayer find good affair recovery.

I would like you to stay present with your feelings to work through them. This will require that you encourage yourself to be accountable for your own life. As you learn to manage and co-manage your feelings, you will look for your own inner guidance system to tell you what you may need to focus on next.

COMMUNICATING FEELINGS IS CRUCIAL TO RECOVERY

To the Betrayer: You learned that you needed to be present with your feelings so you can develop empathy. Both you and your mate should make a regular practice of spending five to ten minutes linking up your thoughts and feelings with the day's activities and your interactions with others. Let it be the compass for what you need for yourself and from each other.

As you identify your primary feeling, you may find that it correlates strongly with guilt and shame. When you do the hard relational work and watch your spouse agonize about what has happened, it is easy to go into a shame cycle. When this occurs, go to Chapter 13 to find an affirmation that you can tell yourself to put things back into perspective. Many of my clients report that they use Principle #6, which reminds them to practice saying, "This is not who I am today; this is the consequence of my past actions. I need to realize that I can only stay healthy and support my partner properly if I stay focused on who I am today."

It can feel like a juggling act to practice good recovery, help the betrayed heal, and stay out of the shame cycle, so I would encourage you to re-read the "7 Principles of Conflict and Shame After Betrayal" (found in Chapter 14) and customize them based on what you need to stay strong as you continue to do this important relational work with your partner.

SAMMIE & TARA: THE LOVE ADDICTION PURSUIT USUALLY STARTS WITH EARLY CHILDHOOD WOUNDS

Sammie and Tara met at work. She was very intrigued by Sammie because his background was Jamaican, and he had this captivating demeanor that made her feel like "she was the only girl in the room." She said, "I had never felt anything like that before, and I remember telling my girlfriend that I felt like I was the star of a movie." They felt an immediate attraction toward each other, and she began to feel like she would not be able to exist without his attention. She knew this was a dangerous attachment but found herself craving more and more time with him.

There were two red flags in the relationship. Six weeks into the relationship, he confided that he was married and separated from his wife but not officially divorced. He explained that they lived in different states and that he had "just not gotten around to filing for divorce." He blew off her requests to get the divorce even though she had printed out two legal copies and filled one out for him. She was making it easy for him, yet he ignored her requests repeatedly. It was obvious that he had no desire to do this for her, and she could not understand how their relationship could progress with another relationship in the mix. She spent a lot of time convincing herself that it didn't matter as it was obvious that Sammie loved her; after all, she rationalized that "there was no communication between the two of them." She chalked it up to Sammie just being lazy.

The second red flag was that Sammie had gotten another job after she had embarrassed him at work. There were many times she witnessed Sammie flirting with other coworkers, and it mirrored the beginnings of their relationship. She found herself to be extremely jealous and would rage at him when he was giving women excessive amounts of attention. They had talked about her need to, as Sammie put it, "Calm it down," but she would retort that she would "calm it down" once he stopped flirting with other women. He kept telling her, "They are my coworkers and just friends." He would then say, "Girl, I just can't please you. I think I need some time off."

At best, it looked like Sammie was having an emotional affair with these women. Tara felt that Sammie was being disrespectful to her and their relationship, and Sammie would act oblivious to his behavior or to her needs. Sammie didn't want to work on their behavior; he just wanted to find a place to hide. And that he did. He informed her that he couldn't take the harassment and found another job across town to get a little space from the drama. This devastated Tara as she wanted to spend every waking moment with him, and he was needing more and more distance.

Then the inevitable happened: Tara found out that she was pregnant, and she felt more desperate to make things work. The harder she pushed, the more avoidant he became, and he was disappearing more and more despite her need for companionship and comfort. When they were together, they would fight non-stop, and Sammie said that he was setting limits because he could not take it anymore. Tara got very desperate and begged Sammie for one more chance, and she told him she would go to couples therapy to learn how to manage her anger.

With much reluctance, she got him to go, which was a sign to her that he "really did care." But from the start, couples therapy did not go well. When they went to therapy, the therapist would side with Sammie and tell them both that because they were not married yet, it might be better to dissolve the relationship. The therapist explained that Tara suffered from an anxious attachment while Sammie seemed to have a dismissive one. The therapist was not helping them to find closeness and connection. She told them that they were both immature.

Tara felt ganged up on and misunderstood in the therapist's office, and yet she acknowledged that it was the only time they could talk. She explained that even though she wasn't heard, she tricked herself into believing that she could feel heard. She felt a dread for herself and for her baby. At seven months pregnant, she could feel Sammie pulling away, and her heart ached for a baby that might grow up without a father, just like she had.

Another blow to the relationship was that she had received a Facebook message one day from his estranged wife. Tamara contacted Tara and said that their property taxes were due, and Sammie was not returning her calls. After a two-hour-long conversation, she learned that Sammie had a history of infidelity and had cheated on Tamara multiple times. They had very little contact, but he promised to support his family financially as he worked on himself. "Family?" Yes, Sammie had a two-year-old son with Tamara, and he was supporting them both.

When she confronted Sammie, it seemed to be rationale for more distance. She remembers that after 12 days of being MIA, he seemed to have pulled out of the relationship altogether. He had said that they were done, but he had said that many times before. Not only did he stop answering her calls, but he did not appear to be staying at his home. Tara found herself going to his house and waiting for long periods of time just to get to talk to him.

One night, as she stood outside in the pouring rain, nine months pregnant, waiting for him to come home, she wondered what was wrong with her and why she would stand for this abusive behavior. She had been listening to podcasts on women who loved too much. She admitted to herself that she sounded like a "love addict," and she wondered why Sammie's unfaithfulness would, in some ways, end up pathologizing her. A healthy person would not stand for this, but instead of contemplating what she would need to do to leave the relationship and take care of herself and her baby alone, she kept defaulting to what she would need to do to captivate him again.

When he came home, she was shivering and soaked, and he took one look and headed for the door without even acknowledging her. She ran up to him to shake some sense into him, and he started to become physical with her. This made her more determined to remind him of what they had. As he fumbled with his keys, she started to beg and plead, but as he ignored her and started to walk into the doorway, saying that she was "f—king crazy and deranged," her tears turned into rage. She knew it was over, but she also believed she could not live without him. Tara hit a wall emotionally. She couldn't eat, sleep, or function. Her OB insisted that she go for counseling, and that is when Tara showed up in my office. She was a skeleton of a person, and her baby in utero was in great danger.

I talked to Tara as if Sammie was her drug. Her body had broken down, and she was so physically compromised. All she wanted was for him to come back, but he had moved on. He had been so intoxicating initially, but now he had turned lethal. We couldn't deal with the infidelity because we had to deal with the withdrawal first.

Many women who discover infidelity, betrayal, and trauma begin to wonder what in their life was real. Although Tara's reaction to Sammie's rejection was extreme, her body's reaction was not. Looking at her from the outside, you might have said, "Wow, that is a very insecure, unsure, needy woman who is mentally unstable." And you would be absolutely right, as Tara was experiencing what we call a clingy mind state. (See Chapter 11 on Mindfulness and the Unskillful Mind States to figure out what your mind state might be).

She wanted something so badly that she clung to the perception of what she wanted. The clingier she was, the more he pushed her away. The more he pushed her away, the more she wanted the illusion of what she thought she had. She clung onto the delusion of what she wanted and what she had thought she had. But that mind state kept her in a state of immobilization and fear. It actually kept her from finding what she needed. Tara needed to do some deep psychotherapy to heal her OLD wounds.

On a cellular level, she was experiencing traumatic stress. The changes in the nervous system were caused by kindling. When trauma victims experience extreme stress, their central nervous system is more prone to reactivity and excitability, which then causes the cells to begin to fray. On a cellular level, this means the cells are not as strong and become more excitable, which then results in the nervous system becoming an antagonist on a cellular level. The weaker the cell structure becomes, the harder it is to regulate, and the compromised cell state becomes its own source of provocation. When she walked into my office depressed, dejected, rejected, and abandoned, I knew that we had to find that place deep inside of her who would be willing to give to her baby what she didn't have for herself. As she became more focused on her own inner child and the severe neglect she experienced as a child, she was able to see through the eyes of her daughter what she needed to get healthy.

Infidelity causes such huge wounds, and in Tara's case, she had complex post-traumatic stress from living homeless with her mother, seeing her father shot over a bottle of cognac, and being molested multiple times by a multitude of junkies who spent time with her mother. It made sense that the initial meeting with Sammie produced such a huge hit of dopamine like no other drug, and she wanted that hit again and again.

We spent several years working through the terror and trauma of living in that hypervigilant state of wondering what lurked around the corner and how she could stay safe in an unsafe environment. As we created more safety in the therapy office, she began to develop more ego strength, which helped her be a better mother to her child and herself. She had officially detoxed from Sammie and recognized that she needed to love herself before she could ever receive love from someone else.

When a person experiences significant childhood loss, they must work on themselves whether they stay with the betrayer or not. It is important to develop a way to trust oneself again, and that means one needs to have a strong sense of self. You will learn later that you assess the world by attending to what you think, how you feel, and what you know, which is really your intuition. Understanding your feelings is the gateway to trusting your intuition again.

This seems elementary, but once you have been deceived, it is hard to know what is real, what is feared, how your mind might be seeing something that is not really there, and what your intuition might be sensing that continues to be off-putting. This is perhaps the toughest thing to discern because your mind and body are on high alert, and you are watching for any sign that says that you are in danger. Tara had learned early as a child not to trust anyone or anything, and yet she continued to repeat trauma repetition because it was in her DNA and felt familiar.

As Tara got healthier and found safe people to talk to, she started to attend Love Addiction Anonymous and learned healthy boundaries that kept her safe. I knew she was healthy when she said and followed through with behavior that was congruent with the Love Addiction Model. She said she had committed to staying out of relationships for a minimum of one year so she could explore how to love herself.

Learning about feelings and getting to know yourself is the foundation for self-love. That being said, I would like you to stay present with your feelings in order to work through them. This will require that you encourage yourself to be accountable for your own life. As you learn to manage and co-manage your feelings, you will look for your own inner guidance system to tell you what you may need to focus on next.

I am happy to announce that Tara started that journey, dealt with the severe feelings around her own abandonment, worked with me to explore what a secure attachment might look like, and began to pursue her own inner guidance system to find healthy men and women she could count on. By the time her child was in middle school, she began to date a committed and consistent man who adored and respected her. She waited three years before she married him, and every year, she sends me Christmas cards of the family.

A STRUCTURED TIME FOR FEELING IDENTIFICATION

To the Betrayer: You learned that you needed to be present with your feelings so that you could develop empathy. Both you and your mate should make a regular practice of spending five to ten minutes linking up your thoughts and feelings with the day's activities and your interactions with others. Let it be the compass for what you need for yourself and from each other. (Later in this chapter, you will learn about Connection-Shares, which is a comprehensive way to assess how you both are doing.)

As you identify your primary feeling, you may find that it correlates strongly with guilt and shame. When you do the hard relational work and watch your partner agonize about what has happened, it is easy to go into a shame cycle. When this occurs, go back to Chapter 13 to find an affirmation that you can tell yourself to put things back into perspective. Again, many of my clients report that they use Principle #6, which reminds you to practice saying, "This is not who I am today; this is the consequence of my past actions. I need to realize that I can only stay healthy and support my partner properly if I stay focused on who I am today."

It can feel like a juggling act to practice good recovery, help the betrayed heal, and stay out of the shame cycle, so I would encourage you to re-read the Seven Principles of Conflict and Shame after Betrayal and customize them based on what you need to stay strong as you continue to do this important relational work.

For the Partner: Most people report that they feel most stuck because their safety has been compromised. Does it affect your sense of safety? If so, how does that make you feel?

_____

_____

_____

_____

_____

_____

_____

For the Betrayer: How do you feel about having robbed the person you love of their sense of safety? Do you go into sadness or fear? Or does it catapult you into guilt or shame? What do you do when you feel guilt or shame? Do you feel discouraged? Do you feel like you will never be proactive enough to stay ahead of potential triggers that take your partner down the spiral of fear? Does it throw you in a shame cycle? Does it make you feel unworthy? What is the primary feeling that links up to "unworthiness?"

_____

_____

_____

_____

_____

_____

_____

We teach betrayers that guilt is a healthy emotion that reminds them of the wrongdoing, but shame keeps them immobilized in self-loathing.

To the Partner: Has the betrayal shattered your sense of the world? What feeling does that evoke in you? Have you generalized it to not trusting anyone or anything? Has it morphed into not trusting your family, your community, your work environment, your religious community, or God? Which feeling is the most overwhelming as you both think of the betrayal? The two feelings that frequently come up in our sessions and typically stop people from moving through their issues are fear and sadness. My experience is that the betrayed feel fear, and betrayers feel sadness and loneliness. Regardless, it is imperative that you identify what feelings are immobilizing you. Spend some time sharing your feelings with your spouse.

You may be flooded by your feelings, which makes it feel impossible to sort through them. Your brain is trying to process normally but is in shock, and you are feeling a whole host of feelings that can seem overwhelming. This is a normal reaction to partner betrayal, and what you need to do is self-regulate and co-regulate together!

There are many ways to self-regulate when you feel flooded by your feelings. Part of doing your own work is to learn how to ground yourself and find resources that diminish the terror that can naturally occur when you are flooded (otherwise known as resourcing).

Partners report that there are many things they can do to honor their feelings and process them to move forward on their journey. Some examples are:

Prayer	Meditation	Journaling
Therapy	Support Groups	Coaching
Mindfulness	Intentional Self-Care	Retreats

In the recovery world, there is a slogan that encourages a person to "face your fears head-on." This encourages you to accept them for what they are but not be controlled by them. It is important for you to sit with your feelings to ascertain what they might be telling you. When you are in trauma, you are flooded with feelings, but now that you are resourcing, I want to reinforce how you can use your feelings to motivate you to make some needed changes in your life. Let's practice looking at some tough situations and looking at how feeling identification can motivate you. I would like you to explore some situations that have felt problematic and observe what they might be telling you.

IDENTIFYING THE POWER OF FEELINGS

1. What situation have you encountered and felt personally overwhelmed by?

   _____

   _____

   _____

   _____

   _____

2. What was the primary feeling, and how did it affect your choices?

   _____

   _____

   _____

   _____

   _____

3.   How could you use this feeling to motivate you to make some needed changes?

_____

_____

_____

_____

_____

4.   What is another situation that you have encountered and felt personally overwhelmed by?

_____

_____

_____

_____

_____

5.   What was the primary feeling, and how did it affect your choices?

_____

_____

_____

_____

_____

6.   How could you use this feeling to motivate you to make some needed changes?

_____

_____

_____

_____

_____

I will share some examples of how other partners identified how sitting with their feelings contributed to some forward movement.

1.   One partner used her anger to create boundaries that would empower her. She might not have been able to control his frequent slips, but she certainly could make her bedroom a safe haven by explaining that she had no desire to be around him when he didn't prioritize better recovery. As a result, she took over the bedroom and excluded him from the opportunity to be close to her. She explained that she needed ongoing distance to process her anger.

2.   Eric sat with his feelings and felt deep sadness. He felt that he and Brad had the perfect life. When he sat with his grief and journaled about it, he recognized that his sadness kept him from grieving his fear about his sexuality. He still had many issues to face about his own guilt about coming out. When he found the "perfect relationship," it calmed his fears about his own insecurities, and now that Brad had been living a life of deception, he questioned whether anything about his life was real. This also made him question his choices. Journaling his feelings brought clarity. It strengthened his reality that he was gay and had every

right to find a loving relationship! He needed to grieve to move on with his life and move beyond his fear of judgment.

3. Another partner recognized that her loneliness was a sign that she needed more connection, so she purchased not one but two French bull terriers to love on. The puppies were no substitute for a healthy husband, but they distracted her from focusing on him. A secondary gain was that she and her husband, who was working diligently on recovery, would walk the dogs together, which inadvertently brought them closer.

4. Many partners complain that they are flooded with feelings. But as they sort through them, they identify that the primary feeling was fear. As Suzy sat with her fear, she recognized that she needed to calm down her emotions. She felt disoriented because of the dysregulation. She committed to spending more time looking at her fear as a gift instead of "the enemy." This resulted in her asking herself, "What is fear trying to show me?" As she power-walked each day, she would ask God to reveal to her what she needed to know most about the fear. One day, she clearly heard God telling her that her fear had more to do with not trusting herself. She started to weep and recognized that she had lost her connection to herself. She committed to focusing on intentional self-care to get to know herself again and separate from the betrayal. She spent extra hours in yoga classes learning how to slow down her mind. She felt more control in her body and began to get her intuition back. She also decided to resume playing the piano, which she had abandoned in adolescence. She committed to taking lessons so that she could practice thinking about something else instead of the betrayal. She found it liberated her from the old fear and reminded her that her feelings could be used to guide her toward something that empowered her instead.

5.   Tom used his fear differently. He journaled about his fear daily and asked God why he could not move out of it. After several days of journaling, God conveyed that Tom was afraid of being alone and that actually Tom was not relying upon God enough to know that God would walk beside him while he worked through the pain of being betrayed by his wife. He nudged Tom to go to a male support group and start talking about the betrayal. He also prodded Tom to come back to church and let the church embrace him with scripture. Tom told God that he was afraid because he felt that Diane was not going to be there for him, and his intuition was to leave her. He heard God reminding him to look up scripture on adultery for comfort. This gave him a special sense of comfort because what Tom feared most from his community was being judged.

To the Betrayer: Feelings have always been hard for you, too. Your deception has interfered with "feeling development." There is much research that suggests that acting out helped to medicate your feelings. This meant you never fully were able to understand them, nor could you feel them because your goal was to suppress them with your addiction. We are doing a deep dive into these five simple feelings so you can become more comfortable identifying them for your benefit and recognizing them in your partner. You must recognize feelings to have empathy for yourself and for others. I want you to list the earliest time you felt each one of the five feelings. After you have completed this exhausting list, I would like you to share it so that your partner can understand the evolution of your feelings. This may bring up vulnerable emotions for you, which may act as a detour to expressing them, but push through them anyway. As you do this work, you will want to find opportunities to express your vulnerability. The act of vulnerability is a "trust builder."

- The first time I felt anger was...

  _____

  _____

  _____

  _____

  _____

- I dealt with the anger by...

  _____

  _____

  _____

  _____

  _____

- The messages I received from my parents/caretakers about anger was...

  _____

  _____

  _____

  _____

  _____

- The first time I felt sadness was...

_____

_____

_____

_____

_____

- I dealt with the sadness by...

_____

_____

_____

_____

_____

- The messages I received from my parents/caretakers about sadness was...

_____

_____

_____

_____

_____

- The first time I felt anxious was...

_____

_____

_____

_____

_____

- I dealt with the anxiety by...

_____

_____

_____

_____

- The messages I received from my parents/caretakers about anxiety was...

_____

_____

_____

_____

- The first time I felt lonely was...

  _____

  _____

  _____

  _____

  _____

- I dealt with the loneliness by...

  _____

  _____

  _____

  _____

  _____

- The messages I received from my parents/caretakers about loneliness was...

  _____

  _____

  _____

  _____

  _____

- The first time I felt happy was...

  _____

  _____

  _____

  _____

  _____

- I dealt with the happiness by...

  _____

  _____

  _____

  _____

  _____

- The messages I received from my parents/caretakers about happiness was...

  _____

  _____

  _____

  _____

- Were there any common themes in how you experienced your feelings?

_____

_____

_____

_____

_____

- What were the messages that your parents/caretakers gave you about feelings and particularly your feelings?

_____

_____

_____

_____

_____

- How did each parent express feelings?

_____

_____

_____

_____

- Which feelings are you the most comfortable expressing?

  _____

  _____

  _____

  _____

  _____

- Are you afraid to express feelings? And if so, do you know why?

  _____

  _____

  _____

  _____

  _____

⚜

Now, let's look at present-day circumstances that involve your ability to identify, process, and express feelings. Let's take a hard look at how you express them when you are around the people you love. I realize this might involve some real excavation of what causes your feelings and how you express them. You may also notice a relational pattern of not expressing your feelings. To create connection, you must learn to share vulnerable feelings. Once you are done with them, you will want to share them.

- The last time I felt anger was...

  _____

  _____

  _____

  _____

- I dealt with the anger by...

  _____

  _____

  _____

  _____

- The messages I received from my partner about how I dealt with my anger was...

  _____

  _____

  _____

  _____

- The most recent time I felt sadness while I was with my spouse was...

  _____

  _____

  _____

  _____

  _____

- I dealt with the sadness by...

  _____

  _____

  _____

  _____

  _____

- The messages I received from my partner about how I dealt with my sadness was...

  _____

  _____

  _____

  _____

  _____

- The most recent time I felt anxious with my spouse was...

  _____

  _____

  _____

  _____

  _____

- I dealt with the anxiety by...

  _____

  _____

  _____

  _____

  _____

- The messages I received from my mate about how I dealt with my anxiety was...

  _____

  _____

  _____

  _____

  _____

- The last time I felt lonely and was with my partner was...

  _____

  _____

  _____

  _____

  _____

- I dealt with the loneliness by...

  _____

  _____

  _____

  _____

  _____

- The messages I received from my partner when I expressed loneliness was...

  _____

  _____

  _____

  _____

  _____

- The last time I experienced happiness was...

_____

_____

_____

_____

- I dealt with the happiness by...

_____

_____

_____

_____

- The messages I received from my partner when I showed my happiness was...

_____

_____

_____

_____

To the Betrayer: As you get more and more comfortable sharing your feelings, you will be better able to contain your partner's pain as they describe their feelings. This process is called co-regulation. For it to be effective, it must build on the foundation of your being able to process and express your own feelings. Co-regulation is when you help to regulate your partner's emotions. This can be done with the two of you following the formula in this book, but you may want to use a specialist who can co-facilitate and create a structure that will help both of you feel safe as the partner begins to share feelings. Your spouse is in a traumatized state; it may require small doses of communication (it may even require small doses of time together initially).

To the Betrayed: When you express your fears, anger, sadness, and grief, the BT can hold them for you. You are much more likely to manage them because you are not suppressing or repressing them.

What is suppression and repression? Suppression is when you stuff your feelings away and try to ignore them because it does not feel safe to express them. You may have learned this early in your childhood, and now that this betrayal has occurred, you have gone back to using suppression as a natural defense mechanism to keep yourself safe. It is not good to suppress or stuff your feelings because the body keeps score, and these feelings will cause you great distress later.

Repression is when you bury your feelings and thoughts so deep that you no longer consciously know they are there. This is an extreme form of denial. Even though it may feel like it is serving you to have amnesia, shielding you from the effects of the feelings and the events from your past, it will play out in how you function, your mental health, or even your physical health. "What you resist persists" in one form or another, and that is why you are so brave for facing your fears head-on and working to assess your current situation and the state of your relationship.

Both betrayers and the betrayed have been known to repress feelings. If you are a partner who has repressed your feelings, you will likely be unable to find connection no matter what the betrayer says or does. Although your defense mechanisms are there to protect you, they can be problematic. When defense mechanisms are used too frequently or with too much intensity, they can end up blocking you from restoring your relationship. You may even find that they rob you of enriching relationships in business, at church, with other family members, or in life.

Betrayers suppress and repress feelings, too. If you are a BT who feels numb and does not believe you have any of the five feelings, you will want to work on this with your therapist with great determination. The truth is that if you cannot identify and express your feelings, you will be a shell of a person. Your partner needs to know how you are feeling and needs to know when you are feeling one of the five primary feelings. You may avoid fear because when you are afraid, it triggers your feelings that the BP might leave you. When you are afraid, you are not good enough, and when you are afraid, the relationship may not heal. When you express those feelings, this will more than likely start a dialogue where you may find your partner reassuring you that there is a desire to know your feelings. Sharing your feelings helps others to connect to you. Vulnerability is honest and authentic.

CONNECTION-SHARES ENHANCE SAFETY AND CONNECTION

To the Betrayed: You may ask, "What if I don't feel safe sharing my thoughts and feelings?" Maybe the BT does not seem to be working hard enough, so you don't want to be that vulnerable. When couples go through that impasse, I encourage them to make sure to talk about their feelings in a check-in since that is a structured process that allows you to identify the number one feeling you are having. You will learn more about check-ins in Chapter 13. The important thing is that both of you own your feelings. It is a natural defense mechanism to put them on the back burner and hope that a time will come when you feel comfortable enough to share them, but if you do not start sharing them now, that time may never come.

Often, partners who have been through the discovery of infidelity are unable to express themselves in this crisis state. Partners report that since discovery, their minds are no longer clear, and they have trouble communicating clearly. They cannot find the right words, and sometimes they cannot speak at all. Trauma affects the part of the brain that receives and expresses communication. Your frontal lobe has functions linked to speech production, and Broca's area of the brain serves a vital role in the generation of a speech network. It is no wonder why you are having trouble producing words to describe how you feel or what you think! You are not going crazy; your brain has been compromised!

As you work through your trauma and BT helps you to co-regulate, you will be able to gather your thoughts together and work toward expressing yourself slowly. As your brain heals, the words will come back as well. But after recognizing how the trauma has impacted your prefrontal cortex, you have even more reason to move slowly into safety and trust your intuition to know how much of your feelings to share.

If you are having trouble expressing yourself and cannot find the words to convey what you are feeling, I would encourage you to go slower and find somebody very, very safe to share your feelings with.

If you are a female betrayed partner, a group like Betrayal and Beyond is a safe place to start the process, coupled with a specialist who understands betrayal and the accompanying trauma. If your fears are preventing you from grounding and resourcing, then it may be time to do some processing on an unconscious level. Brain spotting, EMDR, and somatic experiencing are all extra resources to use when processing your wounds and the wounds of your childhood, and doing so may free you up from your tendency to always appear in control. When you process beliefs and reactions that may be tied to childhood issues, it frees you up to live in the present. Doing this will motivate you to take care of yourself differently.

LEANING INTO TRUST

As you work as a couple to heal, I am going to ask both of you to lean into trust. I know that feels impossible, but you must let a sliver of hope and light in to continue to strengthen yourself and the coupleship. This process of trust begins with trusting yourselves on an individual basis.

To the Betrayed: You must begin to believe that this relationship is worth fighting for and that you are the reason your spouse is fighting so hard. I know it feels scary and even humiliating or shameful to begin to trust again. You wonder if other people doubt your judgment and secretly think that you are crazy. You have some naysayers telling you that you are too good to put up with "the garbage," and they do not want you to be a "sucker."

Do not let their criticism confuse you and make you doubt your feelings. Identify them and then use them to propel you toward your desired transformation. Making the decision to stay together and to work on rebuilding the relationship is your choice. Although other people can be concerned and protective, they do not understand the nuances behind your relationship. They cannot put themselves in your shoes and reckon with the thought of divorce, the importance of your vows, or splitting time with the kids or grandkids. No one can know the sacrifice you have been through or the love you have in your heart for the partner you hope they can begin to be.

Let me remind you that when a betrayer is in good recovery and practicing the principles, they are healthier than 85% of married men or women out there! Understandably, there must be a part of you that wants to take advantage of a renewed commitment with integrity. It can really help to have a partner-sensitive specialist who can also support you as you work through your fears and help you find yourself again. The more support you have, the more you will be able to use those feelings as a compass to point you in the direction that is best for you. You will become confident in your own intuition and make decisions that work best for you.

I have had so many couples hold back from sharing their feelings because they are afraid they will be rejected or their feelings will be used against them. It is understandable that during the crisis of infidelity, sharing feelings comes at a high cost.

As the unfaithful partner, you fear that you and your feelings will be rejected. Many people have even said to me, "I have no right to share my feelings because of the atrocities I have caused." This is a negative mind story that you tell yourself. Depending on the wounding, the hurting partner may not acknowledge, validate, or trust your feelings, but deep down inside, there is a place inside of the BP that does want to know how you are feeling. The hurt partner yearns to know the real you but fears that you are not capable of being honest since you have lied for many months or years. Reconnecting can feel terrifying for both of you. If you need more support, have your therapist use this book as a guide to support you in your desire to heal together. Having a neutral person to provide structure can be a key ingredient to your healing.

Chapter 9

The Ultimate Goal of the
Early Recovery Couples Empathy Model (ERCEM):

Restore Safety, Trust, and Intimacy Through Empathy

ERCEM was designed to set up a structure for you to begin to feel safe and work through the anger and grief of learning that the person you loved was unfaithful. In working with couples, I could see that you both wanted to help, but the unfaithful partner did not know how to respond since they were the perpetrator of your pain.

You, as the partner, may not want to be vulnerable because the unfaithful was not worthy, nor have they earned your trust. You are devastated by the betrayal and fear that your relationship will never be restored. You have not felt safe enough to even begin to share your true feelings because you do not know who your spouse really is. In the last chapter, you learned to look at your feelings a bit differently, and hopefully, you have been encouraged to identify and express them to begin the process of allowing the BT to create a safe haven for trust. Remember that this process cannot be accomplished quickly, but every day that you work on letting him help you heal is another day that renews trust.

Janice Caudill and Dan Drake explain in their books *Full Disclosure: How to Share the Truth After Sexual Betrayal* and *Full Disclosure: Seeking the Truth After Sexual Betrayal*, that "Intimacy is the highest point on the intimacy pyramid. It is built on a foundation of vulnerability, trust, safety, and, ultimately, honesty. With these components, relationships flourish in love and health. They are satisfying and connected." Dan Drake, Joanna Raabsmith, and Matthew Raabsmith have updated this pyramid, placing honesty at the base to reflect intentional action steps taken to provide truth.

If you look at this diagram that Janice Caudill and Dan Drake use in their book, *Full Disclosure (Volume 1)*, you can see that you must know the truth to determine if you can increase your sense of safety. You are suffering from a relational trauma, and there are no guarantees that the relationship can rebound from it. Unfortunately, when couples are devastated by sexual betrayal, it is not just their intimacy that suffers; it is the whole pyramid that crumbles, starting with the foundation of truth. The relationship the betrayed partners thought they were building for weeks, months, years, or even decades shatters when lies and sexual secrets are discovered.

THE INTIMACY PYRAMID ©

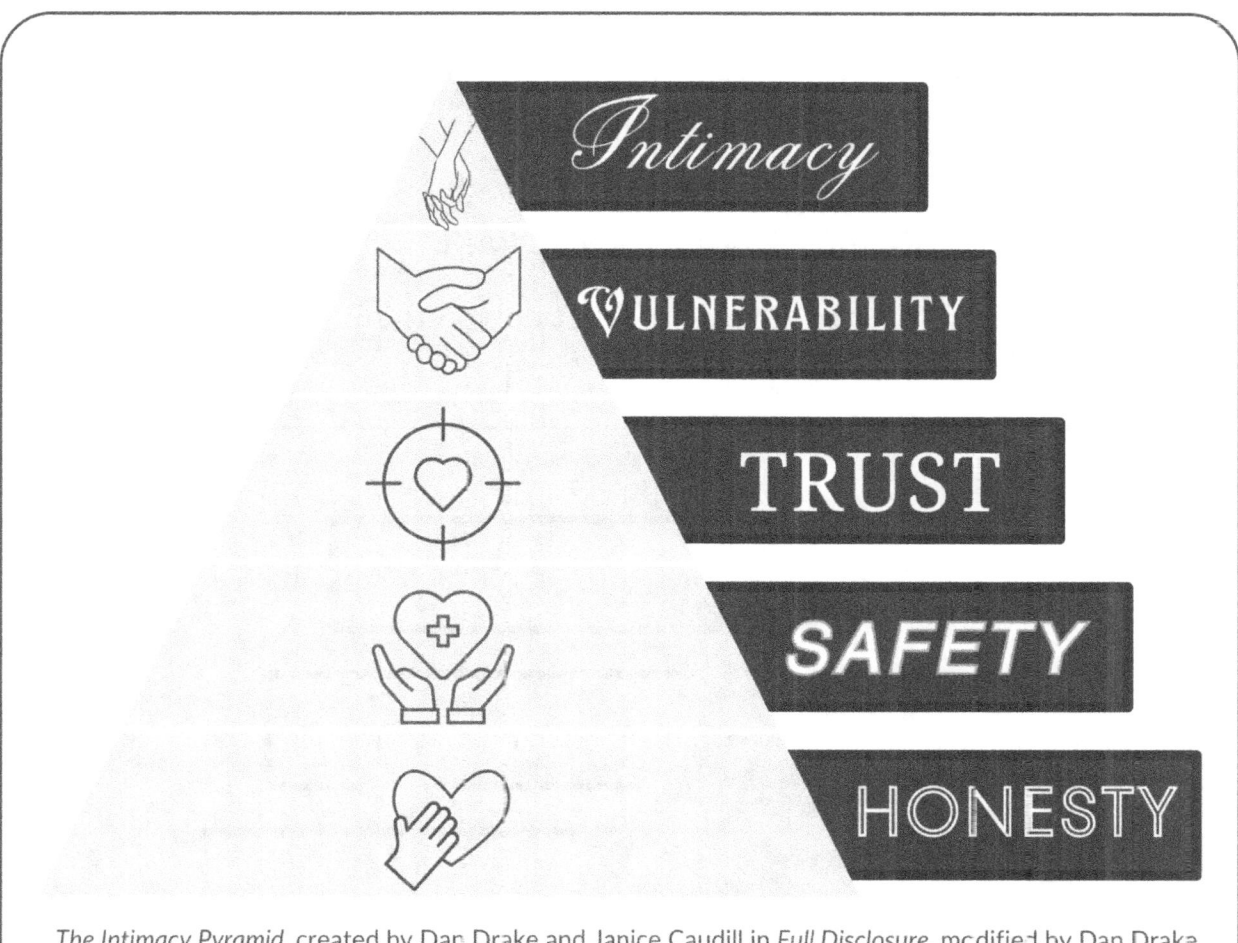

The Intimacy Pyramid, created by Dan Drake and Janice Caudill in *Full Disclosure*, modified by Dan Drake, Joanna Raabsmith, and Matthew Raabsmith in *Building True Intimacy*.

Note to the BP: We do not expect you to initially put yourself into a vulnerable position, as safety is your number one concern. It is, however, important for you to notice the BT's ability to be vulnerable because that is part of his treatment requirements. It is not imperative that you acknowledge it, but it is helpful. If you have been working on the relationship either through a couple's recovery group or with a therapist, it would benefit the BT and the relationship if you could acknowledge the changes that are being made with others and the BT's attempts at sharing his feelings and being vulnerable.

As you recognize change, you will be more likely to work toward trust, vulnerability, and increased intimacy. Intimacy can be increased in many ways, and you will learn in Chapters 10 and 14 how to increase behaviors that work toward more closeness and connection.

YOUR INTIMACY PYRAMID—CAUDILL AND DRAKE

Create your own *Intimacy Pyramid*. What do you think you both need to create more closeness?

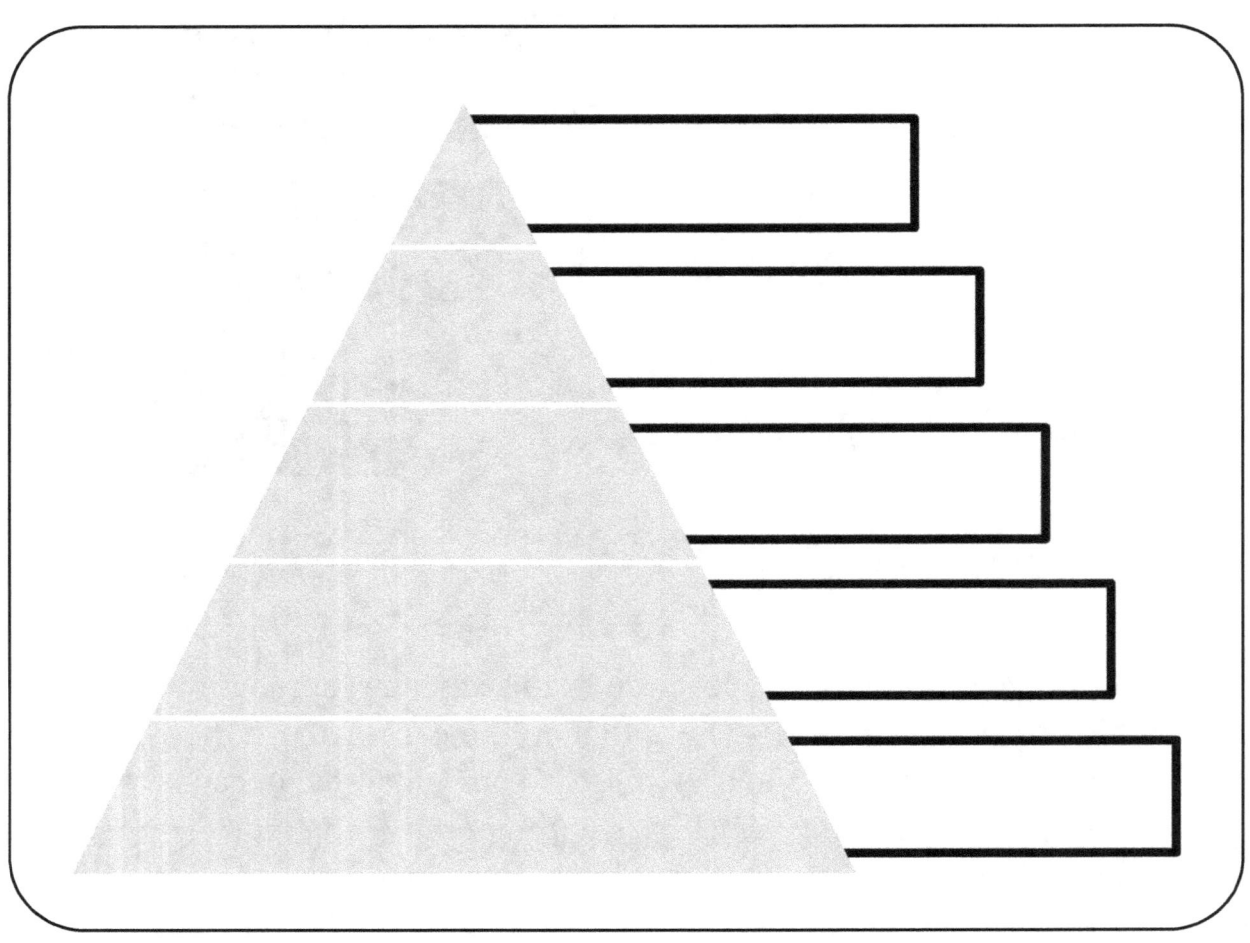

What values are important to you that you might want to include in your intimacy pyramid? You, as a couple, need to agree to authenticity, honesty, and transparency for how you feel, what you need, and what you believe is important for the coupleship.

Make sure to include a value that incorporates how to express conflict. You must know that you can get through the conflict and get closer as a result because conflict breeds intimacy if you are working on creating a healthy relationship.

As I thought about the ERCEM pyramid, I wanted it to embody empathy because taking each other's perspective is so important in a relationship.

THE (ERCEM) INTIMACY PYRAMID

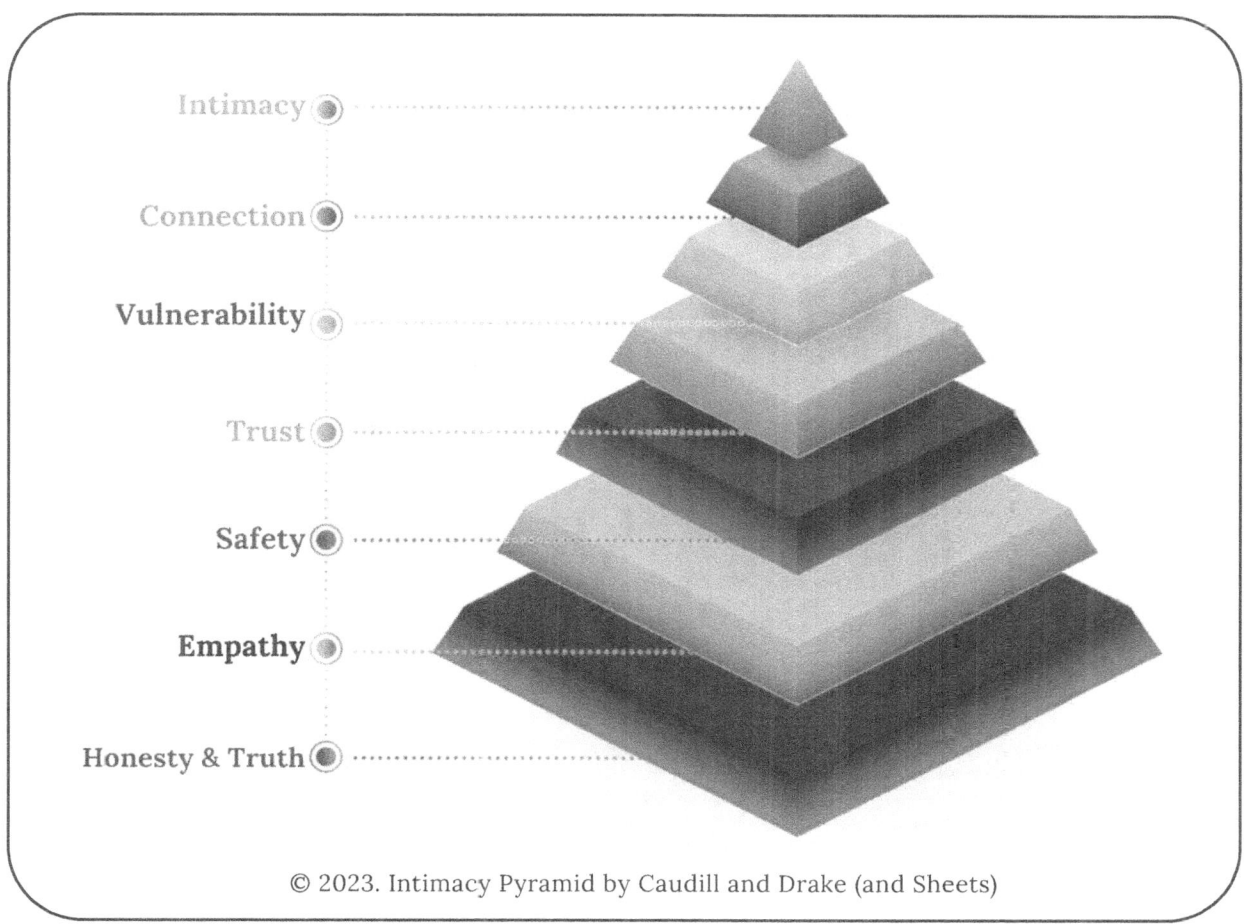

© 2023. Intimacy Pyramid by Caudill and Drake (and Sheets)

After I created the ERCEM pyramid, I realized I had left out faith or spirituality and the word consistency—two very important values! You may alter your pyramid from time to time as you recognize new values you want in your coupleship. This exercise will help to reconstruct what values are important after infidelity has occurred and it will help to redefine what you need to regulate the traumatized brain.

HOW TRAUMA IMPACTS THE BETRAYED PARTNER

It is important that both of you know what can happen to a partner once they have experienced the trauma of the infidelity discovery. Although not every partner experiences a trauma response, most partners experience at least 10 out of the 20 symptoms below. Janina Fisher is an expert on trauma, and she has created a graphic that really depicts the many symptoms of trauma. Can you circle the many trauma responses that you might be dealing with because of the betrayal?

For the Couple: It is important for you, the partner, to share the many trauma responses that you may be experiencing intermittently with the BT.

To the Betrayer: We will talk about what you can do to help stabilize the partner, but first, you need to acknowledge the trauma you caused.

"I WOUNDED MY PARTNER" EXERCISE

In this book, we will expect the BT to work on doing whatever is possible to help you stabilize, but that is no easy feat.

To the BT: Now that you have most likely established more safety by going through this truth-telling process, you must begin to understand all the different ways you have caused pain to your spouse. The "I Wounded My Partner" exercise helps you to identify the wounding you have induced. You will be using it to show that you see the pain and know you generated it. You immediately hold yourself accountable by taking ownership for the pain. When you can correlate your actions with the impact it has had, you are more likely to understand how the partner feels, and it is the beginning of building that empathy muscle. I know that as you examine the damage that your infidelity caused, it can leave you feeling shame and guilt. But I promise that as you begin to see the damage and hold yourself accountable, you can feel the growth of the person you want to become. As your spouse sees that you understand the pain, it will reinforce the belief that there may be a chance to rebuild the relationship and create a new marriage or partnership built on the foundation of trust, honesty, and true compassion for your relationship.

> "I Wounded My Partner" develops an empathy perspective.

I would like you to take it a step further. I want you to think of all the ways that you have hurt your partner:

- Emotionally

- Physically

- Socially

- Intellectually

- Spiritually

Please write out ten ways you have wounded your partner in all these areas. First, describe how you have wounded your partner in all these areas, starting with how you have wounded your partner emotionally.

1.   I wounded my partner emotionally by causing the BP to question the love I have for him or her.

2.   I wounded my partner emotionally by causing self-doubt.

3.   I wounded my partner emotionally by flooding their brain with feelings that are overwhelming.

4.   I wounded my partner emotionally by...

_____

_____

_____

5.   I wounded my partner emotionally by...

_____

_____

_____

6.   I wounded my partner emotionally by...

_____

_____

_____

7.   I wounded my partner emotionally by...

_____

_____

_____

8.   I wounded my partner emotionally by...

_____

_____

_____

9.   I wounded my partner emotionally by...

_____

_____

_____

10.   I wounded my partner emotionally by...

_____

_____

_____

Now, do the same for how you have wounded your partner physically.

1. I wounded my partner physically by endangering the BP's health by exposing him or her to sexually transmitted diseases.

2. I wounded my partner physically by risking them, including our unborn child to disease.

3. I wounded my partner physically by causing their brain trauma.

4. I wounded my partner physically by...

    _____

    _____

    _____

5. I wounded my partner physically by...

    _____

    _____

    _____

6. I wounded my partner physically by...

    _____

    _____

    _____

7.   I wounded my partner physically by...

_____

_____

_____

8.   I wounded my partner physically by...

_____

_____

_____

9.   I wounded my partner physically by...

_____

_____

_____

10.   I wounded my partner physically by...

_____

_____

_____

Now, look at how you wounded your partner socially.

1.   I wounded my partner socially by making the BP doubt who in our community may have known about my deception.

2.   I wounded my partner socially by making them wonder if the women/men they saw in the grocery store may have been old acting out partners.

3.   I wounded my partner socially by possibly causing our friends to think less of my spouse for staying with me.

4.   I wounded my partner socially by...

_____

_____

_____

5.   I wounded my partner socially by...

_____

_____

_____

6.   I wounded my partner socially by...

_____

_____

_____

7.   I wounded my partner socially by...

_____

_____

_____

8.   I wounded my partner socially by...

_____

_____

_____

9.   I wounded my partner socially by...

_____

_____

_____

10.   I wounded my partner socially by...

_____

_____

_____

Now, it may be difficult for you to imagine how your sexual behavior wounded your partner intellectually. Adultery impacts the partner's brain, and it affects your partner's ability to reason, make decisions, speak, or problem-solve. Your partner is in a state of shock, and the brain is flooded with chemicals preventing your partner from thinking rationally. This ordeal has caused temporary brain dysfunction.

As you think about the impact of your choices, complete the following:

1.   I wounded my partner intellectually by causing days of sleeplessness.

2.   I wounded my partner intellectually by causing the BP to have impaired functioning at work.

3.   I wounded my partner intellectually by causing my spouse to take off several days from work.

4.   I wounded my partner intellectually by...

_____

_____

_____

5.   I wounded my partner intellectually by...

_____

_____

_____

6.   I wounded my partner intellectually by...

_____

_____

_____

7.   I wounded my partner intellectually by...

_____

_____

_____

8.   I wounded my partner intellectually by...

_____

_____

_____

9.   I wounded my partner intellectually by...

_____

_____

_____

10.   I wounded my partner intellectually by...

_____

_____

_____

Most partners report their spiritual lives have been compromised because of the betrayal. They now question their relationship with God and themselves. Put yourself in your partner's shoes and imagine how this might be true.

1.   I wounded my partner spiritually by causing him or her to question where God was when I was cheating.

2.   I wounded my partner spiritually by causing confusion as to why God did not get me to repent when my partner had been such a faith-filled believer.

3. I wounded my partner spiritually by wondering if trust can ever be established again.

4. I wounded my partner spiritually by...

    _____

    _____

    _____

5. I wounded my partner spiritually by...

    _____

    _____

    _____

6. I wounded my partner spiritually by...

    _____

    _____

    _____

7. I wounded my partner spiritually by...

    _____

    _____

    _____

8.   I wounded my partner spiritually by...

_____

_____

_____

9.   I wounded my partner spiritually by...

_____

_____

_____

10.   I wounded my partner spiritually by...

_____

_____

_____

You will need to work on yourself to increase your recovery while beginning to communicate and connect with what your partner needs. Your partner's brain is in a very traumatized state, and you will have to be very consistent. Your partner will not be able to trust you, yet it will instill a feeling of hope.

Note: The two of you can do this work in the privacy of your own home. but it can be helpful to have a professional to support you as you work through this process. You may decide that this would be a good exercise to present to your therapist so you can do the work together in a safe environment.

Now that you have established how you have wounded the BP, it is time to demonstrate how you can support your partner to experience increased safety and stabilization. Many partners express that they want to see signs of going "above and beyond" to put them first! This is why the willingness list is so important. It is a vehicle to show what you are willing to do to be open and transparent and begin to restore trust.

To the Partner: Is the BT willing to do WHATEVER it takes to make you feel safe? To increase awareness and empathy, I ask the betrayer to write down 20 things or ways to make you feel safe. The BT can get that list out and share it with you in a check-in.

It may look like:

- "I am willing to give you all my passcodes to my devices."

- "I am willing to quit my job so you no longer have to worry about the affair partner whom I see daily at the office."

- "I am willing to talk to your family so they can support you through the stress."

THE WILLINGNESS LIST—CREATING SAFETY

List 20 things you are willing to do to create safety. Write them out here.

1. I am willing to _____

2. I am willing to _____

3. I am willing to _____

4. I am willing to _____

5. I am willing to _____

6. I am willing to _____

7.   I am willing to _____

8.   I am willing to _____

9.   I am willing to _____

10.   I am willing to _____

11.   I am willing to _____

12.   I am willing to _____

13.   I am willing to _____

14.   I am willing to _____

15.   I am willing to _____

16.   I am willing to _____

17.   I am willing to _____

18.   I am willing to _____

19.   I am willing to _____

20.   I am willing to _____

Now, I would like you to read this list to the partner, but to do that, you must be in the proper position. You must sit facing each other with your knees touching each other. Look into their left eye as it increases laser focusing, which we will talk about in Chapter 12. Share your willingness list slowly so the BP can hear and process it. Read one statement at a time and watch for reactions. Give time to respond, as it may take the partner some time to process it. Be open to your partner critiquing your list. You may have said that you are willing to take polygraphs once a year, and the BP responds, "I will need two tests a year for my sense of safety." After the list has been critiqued, the BP is given the assignment to create additional things needed for safety.

To the Partner: You have three options.

1.   You can request the list, take some time to contemplate how you might add to it, and bring it back to the BT to share it.

2.   You can begin to dialogue and discuss what you need additionally in the here and now.

3.   Your third option is to share the assignment with your therapist and do it in the office so that the therapist can be a third set of eyes and ears and help guide you through this process. Sometimes, there are things that the BT is already doing that are no longer needed in your life.

Betrayers may say they are willing to do screenshots and pictures at the partner's request, and the betrayed spouse may say that this is no longer needed because the BP wants to start building trust without the safety prompts. I had a couple do this assignment, and Tom, the BT, had added that he planned to tell Harry's family everything about the infidelity. Harry thought long and hard about it and responded by saying that this was not needed because Harry wanted the family to stay non-judgmental, so there was no need to divulge the infidelity. Not only does this exercise show the betrayer's willingness to do the right things, but it also opens the dialogue for what partners need out of the relationship for healing.

Note to the Unfaithful: I forewarn you that if you commit to doing something on this list and do not follow through, it will feel like another betrayal. Spend time talking about an action plan if the list involves complicated situations like telling the kids, changing jobs, or moving to new cities. Again, you might want to use an ERCEM specialist who understands the nuances of these important and complicated issues.

If your list includes doing regular check-ins and you begin to get lax on follow-through, it will further deepen the wounds. Good relational recovery involves following through with your word. Your integrity is at stake here, and so is your partner's safety! Don't make promises you can't keep.

To the Betrayed Spouse: Sometimes your willingness requests will change. One of my clients told her husband, "You no longer need to do polygraph examinations because you have been in really good recovery, and I want to start trusting you without the accountability tools." Then, a year and a half later, she confided to me, "I need him to take a test because, as I was working with my support group, one woman felt it was good accountability for her husband to be obligated to take the test, and I keep ruminating on that point. I want him to know I will intermittently need this from him just to give him extra incentive to do the right thing." I assured her that it was always ok to change her mind and that, from time to time, her safety needs would change.

This exercise helps you both clarify what you need for safety. This allows the BT to show empathy and do whatever it takes to increase your safety. You are also expressing your vulnerability. You both are being very courageous.

Note: Brené Brown also says people must earn your vulnerability. The Willingness exercise is a way BT's can show you how important it is to earn your trust.

What things might you like the BT to add? Is it time to talk to your pastor together? Is it time to tell the kids?

WHEN SHOULD YOU INVOLVE THE KIDS?

Oftentimes, kids hear things in the background and come to their own conclusions. How much do you tell them? What do you tell them? I would ask you what the purpose or reason for sharing is. What do you hope to accomplish? Do you know what age-appropriate information might be shared? A good rule of thumb is to share the least amount possible so they don't take on your problems. If they ask questions, be sensitive to their need to put the puzzle together and yet send them a strong message that the details are for the adults to work out, that both of you are working on this, and that you will keep them posted on your progress in the relationship. *Infidelity is for the adults to deal with, and although kids can be curious, it can be problematic to overshare.*

Showing that you are willing to work on your own relational skills can increase connection and safety. The following script that Dorit Reichental created will also show both of you how to increase safety. Both of you should practice using it with each other.

SAFETY AND RELATIONSHIP EXERCISE FOR AWARENESS AND BOUNDARIES

In order to keep our relationship safe, when you say/do _____

_____,

it makes me feel _____.

The impact it has on me is _____,

and I will _____

until you can say/do _____,

and I can see that you understand the impact it has on me.

That will help me to feel _____,

(*loved, valued, respected, cared for*)

As a result of feeling truly seen and heard, you have given me the gift of restored trust and safety.

You do not have to follow the script exactly—the exercise may look like:

> *In order to make our relationship safe, I would like you to initiate Connection Share check-in's before 6 PM daily. This will remind me that you want me to feel "in the know" and the impact it will have on me is that I will feel closer to you.*
>
> *If you become complacent or don't prioritize initiating Connection-Shares, I will likely spend less time with you to keep myself safe.*
>
> *If you prioritize my needs for safety and connection, it will show me that I am your priority and this will help me to feel safe, connected and cared for.*
>
> *As a result of feeling truly seen and heard, you have given me the gift of restored trust and safety.*

To the Betrayed Spouse: Couples need to make each other feel safe. You, as the partner, may have experienced such turbulent and unstable behavior in reaction to infidelity that you may want to create your own willingness list to show your spouse what you are also willing to provide more safety! Trauma brain can result in erratic and volatile behavior, so you may also want to participate in your own safety and awareness contract.

Safety is of the utmost importance, and these exercises will help you see that the BT is looking at the pain that was caused and building the empathy muscle needed to build your safety quotient.

Chapter 10
The Brain Science of Triggers

As a betrayed partner, you are struggling with much right now. Not only are you reeling from the realization that the BT was not who you thought they were, but you are now struggling with the fallout from sexual betrayal The BT never meant to traumatize you but did, and now your mind and body are on full alert. You are waiting for signs that you are not safe when you are also looking for signs that you are.

This book is going to help you both find ways of coping with this tragedy and grow stronger from it. You are both going to learn to lear into the trauma when your triggers are activated.

Triggers are the byproduct of trauma. They can feel frightening and uncontrollable, but they are there to help you stay safe. It used to be that when a BP was triggered, it left a feeling of isolation. ERCEM suggests when you are triggered, you should work on defusing the trigger together. This means that BT needs to be astute at noticing when you are triggered so that the BT can sit with you as the trigger passes.

To the Betrayed Partner: When you are triggered, you need to be able to tell the BT when you are in that triggered state. In most cases, when a couple experiences the trigger together, it decreases the intensity of the trigger. It is totally your choice whether to include the BT, but why should you have to deal with it alone?

Many people will complain that they do not understand their triggers. They realize that some of the triggers are linked to specific dates like their marital anniversary, the date of discovery, a love song that was "their song" but no longer has the same meaning, a hotel where the betrayal happened, or the make and model of the car the affair partner owned. These triggers can be identified and understood. They have been consciously linked, and you can make sense of them. Yet, some triggers are locked in the unconscious part of the brain. They are stored there for safekeeping. There is no recollection of what they are or why they are stored in the brain. These triggers haunt you because you never know when one will occur or why you are having one. You feel hijacked by them!

ALLY & MAX: *TRIGGERS CAN LOOK LIKE THEY HAVE DERAILED THE RELATIONSHIP...BUT THEY HAVEN'T*

Ally and Max had been working through the pain that Max's affair had caused in their relationship. They credited the empathy that Max had learned through the ERCEM model. They had been doing really well in early recovery couples work, and Ally had finally achieved a sense of safety in the relationship. Max was working good recovery and had made it his job to put Ally first. He continued to remind her that he was so thankful that she had given him another chance and that he would never forget the wounding he had caused. He nudged her when it was time to do check-ins and did them faithfully, even when she was tired from a long, hard day of teaching. He would gently ask if he could check in with her so that she would stay "in the know" and that she could listen to his check-in while he rubbed her feet. Even though this exercise is done knees-to-knees (pages 205-215), I secretly smiled as I heard that Max was attending to both her needs for safety and safe physical touch.

That night, they both felt a real closeness to each other, and Ally shared that she could tell that she was healing. She told Max that she appreciated his hard work and his trying to do the next right thing even when he felt exhausted, too. She knew that he had changed his life and his values, and she felt secure in their progress. She proudly acknowledged that she was feeling that she was partially in post-traumatic growth. As Max spooned Ally that night, he thanked God for their progress and her recovery.

They got up the next morning, had breakfast together and went over their day. Ally reminded Max that she was accompanying her class to a children's museum, so she might be home a little late. Max told Ally that he had a few errands to run, but he would wait for her to do their "before dinner run." That morning seemed so normal, so Ally was surprised to be caught off guard by a trigger that totally took her breath away. As she accompanied her students to the museum on the bus, she saw out of the corner of her eye the hotel where her husband had taken his affair partner. She immediately felt her body get hot all over, she felt nauseous, and her gut began to spasm as if she was going to lose control of her bowels or throw up or possibly both. She wondered if she could navigate herself to the bus driver and ask him to pull over at the next gas station. She felt scared and humiliated. She felt so angry at Max, who had put her in a compromised physical condition. How could he have cheated on her for almost two years? How could he have broken their marital vows? How could he have lied to her in full deception?

Somehow, she was able to get up to the front of the bus, and she asked one of the students to trade her seat as the bus driver drove to the closest gas station. She got off the bus and hurriedly got to the bathroom in time to vomit without anyone noticing. She cleaned herself up, looked at herself in the mirror, and wanted to cry, but she forced herself to shut down her tears because she had 80 kids and two teachers waiting for her to return. As she got back on the bus, she felt the familiarity of demonstrating that she was just fine when in reality, it felt like she had just been hit by a two-ton truck.

The rest of the day was a blur, but she managed to get through it. When she got home, she curled up on the couch and said to herself, "Nothing in my life is better. I am never going to feel better. I hate my life, and I hate what Max did to me, to us. I am not sure I can survive." When Max returned, he could see that Ally was noticeably distant and distressed. He tried to engage her, but she was almost non-responsive. He sat on the couch with her and asked her how her day had gone. They had had such a good evening the night before that he assumed her angst was about one of the kids at school. He pleaded, "Please tell me about your day. I can see that you are not okay, and I want to be there for you when you have rough days at school." She was shell-shocked. *School*, she thought, *I wish this was about school.* But she said nothing other than, "I am going to take a nap." He started to rub her feet, and she looked at him and said, "Don't touch me!" And then she pretended to fall asleep.

Max felt so confused. Her reactions signaled that Ally was really mad at him. But what did he do? He went through their previous night and their morning, and Ally seemed so content. Now, she looked totally wiped out, and he wondered what had happened. He remembered that in our session, we talked about the mood swings that could occur because of flooding. He remembered that I had told him, "Always lean into the pain...not away. Don't ignore what you see. Describe it, and ask Ally if you are the source of the pain."

He thought to himself, *But it can't be me...I didn't do anything.*

When she got up from her nap, he moved toward her and said, "I don't know what happened today, but I can see how angry and hurt you are and am wondering if I am the source of your pain." She looked at him with contempt, nodded, and said, "I don't know if I can live with this pain." He wanted to get defensive and tell her he had not done anything, but instead, he said, "I don't know what happened today, but I am so sorry I have caused you this pain. I love you. I don't want to pressure you, but I do want to know what happened so I can comfort you if you let me."

She realized that the triggers felt so great she wondered if she could even stand to look at him. She doubted if he was really capable of change. As she looked at him, shaking her head, she remembered back to one of our sessions where I had told her that she might not be able to stop the triggers from occurring, but she did not have to be held hostage to them. I had asked her to practice assessing not what the past was saying to her but what was happening in current time.

Triggers are about being tethered to the past, and yet she can untether by staying in the moment and asking herself what is happening to me in current time. Even though the pain feels so real and overwhelming, I asked her to use the model that Byron Katie teaches in her revolutionary book, *Loving What Is.* In that book, Byron instructs her followers to ask four questions to seek clarity and reinforce their ability to stay in the moment. Staying in the moment keeps you from living in the past and is a clear conduit to observing the realities of living in the here and now.

THE WORKS BY BYRON KATIE

The Works asks for basic questions that people who have been betrayed can use to assess safety. The four questions are:

1. Is it true?

2. Can I absolutely know that it's true?

3. How do you react—what happens—when you believe that thought?

4. Who would you be without that thought?

Now, let's look at how Ally decided to work herself out of her triggers and fear and come back to the reality of how she had been living before she was so horribly triggered.

Q1. Is it true? She answered that her distress and reactivity were absolutely true to Max's acting out. And her fear that she might not be able to live this way was also true. However, when she thought about the many months that Max had been a different man and worked so hard on being a man of integrity, she realized this was also true.

Q2. Can I absolutely know that it is true? This question encouraged her to look at reality as opposed to her fears. As she redirected to his hard work and thought about how faithful he had been, she could begin to feel her parasympathetic nervous system settle, and she began to feel a little less triggered and angry. She then evaluated that she, too, had done good work and that she could choose where to place her energy.

Q3. How do you react—what happens—when you believe that thought? When she believed the thought that she had noticed a real change in her husband and how hard he was working on building the relational skills of empathy, honesty, and authenticity, she began to feel hope come into her body like oxygen, and she could breathe again. It felt right to want to have faith in the relationship they were actively building. She realized the trigger was about the past, and the hope was in his progress and his focus. Instead, it readjusted her confidence in her husband but, more importantly, in herself. It reminded her of the months that she had spent seeing his progress, and it touched that place inside of her where she felt she was getting a better version of her husband than she had had pre-discovery of the affair. And then she thought, "I deserve that!"

Q4. What would you feel without the thought? It WAS scary to return to the future and leave those terrifying triggers behind, but she knew without the weight of the PAST triggers, she might have the relationship she was working so hard toward rekindling.

When we change the way we look at things, the things around us change, and since Max had been doing such good work, **she gave him the gift of grace.** But she needed the tools to manage the triggers, and she had rejected his many attempts to lean into them with her. Infidelity causes a lot of fear and anxiety, but the more tools the BP must use together and apart, the healthier she will be.

Byron Katie explains, "The Work is a Practice. Every time you do The Work you are becoming enlightened to who and what you are—the true nature of being." It is a method of inquiry born directly out of her own suffering, and she has been teaching for three decades a way to liberate you from your fears. This practice allows you to access the wisdom within you.

In *Help. Her. Heal.*, my book on compulsive sexual behavior, I wrote about a woman who could no longer tolerate going to her favorite restaurant, and she did not know why. She would go with friends, feel claustrophobic, and would need to leave. She felt like she was going crazy. One morning, as she was slowly waking up, her memory moved from unconscious to conscious, and she realized that she had learned of her husband's acting out with prostitutes in their yellow kitchen. That yellow was triggering to her, and her favorite restaurant had colorful, bright yellow walls. As she was waking up, she made the needed association as to why she felt so uncomfortable there. She had no previous understanding of the association, but her body had kept score and was telling her to beware of this yellow building because it could hurt her like the other yellow room had.

Sounds crazy? Well, that is trauma. When BP's make a choice to go back to staying in the moment, they empower themselves not only not to be held hostage by the trigger but also to choose self-compassion as their antidote to the old pain!

To the Partner: As frightening as it can feel, I want you to know that triggers are your mind and body trying to keep you safe. When you experience an unknown trigger, you can take pause and look for an identifier, and if nothing comes up, you can silently remind yourself that nothing bad is happening in the here and now. Some even thank their triggers for being so protective.

To the Couple: Here is how you can work on trigger-busting together.

When the partner is triggered, it is easy to become activated. Often, the betrayer can see that something is wrong, but the BT is unsure about the origin.

THE BRAIN SCIENCE OF TRIGGERS

When the BP is triggered, the left part of the brain goes offline while the right brain takes over. The BP is flooded with emotions and feels a sense of being out of control. Although a BP can work on regulating the trigger, it can be more effective if the spouse guides the BP back into the "Window of Tolerance" to decrease the helplessness and confusion felt by the triggers.

To the Betrayer: You can assist the BP in feeling safe when the trigger is experienced, but you must be patient and present as the triggers are processed. When you acknowledge that the BP is triggered, you show that you recognize the pain of the trigger.

To the BT: In this chapter, you will learn how to help co-regulate triggers. When you notice the BP is unexpectedly different, you will want to ask if they are triggered. This seems like an obvious assumption, but many betrayers avoid asking questions because they fear it would make things worse. They sense that something is wrong because the BP has gotten markedly angrier or has withdrawn for no apparent reason, and it is a typical reaction for the BT to leave the room to give the BP space, not realizing how alone and frightened the BP feels. They do not know they can help by sitting through the trigger and helping the BP co-regulate until the trigger has subsided.

Trigger-busting is a process you will both need to learn to work through together.

To the Partner: I am sure you have noticed that the BT is working hard to help you heal. It can take a lot of emotional maturity to sit with you when it is obvious that you are visibly in pain, and the BT knows that past behaviors have caused it. When you notice the BT is staying present and watching your pain, you might remind yourself that you see the change that is being made and the effort the BT is making to help you heal. When you appreciate the effort, it can defuse the trigger that has occurred involuntarily.

You may feel indignant that I would even suggest that you appreciate your spouse for helping you through the very event that the BT is responsible for having created. Yet your trigger is holding you hostage to the past, and if you want to break the effects of your triggers, you must stop hating your spouse for being the cause of these triggers, just like Ally did. This will release you from the current-day trauma and cause you to feel more at peace with what is occurring for you in the moment.

To the BT: Having worked with thousands of partners, it has become apparent that all a spouse wants to do is feel safe again. Whether your partner felt they had a good marriage or knew that the relationship had problems, your partner had no idea you were living a dual life that entailed lies, deception, and secrecy. As a result, this trauma has deeply affected the brain and sent it into overdrive.

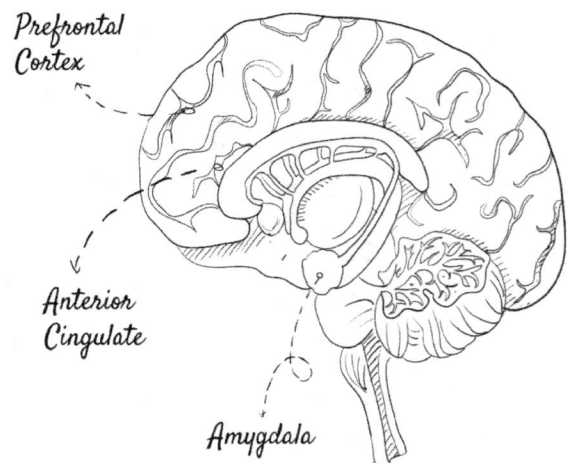

Prefrontal Cortex

Anterior Cingulate

Amygdala

This information has impacted the amygdala, which exists at the bottom of the brain above the brainstem. This part of the brain stores and processes information, and its main function is to keep your spouse safe. Therefore, it guides your partner to react to the pain, anxiety, and anger by going into fight, flight, or freeze mode. If the protective mechanism moves toward fight, your partner will go into "attack mode" and say mean and hurtful things. The BP may become physically aggressive—pushing, shoving, and hitting you as the emotions feel more and more intense. Many partners tell me they are reacting to their emotions in ways they could never have conceived. They wonder if they are going crazy because they have never resorted to name-calling or aggressive behavior in the past.

To the Partner: Have you felt like you were going crazy? Has your normal functioning been compromised? Are you having trouble remembering words, dates, and simple tasks that have real impact on your daily functioning? Are you experiencing emotional highs and lows that seem insurmountable? Are you having trouble with impulse control and wanting to yell or cry all the

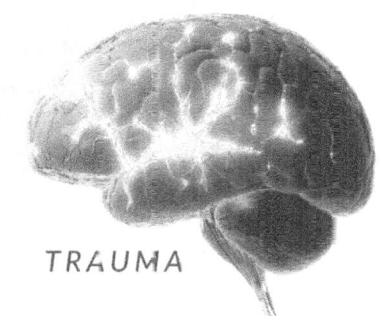

TRAUMA

time because of something they have done or not done? Your brain is being hijacked by trauma. Unfortunately, you are experiencing a trauma reaction that can feel uncontrollable. It will be necessary for you to calm down your brain and work on lots of grounding and resourcing to bring some safety and sanity back into your life. I will show you how to manage the triggers you are facing because of partner betrayal.

To the BT: It can feel scary when you notice your partner is triggered. One minute, they may be fine, and then BAM, they appear to be struggling with thoughts and feelings that have overcome them. Neither of you necessarily knows why they've shown up.

It is important that you understand what happens when partners are triggered so that you can empathize and spend time using empathy exercises or trigger-busters to help ground them. You will be learning about empathy in the next chapter, so for right now, let's focus on how to deal with the triggers.

TYPES OF TRIGGERS

Triggers may have origins you both can trace.

1.   You came home and told your partner you were overcome by shame as you saw another adult bookstore going into the strip mall. You questioned what impact this would have since you both travel this busy highway every week.

2.   You may have taken your daughter to an ice cream social at school together, only to run into an affair partner from the past.

3.   You both drove by a hotel or massage parlor where you acted out. You try to distract your partner, but you easily see the affected, compromised emotional state and feel really bad.

Triggers can occur anytime and are everywhere, and your partner's brain goes into immediate overdrive. There may be an awareness of the anniversary date of the first discovery. In other words, there may be an actual connection to a person, place, or thing that triggers your spouse. There may be sensory triggers. Your partner sees a billboard on the highway that advertises a hotel where you have acted out, and their brain goes directly to the past. It may be auditory, and the trigger is the ding of a text on your iPad because a text from the affair partner was the origin of discovery. It might be olfactory, and the trigger is the smell of the Italian meal that was being prepared for you when the phone call occurred from the affair partner. Those types of triggers, once identified, can help you both decide how you are going to manage them.

Since the betrayal, it is your responsibility to let your partner know if a trigger is coming up—that way, you can pre-plan how you can deal with the potential trigger together.

However, sometimes, the triggers are not associated with anything conscious. Triggers may occur without any direct link to a situation that is associated with your acting out. What we know about trauma is that there can be associations that are unconscious. Many times, as I mentioned, triggers are associated with the five senses, but unfortunately, they can be stored unconsciously, too. Just like the woman who was triggered by the color yellow, the partner may be triggered for no known reason, which is all the more reason for you to realize a shift in your partner's behavior and ask, "Has something triggered you, or does it seems like you are triggered?"

Partners may not tell you when they experience triggers, but they seem angry, cold, or distant. And you can tell that something is off, but you do not know why. Can you imagine how scary that would be not knowing why your brain has gone offline? One minute, your partner is going through a normal day, and then instantly, and for no apparent reason, the BP is thrown back into post-traumatic stress and must navigate through the fear, panic, and fright that accompanies the association.

To the Partner: As you experience the trauma, it may feel unsafe to share what is going on with your mind and body, but I plead with you to be more vulnerable and help the BT know what is going on inside of you. I want the BT to learn how to help you, and it works better if you share your thoughts in present time. I know that you have been hurt beyond belief, but you two are working on rebuilding your relationship. The BT needs your guidance to get better at empathizing with your trauma responses and pain.

Christina Bell has a wonderful chart that helps you both understand what happens as you are being triggered. Please go to sexhelpwithcarolthecoach.com/resources and print it out so you can add to it and begin the discussion of what happens when you are triggered.

I would also recommend that you visit her site at ChristinaBell.net to access her tools for working through triggers. She has a lot of great free tools to help you heal! As Christina Bell exemplifies on the diagram below, it is important to deal with the triggers as a team, and when you assist your partner in working through the triggers, you are building trust. You will need to provide comfort and reassurance to your spouse.

One of the men that I worked with in a Help.Her.Heal group took her chart and made it couples-friendly...Now, that is a man in empathy!

Managing Triggers of Betrayal

1. Trigger
* Partner Inconsistency
* Ambiguous Situation
* Broken Promise
*Media/Outside Influence

2. Alarm/Bomb Goes Off
(Betrayed Spouse)
* Physiological Flooding
* Preoccupation

Fight
* Physiological Flooding
* Preoccupation

Flight
* Avoidance
* "Stuffing" Concerns

3. Betraying Partner is Overwhelmed by Intensity/Reaction

Defends / Minimizes

Shuts Down/ Avoids

4. Escalation of Conflict
(Partner Hurt)

5. Over Time, the Couple Avoids Talking about Issues in Order to Avoid Conflict

* Greater Distance
* Resentments Can Fuel Acting Out

Background Factors
(Ever Present)
* Past Betrayals
* Past Trauma
* Current Stressors

Betrayed Partner Tasks
1. Self-care
2. Emotional Regulation
3. Expressing Needs Moderately

Betraying Partner Tasks
1. Provide Comfort and Reassurance to Spouse
2. Work on Reliability and Thoughtfullness
3. Initiate Repair Attempts
4. Volunteer Information about Thoughts and Feelings

Remember

Triggers are a natural part of recovery.
Managing triggers as a team provides
an opportunity to build trust

MANAGING TRIGGERS OF *BETRAYAL*
(for couples)

1. TRIGGER

- Partner Inconsistency
- Ambiguous Situation
- Broken Promise
- Media / Outside Influence

2. TRAUMA RESPONSE

- Flooded emotions
- Emotions overcome logic
- *Fight, flight, or freeze*
- Partner is outside their window of distress tolerance due to their trauma

3A. BETRAYING PARTNER IS OVERWHELMED

- Shame paralyzes the Betraying Partner (BP)
- BP may deflect w/ anger
- BP may blame partner for the betrayal

3B. OPPORTUNITY FOR HEALING

- BP practices *Reflective and Focused Listening*
- BP employs *The AVR Formula* ©
- BP utilizes *Relational CPR*

4. ESCALATION OF CONFLICT

- Partner is re-traumatized
- Communication breaks down
- Attachment wounds activate for both parties

5. AVOIDANCE & DISCONNECTION

- Couple avoids talking to avoid conflict
- Distance between the coupleship grows
- Resentments may fuel the BP's desire to act out

PARTNER TASKS:

1. Self-care
2. Emotion Regulation/ Distress Tolerance
3. Expressing Needs Moderately

BACKGROUND FACTORS:
Past Betrayals
Past Trauma, Current Stressors

BETRAYING PARTNER TASKS:

1. Provide Comfort and Reassurance to Spouse
2. Work on Reliability and Thoughtfulness
3. Initiate Repair Attempts
4. Volunteer Info About Thoughts/Feelings

REMINDER:
Triggers are a natural part of the recovery & healing process.
Managing triggers together as a couple facilitates rebuilding trust.

So, as your partner heals, it will be important for you to be patient as you watch the frustration, sadness, and anxiety that accompany the triggers. The BP will remind you that your infidelity has been a living "hell." A BT who is not in good recovery will either lash out or go into isolation to avoid feeling the shame that normally accompanies a partner's anger or fear. Of course, the first step is to have good recovery so your partner can begin to trust that you have changed. Then you need reliability—reliability in all you do!

- Therefore, you must be predictable and put your partner first.

- You must be reliable by letting the BP know when you are leaving and coming home. You will need to follow through with promises and commitments.

- You can help by taking over the household duties and kids. You will need to step up and provide a true team approach to your family.

When your partner experiences a trigger, you will need to acknowledge exactly what you are noticing in the here and now. Christina and I believe it is helpful to provide repair attempts, which John Gottman defined as partner requests. In his book, *The Seven Principles for Making Marriage Work*, Gottman defines a repair attempt as any statement or action—verbal, physical, or otherwise—meant to diffuse negativity and keep a conflict from escalating out of control. **Dr. Gottman calls repair attempts the secret weapon of emotionally intelligent couples.**

When an infraction has occurred, it is helpful to ask your spouse, "What can I do for you right now?" or "What do you need?" That might be more space or perhaps more physical comfort. Maybe your partner needs you to go through the trigger together and then find a way to reconnect. Unfortunately, many therapists do not know how to help you both through your feelings of inadequacy, insecurity, and fearfulness. It sets the partner up to wonder when the next one will come, and the cycle becomes auto-exacerbating.

You are likely to go into shame and want to do nothing, but this is the time to move into the process of trigger-busting so you can assist the BP in getting through it. I am going to share a trigger-busters activity sheet that will help you with this process. It takes lots of practice and patience for both you and your partner.

Remember to stay patient and gentle; when your partner experiences triggers, the BP is in full-blown trauma and needs to feel reassured that you can work through them together.

If you are acting out or are in middle-circle behavior, you should not practice trigger busting. Trigger busting, as a team, requires that your recovery is strong and that you are not hiding anything from your partner.

My colleagues Dorit Reichental and Janice Caudill have produced a Trigger-Busters Protocol, which can help you and your partner work through the triggers together.

They have broken it down into four stages:

1. First, calm yourself so that your voice, tone, and demeanor are comforting and soothing. Then, identify what you believe you are noticing with your partner in the here and now. You next ask, "Are you triggered?" and validate what you are seeing, which in most cases is the trigger. You can say, "It makes sense to me that you would be triggered," or if you are confused about the trigger, simply "I can see that you are triggered."

2. Help the BP stay grounded in the here and now by orienting to the present. Remind your partner that nothing bad is happening now.

3. De-escalate the experience by saying something nurturing and safe. "I am not doing anything now that would put you in harm's

way. This is a bad trigger, and I imagine it is reminding you of my past acting out. I am not acting out now. You are safe, and I am right here with you." If your spouse is open to comforting touch, place your hand on her back.

4. Once the trigger is defused, your partner will be able to anchor onto your regulated nervous system and come fully into the present moment to re-engage and reconnect with you. We call this co-regulation. You have gone through the trigger-busters cycle together!

On the following page is Reichental and Caudill's "cheat sheet" for what they call "Relational CPR for Sexual Addiction and Triggers."

TRIGGER-BUSTERS: RELATIONAL CPR

FOUR STEPS TO SAFETY AND CO-REGULATION

Trigger Activation—

Partner: Left brain goes offline; right brain takes over as the BP becomes triggered. The BT must actively help the partner calm the nervous system.

STEP 1: IDENTITY THE TRIGGER

- Clarification: Clarify if spouse is triggered.

    ○ "I can see X, Y, Z. Are you triggered?"

- Accountability: DO NOT defend, blame, shame, minimize, invalidate, judge, criticize, debate, stonewall, correct with irrelevant detail, withdraw, escape, or project anger.

Reichental and Caudill's *Relational CPR for Sexual Addiction and Triggers*, adapted with permission.

- Validation: As soon as betrayer realizes partner is triggered, s/he validates partner.

    ○ "I can see how scared and unsafe you are. It must remind you of…It makes sense to me that you feel triggered, scared, angry, unsafe, etc."

STEP 2: ORIENT TO HERE AND NOW

- The BT gently reminds the partner that s/he is safe and nothing bad is happening right now (triggered partner cannot differentiate between past and present).

- "I am not doing anything now to put you at risk or in danger; it's a bad trigger as a result of something that happened when I was acting out."

- "I am not acting out now. You are safe, and I am right here with you."

STEP 3: DE-ESCALATION, SAFETY, & STABILIZATION USING TRIGGER-BUSTERS

- What does the nurturing/protective BT need to continue saying and doing to help the partner down-regulate? The BT may need to reassure and repeat the message multiple times.

- As the hijacked brain comes back online, the BT empathically attunes to the partner and states:

- "I can see this was a really bad trigger. You are safe right now I am right here with you."

STEP 4: SOCIAL ENGAGEMENT

- Notice the somatic signs that the trigger is being defused. For example, partner's eyes, voice, and face soften as the body begins to relax and breathing regulates. Now, the two of you can have a real conversation. In fact, the partner may even want to connect with you.

To the Couple: You can both defuse the intensity and frequency of triggers if you work together to identify them, decide what safety precautions need to occur, and work together as a team to manage them.

To the Betrayer: It is so important for you to be proactive, inquire about what you are noticing, and validate what you are seeing. Sitting with the BP and going through the trigger with the BP is an act of empathy. When you put your guilt and shame away and show up for your partner during the trigger, it is a reminder that you know that your past actions are responsible for the pain and that you are willing to do what it takes to help your partner heal!

Chapter 11

Couples Need a New Model to Help Them Heal from Sexual Betrayal:

Empathy to the rescue!

In working with those who suffered from infidelity, I noticed that they knew they lacked the skills to make things better. More importantly, they were traumatized by the trauma caused by their partner, which further complicated their inability to know what to do to help them. They reacted in ineffective ways to their partner's devastated state. They were floundering in a relational pool of trauma.

In the beginning, I discovered that they really needed a professional to coach them through the relational tsunami occurring at home. Betrayers reported that the skills were helping, but they wished I could be a guide on their shoulder, assisting them with the next relational piece. That is when I started bringing in partners to talk about what they were learning and practicing. We turned the BT's individual sessions into couple's work and practiced the work in the office. Partners showed me what they needed and wanted for safety, and I customized the assignments for them. The BT experienced much more success, and the partner felt much more safety. I knew that this field needed a new movement that would help couples rebound from this terrible ordeal. That is when ERCEM was born, and I developed the Early Recovery Couples Empathy Model to help professionals work differently with couples who were experiencing sexual betrayal. The major component was finding empathy tools to incorporate into the work and help both of them heal simultaneously.

WHAT IS EMPATHY?

In Brené Brown's video on empathy, she cites Theresa Wiseman, a nursing scholar, who researched empathy and found that people who practiced it exhibited four characteristics that helped them practice empathy. These qualities are:

1. *Perspective Taking*: People with empathy want to know what other people think.

2. ***Identifying Emotional Awareness of the Other Person:*** They are better able to sense emotions and convey curiosity and insight about them.

3. ***Communicating the Feelings of Others***: They can articulate what others are experiencing, helping to validate emotions and create understanding.

4. ***Staying Out of Judgment:*** This means avoiding judging others or jumping to conclusions.

To see a great three-minute of Brené Brown's video on empathy, go to: https://brenebrown.com/videos/rsa-short-empathy

This video is three minutes long and does a great job of describing empathy, so I recommend watching it. When infidelity has occurred, empathy is the ability to show that you, who did the betraying, can see and feel the pain that you have caused your partner.

To the Couple: Know that the betrayer's heart is aching because the infidelity has caused the BT to do despicable things. Betrayers question whether they will ever be forgiven, and they fully understand if they are not. They ruminate about what they have done to you, and they question their own sense of sanity. They never meant for it to get this bad, and **they hate themselves for the pain it has caused you** and the family.

They want to show you empathy, but they are afraid to be close because *they believe they do not deserve your forgiveness.* This makes the process of empathy more difficult because empathy naturally opens the door to connection and closeness. They are fearful of the reaction they will get from you. Often, betrayers will say, I want to show my partner empathy, but my partner doesn't trust it. Why should the BP after all I have done? I fear that trust will never return.

To the Partner: After discovery, you are more than likely coexisting to buy some time in deciding what you are both going to do. It will be necessary for betrayers to work diligently on their empathy skills so they can assure you they not only want connection but know they must act to restore your sense of safety.

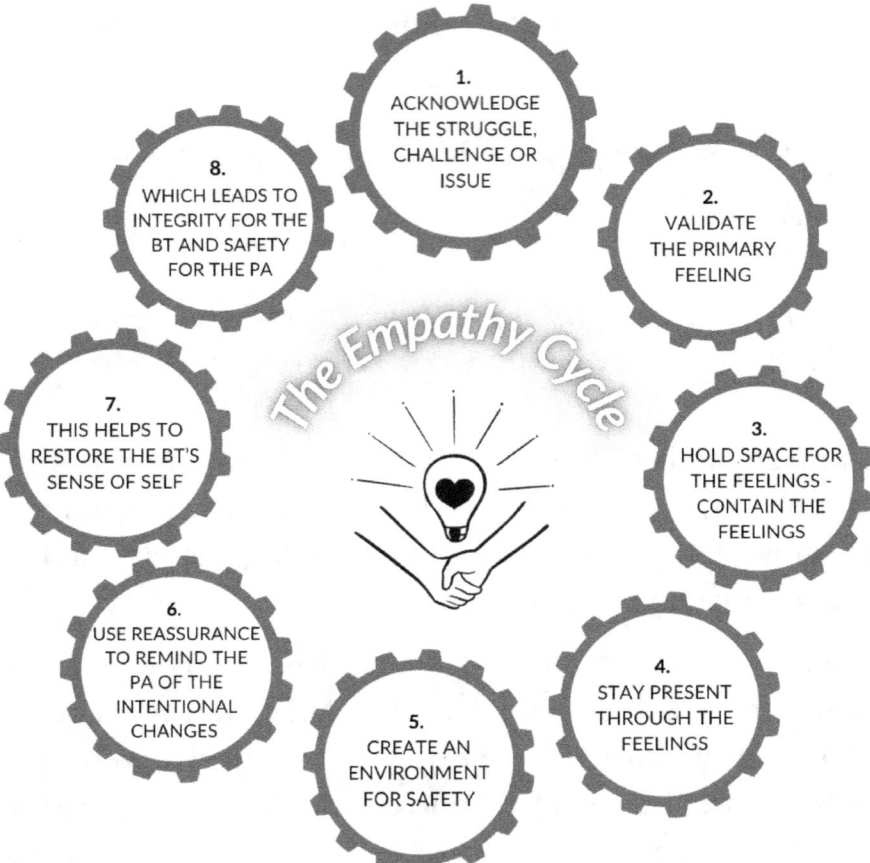

To the BT: Learning the new skill of empathy would be easier to practice if your partner believed you and accepted it easily, but you need to learn the skill of building connection so your mate can begin to trust you again. It is a natural process that will be rejected initially because there is no trust that you are seeing things from the partner's perspective.

I understand that learning this new skill would be reinforced if your partner believed and encouraged you, but you must gain the skills to show the BP you are no longer that dual personality that fed your own needs by sacrificing theirs. You will run into the roadblock of defensiveness on the part of your partner because they are afraid to let their guard down and let you back into their life. Their trauma response is initially involuntary and requires you to continue to address the pain by seeing it through your partner's eyes.

Empathy is a skill you need regardless of whether this relationship survives infidelity. Part of your job is now to make a living amends by showing you are going to be a person of integrity and the person your partner deserves and desires. "Living amends" is a term that originated out of the recovery world. It is the commitment to keep working on those qualities that make you a better person. The betrayer is always looking for ways to heal the relationship and prove their commitment to be trustworthy. Living amends cannot occur unless empathy is at the heart of it.

Developing empathy shows you are in sync with how the other person feels, what they believe, and what they need. This is counter to your old unfaithful cycle, and it will be rejected because the partner fears it is not real. They must protect themselves until you practice empathy long enough that they get comfortable with it and the new person you have become. When that occurs, the empathy cycle will come full circle because then you will feel good about yourself, which will restore your integrity.

HOLD YOURSELF ACCOUNTABLE

Some betrayers will report that they had marital problems before they started acting out and will say, "We didn't communicate prior to my confession or discovery, and we really aren't communicating now that the BP knows about the betrayal." Empathy can be used in those situations, too. Empathy is a form of communication that shows your partner that you heard what was said and that you are noticing the collateral damage. You want to support your partner by being accountable for the pain you caused.

Your infidelity has created a lot of guilt and shame. When you feel your partner starts to reject, criticize, or mistrust you, you may want to revert to the old style of communication where you get defensive, want to check out, give up, or fight back. When you make the conscious choice to use empathy, it can defuse the angry feelings and your protective stance.

Therapists know that problems in a relationship are never the result of "just one person," and yet it is extremely important you remember that ANY problems that you had in your relationship are now secondary to the damage that was caused because of you sexually acting out. You must take full responsibility for the betrayal and consistently show empathy before you can attend to the other normal marital issues that were there prior to the discovery.

Remember, you never want to send the message that your previous problems prior to discovery caused your acting out. Previous problems were the justifications and rationalizations that you used for your being unfaithful. In other words, you will not be able to get to the inherent problems in your relationship until you "right the wrongs" regarding your unfaithful behaviors. This process requires that you show up and develop the skills to right those wrongs, rebuild the trust, reassure them you are new and improved, and consequently take your relationship to the next level.

Can you imagine how incredible the relationship would have been if you had learned empathy, healthier communication, and true connection? Can you envision what it will be like to build a sacred space to give and receive the love you always wanted? I have seen couples achieve this and have the relationship they have always wanted, but they must learn the skills for connection and trust. It is up to you to practice healthy relational skills that will begin the process of a living amends. Empathy is the muscle in that living amends.

Empathy will look like two different things depending on whether you are the unfaithful partner or the betrayed. It will be difficult for you both to be empathetic for a variety of reasons. As the BT, it will mean that you must make a specialized effort to see the world through the eyes of your partner. This requires asking yourself at all times, "How does my partner feel?" I teasingly tell my clients that it is symbolic of the rubber bracelets that Christians wore which said, "What would Jesus do?" This bracelet was a reminder to always act like Jesus. Well, it wouldn't hurt to wear something on your wrist to reinforce the need for constant empathy. I have had couples go out and buy bracelets to remind them to consistently work on imagining how their partner is feeling and what they need or what their spouse would need to feel safe.

Empathy might look like:

- "I have noticed a trigger and need to ask if you are triggered so I can use trigger-busters with you."

- "I know that the anniversary of D-day (Discovery) is Friday, and I need to let you know I recognize that day is coming up. I know it is going to be a hard day for both of us, and I am wondering if there is anything I can do to make it easier for you?"

- Out of the blue, you say, "I just want you to know that it must be hard for you to drive past 'his' (affair partner's) house, and I am absolutely willing to do anything, including moving if that is what you think we need to do to make you feel safe."

- When you create this type of mind state, you are working the relational side of the brain that brings forth understanding, compassion, and responsiveness. It feels good to put the BP's needs first and grow your heart relationally. The secondary gain to this is that it makes you feel better about the person you are becoming, and that increases your self-esteem. You feel good about yourself, perhaps for the first time in your life.

I want to give you hope that this is the person you can be! I want to give your partner that same hope, but that requires you to work empathy with vengeance. Your vengeance is against the unfaithfulness that robbed you of so many things. We know you had no idea about how medicating yourself with another person or pornography would become so compulsive and result in losing everything that ever had meaning to you—your partner, your family, your self-esteem.

Do you believe that you ever had empathy? After working in sexual integrity for many years, I have often wondered if your unfaithfulness robbed you of your ability to empathize. Or did you lack empathy from the beginning but somehow still functioned and provided for your family? Did this lack of empathy feed into your need to self-medicate with sexual acting out?

DID THE INFIDELITY ROB YOU OF YOUR EMPATHY?

For the Betrayer: When you are out of integrity, you must ignore what your infidelity is doing to you and your partner so you can remain unfaithful and live a dual life. You learned to compartmentalize so you could act out your sexual fantasies in total deception and then close that box or compartment to come home to them at night and maintain your old routine filled with love, family commitment, and routines. It also kept you from truly loving yourself because you were holding such a shameful secret. Secrecy feeds the shame that chips away at your self-esteem. When your self-esteem is compromised, so are your relationships. You cannot give what you do not have!

We know that your unfaithfulness interferes in empathy because you could never have participated in incomprehensible behaviors if you had it. Your inner demon stole your ability to put yourself in their shoes because then you would have had to confess and get the help you needed. You were not stronger than your desires. Your focus was to maintain your secret and your acting out. Then discovery occurred, and all hell broke loose!

Now that the secret is out, you have the freedom to commit to empathy. It is imperative to see it from their perspective. You want to put yourself in your partner's shoes to the best of your ability and keep reminding the BP that your compulsive behaviors were at the root of the excruciating pain. In a normal empathetic exchange, a person describes what they believe the other person must be feeling. However, your situation is different because, in many cases, your actions caused betrayal injury, and you can only "imagine" how that could feel. You see it and are witnessing the struggle, and it is causing you great pain to watch it. You are very much aware of the pain, but you cannot know the devastation your partner feels from it. That is the BP's pain to bear alone.

This book is going to teach you the concept and skills of empathy. **This will require that you try to understand your partner's feelings and validate that you know you caused this pain.** This model teaches you to meet the BP where they are. If your partner is unbelievably angry, you will need to acknowledge the anger and convey that you know you caused that pain. It will show that you can hold the BP's pain. When you are in good sexual integrity recovery, you can be the container for the pain to keep from immersing yourself in the shame. This lets the partner know that their choice to share feelings is welcomed in the relationship. This is a huge undertaking and typically requires the assistance of an ERCEM specialist who can help you navigate through your partner's feelings. You have traumatized the BP, and now you must prove that you can meet the emotional needs, perhaps even for the first time in your partnership.

These points are so important that I would like to highlight them again.

1. This book is going to teach you the concept and skills of empathy.

2. This will require that you work on understanding their feelings and validate them.

3. You will need to show your partner you know you caused this pain.

4. When you use this model, it will teach you to meet them where they are and accept all their feelings.

5. Together, we will demonstrate to the BP that you can hold the pain.

6. This lets your partner know that their feelings are welcomed in the relationship and that they are safe.

7.   This is a huge undertaking and typically requires the assistance of an ERCEM therapist who can help you navigate through your partner's feelings yourself and as a couple.

8.   You have traumatized your partner, and now you must prove that you can meet the emotional needs and help your partner heal.

9.   So many betrayed partners confide in me that, yes, they despised the acting out, but even more than that, what they could not live with was the manipulation and "gaslighting" that occurred while their spouse was acting out. They report that the BT made them feel crazy when they asked too many questions or shared their fears that something was not right.

THE #1 SKILL TO PRACTICE TO INSTILL SAFETY AND TO DEVELOP EMPATHY: KNEES-TO-KNEES REFLECTIVE LISTENING

The most important skill I can teach couples, and especially the BT, is reflective listening. It teaches BTs how to learn their partner's perspective.

KNEES-TO-KNEES COMMUNICATION

The basis of empathy work is communication. That starts with following some basic foundational tools. Communication requires focus and listening.

THE SET-UP

When the two of you are talking, I want you to really work at facing each other directly and finding a safe way to physically touch. I recommend touching each other with your knees because it is a safe way to re-establish "safe touch." This is a difficult process for the typical couple, but it can be extremely challenging for a couple that has experienced so much pain.

I call that "knees-to-knees," where you are looking at each other knees-to-knees and attending to each other's posture and facial expressions by looking at the left eye, the window to the soul. You may question what the "window to the soul" is, but research has shown that when you look at the left eye, you are much more able to understand the other person's position, as well as the level of emotion and communication.

Human beings have a subconscious agreement to take notice of the personality in the left eye. Because of the crossover, our left-eye imagery goes to our right brain and looks for a deeper sense of meaning. William Henderson, in his book *The Science of Soulmates*, states, "The left eye is literally the window to the soul and the indicator of the hidden unmasked true self." Most couples therapists do not realize how contraindicated it is to sit side by side and communicate. I never let a couple sit on the couch where they cannot attune to each other's nonverbal skills. Much of the communication you do at home is done "on the fly." There is no deep focus. You are not reading each other. You both will be making a commitment to this work if you set up your communication by attending and attuning to each other before you speak.

DOING KNEES-TO-KNEES WHILE USING REFLECTIVE LISTENING

You have likely heard the adage that the best form of communication is not to communicate verbally but to listen. Reflective listening is the best way to do this because what you are doing is allowing each other to share one's beliefs, thoughts, and feelings. It is so important for a partner to have an uninterrupted voice. And you are listening without any emphasis on explaining or defending your own position. It may be the first time you ever really heard your partner without feeling obligated or compelled to respond.

Partners can typically be very wordy, and as a couple, the two of you will need to work diligently on keeping your communication clear, direct, and succinct. Partners know that it is difficult for betrayers to listen without becoming defensive. Partners need to keep their thoughts and beliefs short and under three minutes to give the BT a real opportunity to hear and understand you. That is the goal of good communication. We want the betrayer to have a renewed sense of who you are, how you have been affected, and what you need for your future, so I want you to practice reflective listening daily.

This can be very difficult for BTs who are in affair recovery because they fear the conflict that they know they caused and can easily go into shame because of a new awareness of the ongoing trauma they have caused. Therefore, they want to avoid communication because they know it could likely bring up more conflict. Partners want to know that BT has really reprioritized their values and is honest, transparent, and authentic. However, conflict will be part of your communication process because there is so much pain! Yet when the couple has worked on self-regulation and co-regulation, they will begin to appreciate the honesty in the share. Both of you will feel more gratified, and the connection will grow.

As you gain more recovery, you wonder what the one thing you can do for the relationship is. Know that the number one skill you can practice every day is empathy with focused listening and communication. When you initiate communication and follow through with the commitments you have made to the relationship, it will exponentially provide the most emotional investment in your relationship. Just know that as your relationship gets healthier, you will be able to experience conflict, and know that conflict breeds intimacy. I know that both of you are craving and longing for emotional intimacy in the relationship. We are not talking about physical intimacy. A close and physical relationship takes time and patience, and there needs to be a solid foundation of emotional commitment, consistency, and transparency.

To the Betrayer: You must create that emotional bond of safety that your partner so desperately needs to redevelop trust. You want to see your partner love you again. You need that, so as you practice empathy, be patient. Know that this is the emotional fuel that is going to fill the love tank. And do not forget to practice patience. Your partner will require a lot of patience because the BP will test you every step of the way. Not only is BP traumatized, but your partner is angry that it has to be this hard. When you repeat back the concerns your partner has, the BP feels heard and will automatically feel less defensive.

Reflective listening takes structure. The next time your partner makes an angry or defeated statement, I want you to calmly request that the BP sit down at the kitchen or dining room table.

1. Move the chairs out about two feet and have them face each other. Ask your partner to please sit down so you can share what you just heard.

2. If your partner will allow it, ask her if you can sit knees-to-knees so that you can find a safe way to connect physically. If the BP will not let you, tell her that it makes sense to you why your partner would not want that closeness.

3. Proceed by sitting down and looking at her left eye, the window to the soul.

4. Repeat back what she said verbatim.

Here is what a couple I worked with said their first experience with reflective listening was like.

CRYSTAL & TOM: WHAT MUST THEY THINK OF ME?

"Crystal, I heard you say that you are exhausted, your mind is racing a mile a minute, and you can't stop thinking that you didn't sign up for this! Did I get that right?"

Crystal shook her head in agreement and said, "I just don't think you know how embarrassing this is. I cannot even walk into the grocery store without wondering who else might know. You have ruined every conceivable place in this town. Not only do I wonder who knows, but I also question what people must think of me. I am embarrassed for myself and for the kids. This is exactly what people love to gossip about, and when I walk into church, I can see the pity in their eyes. No one is asking us to do anything anymore, and I fear that I will live in isolation forever." She burst into tears.

Tom waited for her to stop crying, but his heart was aching because he wanted to hold her and have her sob into his chest. He knew that she would not be able to trust the man who caused her such great pain to be the source of comfort, so he just continued to silently wait for her to stop crying.

Once she started to stop crying, she looked at him and shook her head. She looked so alone, hurt, and discouraged.

Tom asked, "Can I share what I heard to make sure I heard it correctly?" She shrugged her shoulders in quiet resignation. He said, "I heard you say that you just didn't think I knew how embarrassing this has been for you, and you're embarrassed to even walk into the grocery store without wondering who else might know about the affairs I have had in the past twenty years. I have ruined every conceivable place in this town for you, and now you do not even want to face people because they are probably talking about you behind your back. You wonder who knows about the betrayal, and you question what people must think of you and think that they must see you as weak or afraid.

"You are not only embarrassed for yourself, but you are embarrassed for the kids because this is a small town and people talk about stuff like this. This is exactly what people love to gossip about, and when you walk into church, you can see the pity in their eyes. Our relationships have changed, and no one calls anymore. No one is asking us to do anything with them, and you fear that you will be alone forever. Did I get that right?"

She nodded her head in agreement as she looked down at the floor. Tom could see that she was not only devastated but defeated. He said, "Well, I want you to know that whatever you decide to do, I will help you every step of the way because you and the kids should not have to deal with this mess. I hate that I caused you this pain. I cannot take it away, but I am going to do whatever it takes to prove that I will never cheat on you again."

As you can see, there are many great opportunities to use Knees to Knees Reflective Listening to see if she feels heard and understood. It also gives you an opportunity to remind yourself of the hard work that you are putting into your individual and relational recovery.

KNEES-TO-KNEES REFLECTIVE LISTENING PROTOCOL

To the Betrayer: Both of you find two chairs that allow you to touch knees as you both talk to each other.

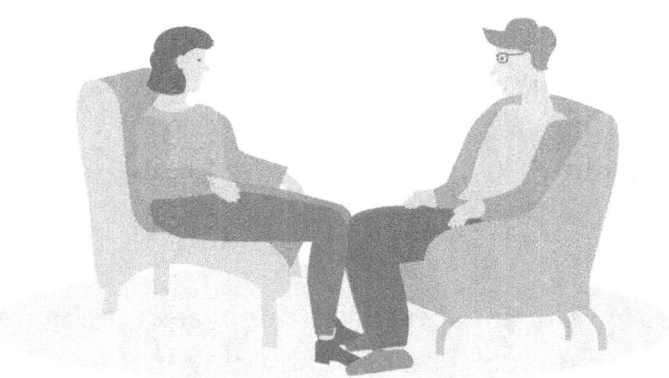

1. Encourage the BP to speak about anything that has been bothersome. The BP will talk about a trigger and share accompanying feelings about your inability to keep your partner abreast of your daytime events and business plans. She may want you to talk to your brother and sister-in-law about your infidelity so that they will understand the excruciating pain. Your spouse can bring up anything related to the infidelity while you encourage the BP to begin to share. It helps if the conversation is limited to no longer than a couple of minutes so you can use reflective listening to make sure you hear the BP's thoughts and feelings.

2. Repeat back verbatim exactly what you heard. There is no need to respond to her because this is an exercise in listening.

3. Next, ask her, "Did I get that right?" so you are assured that you heard your partner completely. (This is an empathy exercise that lets the BP know that you want to hear her and understand her feelings, thoughts, and beliefs.)

4.   When you have completed this process, it becomes your turn to respond.

To the BT: Even though they may ask the same question one hundred times, their questions are always welcome because you traumatized their brain, and they will ruminate with questions until the brain heals. And the healing is dependent on your recovery and patience. This work requires you to be very gentle and patient with your partner. Now that you are in recovery, you will need to learn how to be direct, ask inquiring questions to clarify how they feel, and send them the all-important message that their feelings and needs really matter.

You see, *"in healthy relationships, conflict breeds intimacy,"* so the hope is that you can restore your relationship and bring it into a state of health and well-being. Then, when conflict occurs, you will have the strength to know that even though it feels scary, once it is externalized and you work on your empathy, your partner will feel safe, and your relationship will move toward more connection. This is the goal of empathy and intimacy: to restore the relationship and bring it back into a state of health and well-being. When conflict occurs because of betrayal trauma, you will have the strength to know that it needs to be externalized through empathy, leaving your partner feeling safe and your relationship feeling more intimate.

> *The next most important communication process to follow in order to validate the partners experience:* THE AVR FORMULA©

As I worked with couples after discovery, I noticed how difficult it was for the unfaithful to directly share empathy. When betrayers were face to face with their partners, they lacked the verbiage and skills to convey how they wanted to help them heal. It was then I decided that I needed to break empathy down in a way that could be used consistently. I experimented with different formulas to convey what they were seeing, what they believed their partner was feeling, and what they wanted to do to help their partner heal. Out of these sessions, AVR was born.

For the Unfaithful: AVR helps you acknowledge all the damage you have caused. It may feel counterintuitive because you are afraid that if you identify that you are responsible for the pain, your partner will go on a tirade and be filled with more contempt for your actions. But, actually, nothing could be further from the truth. When you see your partner's pain and acknowledge it, it has just the opposite effect.

> *It brings their defenses down because you have made them aware of your accountability, and it reinforces that you not only recognize the pain and struggle but also know you are the source of that pain.*

It was then that I realized how your acknowledgment was a game changer for helping the partner to heal. So, let's go over this three-part formula that will be the foundation for using empathy.

1. The "A" stands for "Acknowledge." When you acknowledge the current struggle or challenge that your infidelity has caused, you are connecting with your partner on an emotional level. It is so important to remind them at every juncture that you see and hear their pain and that you know you have caused it.

2. The "V" stands for "Validate." When you validate the feelings, it will help you to identify how they must be feeling—which is no easy task due to the trauma they have endured. I encourage you to keep it simple and only include the five primary feelings: anger, sadness, happiness, loneliness, and fear. As you determine how the issue or pain is making them feel, you can begin to understand which feeling is the most predominant, which leads to understanding them better emotionally. You will be checking in and assessing how they must be feeling. When you validate their primary feeling, you are reinforcing that you are connecting with them on an emotional level.

3. Brené Brown says that empathy is "perspective taking," so it will be your job to "take their temperature" so to speak—identifying which feeling appears to be primary and validating it to build that emotional connection.

4. The "R" stands for "Reassurance." In this last part of the formula, you are sharing the changes you have made and will continue to make to be in good recovery both relationally and in sobriety. Secretly, partners want to be reassured you are in good recovery and are making strides relationally to put them first and help them heal. I say secretly because they have been so betrayed and traumatized that they are scared to believe you and believe in you. Their heart cannot take more disappointment, so they stand before you in a guarded position, not sure if they can trust this new reality. Your job is to be consistent, work on the relationship skills in this book to build trust and show that you will "contain the pain," and sit with them as you both work together to heal from this betrayal and the damage you have caused.

5. As you practice looking for opportunities to use AVR or, as I prefer to call it," to AVR your partner," you may question whether it is helping. They may continue to send discouraging messages that they do not believe you, but keep doing the next right thing because they really do want to see you work on relational repair. Partners consistently tell me that they want the betrayer to understand the depths and devastation of their pain. Although the BT is living with the pain they have caused daily, part of the partner's healing process is to be reminded that the betrayer "sees the pain" and can link it back to the "knowing" that the betrayer is the reason for the pain. This process must happen consistently for them to feel safe enough to trust their partner's recovery. They want to believe that you will never do this again, but they have no guarantee. Their heart wants to trust you, but their head and experience are telling them it is not safe to be this vulnerable. So, they will keep their guard up and look for

reasons to reject your attempts at honesty and authenticity. This is going to require you to consistently practice empathy in all sorts of ways.

WHY DOES AVR WORK?

Using AVR assures the betrayed partner that you are linking up your previous actions to their feelings. It also reminds them of what you are doing to rebuild their foundation of safety. Often in Early Couples Recovery Work, the BT needs a formula to help them respond to the betrayed partner in a way that shows they realize the damage they have caused and how the sexual addiction has affected the partner.

We have been trained to know that the quickest way for betrayers to redeem their reputation and prove to their partners they will do whatever it takes to build the trust back is to recognize the pain and remind the partner that they know they caused it. It is then important for the betrayers to validate the partner's feelings, making sure the BT can assess them appropriately, and then to reassure the partner that the BT will do whatever it takes to rebuild the confidence the partner once had. Again, let's break down the formula and look for situations to use it.

THE AVR FORMULA

ACKNOWLEDGING THE ISSUE AND THE PAIN YOUR INFIDELITY CAUSED

- Practicing the **A** in AVR requires that you ***acknowledge*** the situation and accompanying pain. At first, it can seem counterintuitive to bring up the damage your infidelity has caused. Betrayed partners want to know that you remember their pain is a result of your actions. It assures them that you have not forgotten, nor are you in denial. As you are creating your AVR, please keep it short and simple so that the BP can assimilate it into her experience.

  - "It makes sense to me that looking at our Memorial Day picnic pictures causes you great pain..."

- **Validation** of the betrayed partner's feelings using the five primary feelings. It can be difficult to ascertain how a partner is feeling, so it is helpful to focus on the primary feeling (and see if you got it right). If you were indeed able to figure out the primary feeling, you will be able to validate it. Remember to identify one of these five feelings: anger, sadness, loneliness, happiness, or fear.

  o "I can see as you look at the pictures from the Memorial Day family picnic that you feel sadness because now you question the reality of what really happened on that day. It feels like I contaminated the joyful event."

- *Reassurance that you have changed and your top priority is to help the betrayed partner heal.* It will be necessary to share how you are changing and what you are working on to focus on your recovery and your partner's healing. You want to gently remind the partner that you will work diligently to build back their trust in you.

  o "I hate that I have ruined some important holidays for you, but I want to reassure you that I am working a good recovery program and will work on creating new memories that you can trust."

Empathy is putting yourself in the partner's place. You cannot possibly know the gravity of the BP's feelings, but when you are able to look at what the BP is struggling with through the partner's eyes, you are better able to assess what is needed.

To the Betrayed Spouse: I recognize that the AVR formula will sound scripted and rote. I promise you the BT does not know how to empathize and must learn the skills before it becomes natural. I would like to tell you that this process could take three months, but unfortunately, it will be 12 to 24 months before this becomes organic. So please be patient and try to refrain from rejecting the BT for inadequate empathy statements. You can make this process smoother if you acknowledge their attempts—no matter how scripted or feeble.

> *All humans need positive reinforcement, especially when they are working on relational repair.*

Throughout this book, I am going to share situations to which I am sure you will find some parallels or pieces to relate to as you examine your own relationship. You will also see how relational skills help repair the present-day problems that are buried in relational trauma.

SAMSON & TAMI: FROM PORN TO EXTORTION

Note: Pornography is seen by BPs as a form of infidelity. Although I was trained to remain neutral about pornography, after doing extensive work with couples who have experienced compulsive problematic sexual behavioral disorder or affairs, I recognized that pornography use is often the gateway to "other problematic behaviors." I cannot endorse any objectification of men or women who are in pornography because my fear and belief is that there are many people who are forced to partake in pornography and have been trafficked for that purpose. I also believe that pornography exploits the viewers, often hijacks their brains, and causes addiction. I also know that children from ages eight and up are exposed to all forms of pornography, which can be extremely violent, and it is wreaking havoc on their brains and providing confusing scenarios that are setting them up for poor role modeling of the sacredness of sexuality. This next story shows how pornography was a gateway drug and almost destroyed a relationship. Watch as Samson worked a solid recovery program and used empathy and AVR to offset his tendency to be self-absorbed and emotionally immature.

Samson and Tami came to see me after Tami discovered Samson's visits with married women he had met on "hookup" sites. They had been married for 18 years. Samson never meant to be unfaithful to Tami, yet his history was such that he had looked at porn from age 11 until discovery at age 43. He knew that something was not right about porn, but he ignored his discernment and rationalized that looking at it was "boys being boys." Over the years, his behaviors escalated, and his visits to strip clubs advanced to private encounters in the back of the clubs. He knew that what he was doing was wrong, but his brain could not wait for the next encounter. His pornography use was a gateway to wanting more sexual stimulation. In those 32 years, he was able to stop for brief periods of time out of a sense of conscience, but somehow, his compulsion would come back with a vengeance and get stronger.

He met Tami at his work at the hospital. He fell in love with her immediately and spent all his energy winning her over. He loved her children like his own, and after a year, Tami was sure she had met the man of her dreams. They married, bought a home together, and both climbed the corporate ladder at the hospital. They had so much in common and both felt a love they had never felt before. Samson stopped acting out temporarily and convinced himself that he did not need to act out because he had found the love for which he was searching.

And then his compulsion returned. His visits to the clubs became more frequent, and he started to experiment with other forms of acting out. It was as if his addiction had become even stronger than before he had stopped. It escalated, and he got on websites that advertised "hookups with married women." He reassured himself that this would ensure that he did not become emotionally involved. Somehow, he rationalized that if he remained detached emotionally, his sexual acts were harmless. He continued to cheat on Tami until one day, an affair partner started demanding money from Samson. He had initially given her money after she had separated from her husband and could not pay her rent. Her requests became more frequent, so Samson decided to stop seeing her and blocked her calls.

Through social media, she contacted him and threatened to expose him to his wife and the hospital. Samson panicked and gave her $5,000 hush money, but her threats to expose him continued. He eventually went to his wife and shared his infidelity. Tami was in disbelief that he had put both himself and their family in jeopardy. Together, they went to the police, but the police said they could do nothing. They waited together, wondering if she would threaten Samson again. The extortionist did contact Tami through social media and demanded more money. Tami told her to leave them alone or they would have her arrested. The extortionist said that Tami and Samson would be sorry, but then she disappeared from their lives. However, her ghost haunted them for years.

When they came to my office, they appeared to have lost all passion for life. They both wanted help, but they admitted that they were just going through the motions. Tami wanted me to help Samson and was not sure if she really wanted to follow my recommendation to come in for the first session. It was as if she had become a skeleton of a woman and wanted to detach from the horror of Samson's infidelity.

I acknowledged the intense pain that she must be going through. Tami had thought she had met her Prince Charming, who had presented himself as the perfect man. They shared so much together, and now their life seemed ruined. Neither of them had the strength nor the desire to end things. They both expressed a deep love for each other, yet Tami questioned whether she could really be in love with him because she did not know him. She questioned her sanity because she was not ready to end the relationship. It was as if they were both in purgatory and were not sure what might happen in their future. She wanted me to fix Samson, and as the session continued, she realized that she, too, wanted guidance as to how this could have happened and what she should do next.

I talked about the brain science of sexual compulsivity. I explained that she would not be able to determine what she needed next until she knew what she was dealing with. I talked about the intense work Samson would need to do, and he admitted that he wanted to go somewhere to get that intensive help. Together, we talked about treatment centers that could provide him with the time and the treatment to reset his sense of self. Tami admitted that this would also give her the needed space to evaluate what she might need in the future. We sent him to a treatment center specifically for sexual compulsivity and infidelity, and she worked with me and a psychiatrist who specifically worked with trauma to help regulate her emotions. Tami was very bright and had hundreds of questions, so I knew that together, both the psychiatrist and I could help her understand the nature of her husband's problems.

I encouraged her to write out all the questions she would need to have answered, knowing that some of them would be impossible for Samson to answer. The treatment center wanted to do a disclosure. However, I intervened and told them that I would be preparing Tami for the disclosure so they could help Samson prepare his timeline— which, of course, would start from the time Samson was 11 years of age and saw his first pornography video.

I explained to Tami that it was important for her to have lots of preparation and support if she was going to do the disclosure, and I would rather that the couple work with me to ensure that each person was fully supported during it. She agreed to wait for the disclosure until after he returned from treatment.

Tami went out to the treatment center for the week and learned about Samson's compulsions. She found that she had learned how to detach from how he had hurt her personally, and she was able to understand how Samson was unable to stop. She was still devastated, but the 60 days away had given her some perspective. When Samson returned, he remained motivated to stay in recovery and work his program. Together, we worked out the guidelines for the disclosure, and when the day came for Samson to bare all his secrets, he did so with the goal of giving Tami the information she needed to determine how she was going to proceed. He took the polygraph and passed it, and Tami told me at the next session that she felt ready to go on and assess whether they could repair the relationship.

We spent many sessions practicing ERCEM. Samson not only suffered breaches of fidelity, but he also experienced compulsive sexual behavior disorder (sex addiction). This complicated both the intensity of the couple's healing and the treatment protocol to help both of them restore their marriage. ERCEM allowed the couple to learn and use reflective and focused listening. For the next four months, Tami had ongoing questions about "how" he could have led such a double life. She understandably was frequently triggered and honestly disturbed by the reality of what she had gone through. Samson worked diligently on using AVR with her to show her the empathy she deserved as they battled this problem together. As with all my couples, they would come in and talk with each other about the events of the past week and the feelings that accompanied them. They sat in their chairs, knees-to-knees, and intently focused on each other as they communicated their struggles and successes.

The session started with me asking the couple to discuss with each other how their week had been. Samson stated, "Things were better this week, less fighting, although we were really busy."

Tami said, "I tried to be easier on you because it was your birthday."

Samson replied, "Yes, I had a good birthday. I felt very grateful to be with you celebrating it."

Tami retorted, "Yep, it started out okay, but when you pouted at the end, I just wanted to throw my hands up and say I give up." She looked at me and said, "Samson didn't get everything he wanted for his birthday."

Samson started to explain himself, but he realized that he should AVR Tami because she was understandably upset with him. He said:

- **A**: "I realize it hurt you that I was selfish with my high expectations for the evening."

- **V:** "It must have made you angry when I wanted you to lay close to me so we could hug and cuddle with each other."

- **R**: "But I want to reassure you that I am going to keep working on my neediness. The next morning after the party, I berated myself for not having gratitude that I had gotten the most important gift for my birthday, and that gift was you."

Tami looked at me and explained, "I baked Samson his favorite cake and watched a movie with him, so he automatically assumed that we could be close because we were getting along. I knew what he was thinking, but I absolutely did not feel it was fair for him to think that just because it was his birthday, that physical closeness, which might have led to sex, was automatically on the table. So, when I told him after the movie that I hoped he had a good birthday and that I was going to bed, he got sullen, did not thank me for the night, stayed up, and didn't come to bed. I was glad that I stood up for myself, but I was mad that he thought we were normal."

Samson started to explain, but instead, he said, "I wasn't able to process it right away, but the next day, I was disgusted with myself that I automatically assumed that since our night seemed so normal that we would take it to the next level." He looked at Tami and said, "I promise I will get better at sharing my feelings with you when I begin to feel entitled or assume that you might be ready for that closeness."

- **A**: "It had to have put you back in that place of wondering how I could be so arrogant."

- **V**: "You had to have felt very lonely lying in bed that night."

- **R**: "I can only say that I will continue to work on putting that self-interested side of myself away, and I know that I can do that if I continue to put myself in your shoes."

NOW IT IS TIME FOR YOU BOTH TO USE THE AVR FORMULA EXERCISE

The formula is simple, but it takes lots of practice. So, together, I would like you both to get comfortable using the formula. After several months of practice, you can change it up and not follow the script verbatim. But I find that following the script gives a good chance to develop the language behind empathy. Be patient…This stuff is hard for a betrayer!

USE AVR WITH YOUR PARTNER'S FEARS

To the Betrayer: Now it is your turn to think back to some frequent fears your partner has experienced.

Fear/Concern #1:

Acknowledge their struggle/concern/issue:

Validate the primary feeling:

Reassure the BP of your progress or willingness:

Struggle/concern/issue #2:

Acknowledge the struggle/concern/Issue:

Validate the feeling:

Reassure the BP of your progress or willingness:

Struggle/issue/concern #3:

Acknowledge their struggle/concern/issue:

Validate the feeling:

Reassure the BP of your progress or willingness:

AS A PARTNER, WHAT WOULD YOU LIKE TO SEE?

To the Partner: I would like you to channel the BT. If you were the BT, what three fears might you have? Write out an AVR for each one of them. This is an opportunity to let the betrayer know what you wish the dialogue would sound like. It is also a chance for you to see how challenging the AVR formula can be. It will help you to have empathy for the process!

Struggle/Issue/Concern #1:

If you were channeling the unfaithful, how would you like the BT to:
Acknowledge the struggle/concern/issue?

Validate the primary feeling?

Provide **R**eassurance that they are making changes?

Struggle/Issue/Concern #2:

If you were channeling the unfaithful, how would you like the BT to:
Acknowledge the struggle/concern/issue?

Validate the primary feeling?

Provide **R**eassurance that they are making changes?

Struggle/Issue/Concern #3:

If you were channeling your spouse, how would you like the BT to:
Acknowledge the struggle/concern/issue?

Validate the primary feeling?

Provide **R**eassurance that they are making changes?

To the Betrayer: I know that writing these challenges and concerns out can feel laborious, but this is an important process and one that will really make the difference in your relationship. Therefore, you want to get it right and do it well. Remember that you spent a lot of time lying, deceiving, and denying there was a problem. Now, it is your opportunity to be heartfelt, honest, and authentic.

If you are a male betrayer, my experience with working with the male population in general is that men did not learn empathy skills in their childhoods. As a result, this may be the first time you have concentrated on learning and using it, so it will take some work. There is a saying the Twelve-Step community uses: "When you work it, it works!" That saying applies here, so do not shortchange the process!

If you are a female betrayer, you likely had relationship and empathy skills, but your desire for attention and affection trumped your ability to assert yourself and communicate what you needed in the relationship.

To the Partner: This exercise may have come easy for you, or you may have had some difficulty with it. It is not as easy as it looks. Yet, this is a great opportunity for the BT to see what you would like to see during AVR. The secondary gain is that you may begin to develop some empathy for what they are trying to do.

Some people have questioned if ERCEM is teaching empathy to the unfaithful to deceive you further. In my history of working with couples who have experienced infidelity, I have never known the BT who is in good recovery to deceive his partner by practicing this process. It is my experience that they want to help you heal—they just did not have the tools by which to do it. By going through this process together, you will be able to understand the effort behind the outcome, and it will hopefully help you both see the progress that you are making.

AS BETRAYERS GET HEALTHIER, YOU WILL NEED TO SHOW THEM EMPATHY TOO

To the Partner: After discovery, your whole world seems unreal. You are shell-shocked by what you have learned. You wonder who this person is that you thought you knew and how they could have done this to you. You cannot figure out who you are living with, and you question whether you are living with a sociopath, a narcissist, or both. You are not only reeling from the horrible shock while your brain is offline, leaving you unable to think or speak, but you also worry about your future, children, and family as a unit. You have had the wind knocked out of you, and you say repeatedly, "Who is this monster, and why is this happening to me?" You possessed a lot of empathy prior to discovery, but now you are in survival mode. It is understandably all about you. There is no way that it would be safe to empathize with them because you cannot even comprehend what happened, let alone understand in the first few months how the person you loved could live a dual life.

Your hypervigilance, which is a survival skill and a trauma response, watches everything they do. You make a deliberate effort to watch them walk their talk, and when they do so, it will be hard to comment. This is because they have hurt you so badly, and you are not going to reward them for "doing what they should have done all along."

At some point, as they continue to work good recovery and have proven that they want to be a person in solid recovery, they will need your feedback and reinforcement that you can tell they are changing. You will resist this, and you will find a million reasons to push them away. You have been so badly hurt that you could not conceive of trusting them again ever. But as you learn the guideposts for good recovery and assess that they have used the right tools, you will begin to let your guard down.

When this miracle starts to occur, you will begin to do what you have always done, and you will start to acknowledge the changes you are seeing. You will resist this at first because you will not believe that it is true, but then you will see it with more regularity. You will feel the relationship take a turn in the right direction. You will begin to use empathy and identify the good work they are doing in recovery, and you will breathe a bit easier as they continue leaning into helping you heal! (Actually, I see betrayed partners who are able to practice empathy as soon as they see that the BT is practicing the skills diligently. We know that empathy is innate in women, so oftentimes, it is a natural byproduct of their work.)

It doesn't matter where you are with your trust level to begin to practice empathy. It will be harder if your guard is up, but you will still see opportunities to use it. Please practice it so that you will begin to let that huge wall down just enough to really assess the situation. Remember, now that you know what they did, you will be able to protect yourself and still *be able to work on the skills you need to heal.*

Chapter 12

Mindfulness-Based Infidelity and Trauma Work Can Change Your Perspective

I nfidelity requires faithfulness, honesty, and co-regulation. However, the prerequisite for emotional co-regulation is emotional regulation. Betrayed spouses need to learn the art of sitting in distress while they are creating constructive compassion. This chapter is dedicated to teaching a mindfulness practice for trauma and anxiety. While the BP is utilizing mindfulness strategies, the BT is leaning into a supportive position to show empathy and stay regulated, too.

Historically, couples would dive into therapy, but since no one was doing formalized empathy work with them, they floundered and were flooded with treatment modalities that they could not even begin to assimilate. This left them feeling scared, overwhelmed, and shamed. I kept thinking we need to find a treatment modality that helps to quiet the minds of both people in the relationship. It was no accident that I met Darrin Ford, who is the President of Sano Press, my book publisher. Darrin is a therapist who also ran a publishing company and catered to professionals who worked with acting out behaviors and trauma. I must be transparent here; Darrin Ford is a CSAT who I sought out to be my publisher because of his knowledge about problematic sexual behavior. I thought he would well-represent me and the books that I wanted to write because of his knowledge base and sensitivity.

As I got to know Darrin and his publishing company, I realized he had his own story about trauma and trauma recovery. Darrin Ford is the Founder and Chief Executive Officer of *The Mindfulness Academy for Addiction and Trauma Training* (TMAATT.com) and the Chief Executive Officer at *Mindful Centers for Addiction and Trauma Therapy* (MindfulCenters.com) with offices in Long Beach, West Los Angeles, and Newport Beach, California. *Mindful Centers* also sees clients from all over the state of California, Oregon and Texas via telehealth services.

After years of reviewing the work of Daniel Segal, Richard Davidson, and Jon Kabat-Zinn, Darrin has come to the realization that the research supports mindfulness as a necessary step in working with compulsive sexual behaviors and partner betrayal:

> *Our mission at TMAATT is to provide comprehensive, inspiring, research-based mindfulness training to therapists worldwide. We*

are dedicated to helping mental health professionals learn how to incorporate mindfulness tools and techniques as they support their clients in long-term recovery, growth, and healing.

What was especially appealing to me was that his strategies were simple, straightforward, and incredibly effective in reducing addiction and trauma symptoms while improving the overall health and well-being of my clients. His curriculum gave me practical tools to work with betrayers, partners, and the coupleship.

Darrin Ford teaches in his Mindfulness-Based Addiction and Trauma Work that he wants BTs to gain the ability to identify their mind states and mind stories. This allows them to recognize the ability that they must alter their relationship to these states and stories, providing a new perspective that will move them into healthy, non-reactive behaviors. He describes the work with partners as the following:

> *Our goal as therapists is to allow partners to recognize that the trauma has their thoughts, feelings, beliefs, which are all constructs designed for survival. Their minds are seeking the certainty they believed they had in the past before they discovered the betrayal. The betrayal trauma reactions are now causing distress that intensifies uncertainty and discomfort. Their mind's resistance or "aversion" to this uncertainty creates greater suffering.*

You, as the recovering person, are working hard to create safety, which is a new truth. The mind is conditioned to create certainty, which is a survival mechanism. The traumatized partner's mind is on a perpetual search to find more certainty, which can lead to more suffering, and yet it is the survival skill attempting to keep the partner safe." A partner's attempts to find safety can exacerbate fears because the primary need is to feel safe and survive. This can create more suffering because the partner is in that hypervigilant state to know the truth. It can be an auto-exacerbating cycle that results in more pain.

To the Partner: My goal is to teach you how to become aware of your emotionality and identify what emotion is driving your mind state. My job is to help you use constructive compassion so you can surrender to what has happened to you and, through compassion, find an identity that is separate from partner betrayal. When you do this, you decrease reactivity and begin to trust yourself again so that you can appreciate who you are and your own intuition. You develop an improved sense of confidence that allows you to attune to the reality that the betrayer's behaviors affect you but are in no way, shape, or form because of you. Your spouse did not act out because you were not good enough or not worthy of love. You did not cause or contribute to the BT's desire to act out.

A secondary gain of mindfulness is that over time, you can learn to be present with the uncertainty, which is a normal response that is manifested out of betrayal trauma. You will learn to react with less intensity. When you acquire this skill, you will not only survive but thrive because of the self-growth that has occurred because of your trauma.

FORD ISOMORPHIC PATHS TO SELF-INTIMACY AND INTIMACY WITH OTHERS

This next diagram is a game changer for both the BT and BP because it recalibrates your focus and teaches you how to care for yourself with constructive compassion.

For the Partner: The unfaithfulness has naturally made you feel like you need to totally focus on the BT, but as you process the pain, you need to focus on yourself and rebuild a self-intimacy that will reconstruct your sense of trust and confidence in yourself.

Here is an illustration of what needs to happen after the betrayal:

FORD ISOMORPHIC PATH TO SELF-INTIMACY

It is imperative that you begin to refocus on yourself again, and yet your brain is screaming trauma. It is as if you do not have the capacity to quiet the mind to allow for that shift from the BT to you. Darrin explains that to gain self-intimacy, you must practice distress tolerance and be present with the uncomfortable emotions because it is an inevitable outcome of partner betrayal and, on a larger level, our humanity.

1. He suggests that when you begin to feel the emotional flooding that accompanies partner betrayal, you reframe it as an awakening to what is occurring inside of you.

2. He then encourages you to identify the emotions to better understand their gifts.

3. He wants you to explore the questions "What might the mind stories be telling you about yourself?" and "What maladaptive thoughts are co-created out of the rejection you are understandably feeling right now?"

4. He asks you to practice mindfulness to improve your ability to manage the distress.

5. He states that the distress is a signal to practice "constructive compassion" and to find interventions that the BT or BP can utilize to gain the ability to remain present.

6. This will allow for less reactivity which promotes more serenity and equanimity with self. There is more certainty and less fear as a result!

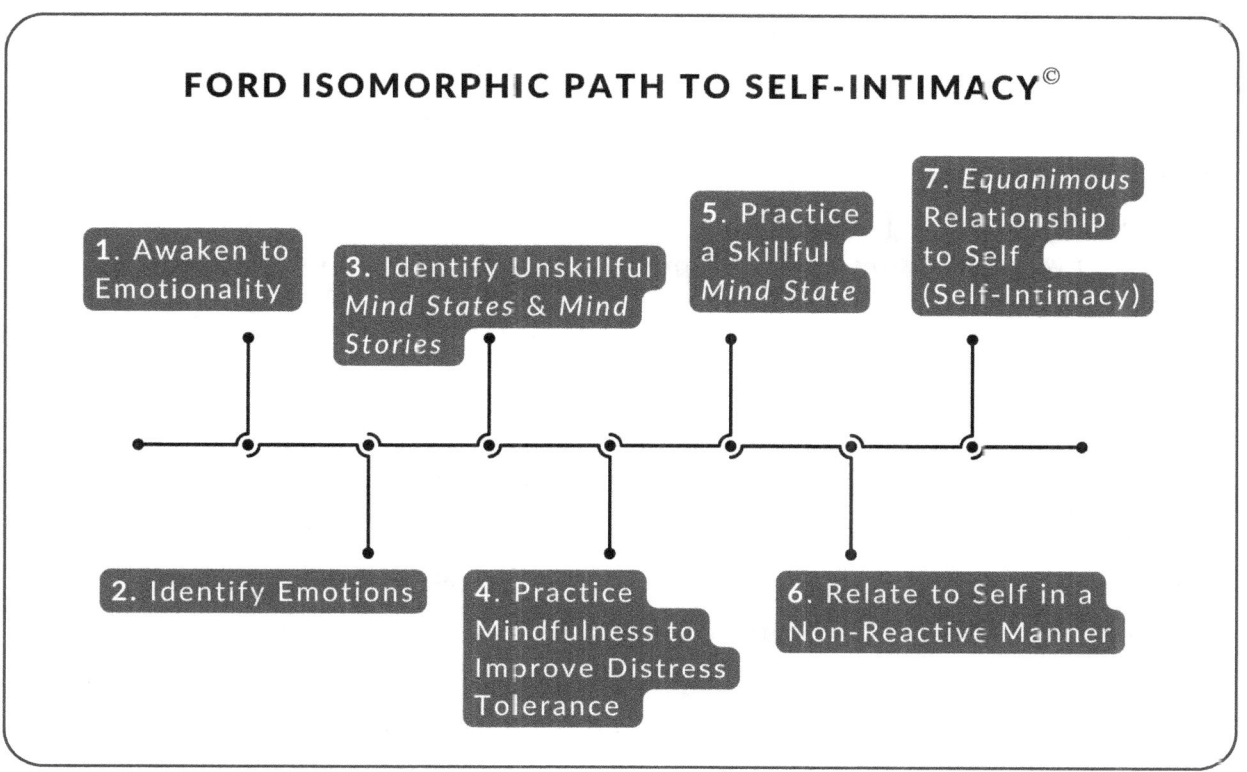

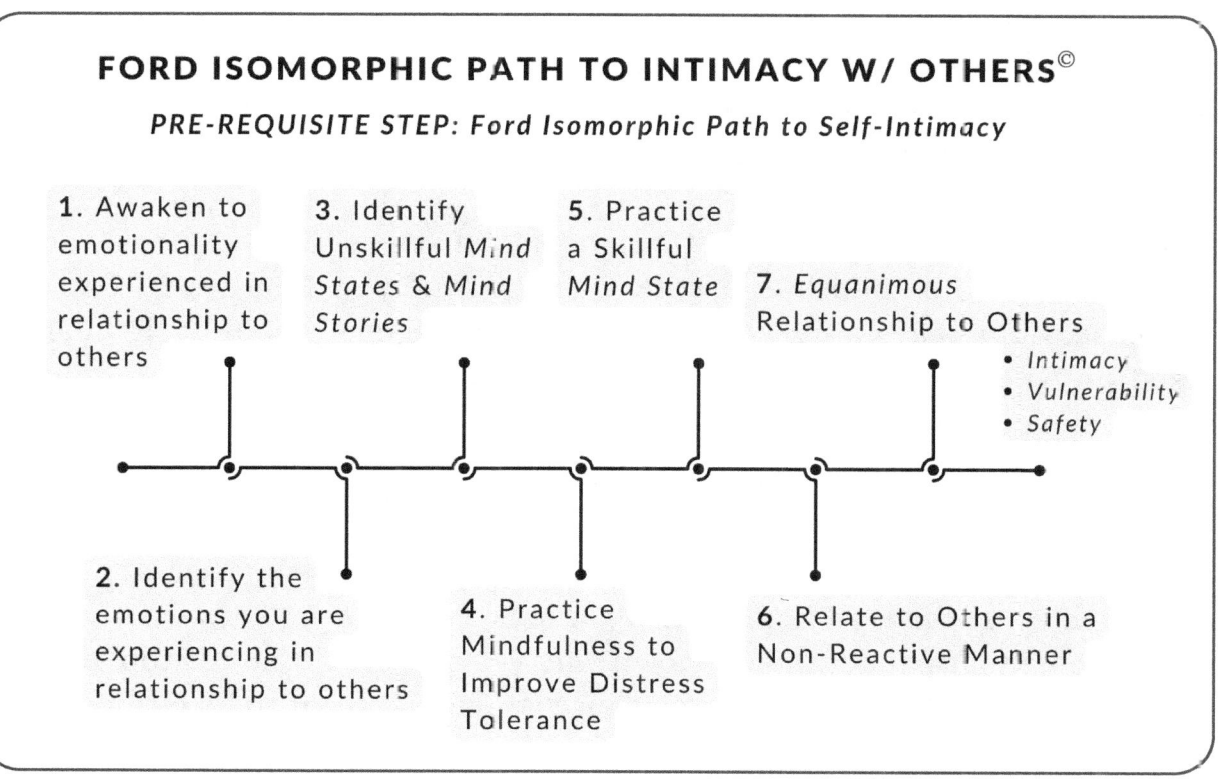

Ford believes it is imperative we assist partners in knowing that they will experience distress for a significant amount of time and that they can regulate it by recognizing it, practicing skillful mind states, noticing the stories that arise from those mind states, and increasing constructive compassion. This will promote a reduction in the impact of distress and will be a signal to treat yourself with kindness and compassion.

The secondary gain is that doing this for yourself allows you to have more compassion for others.

Ford explains in his *Isomorphic Path to Intimacy With Others* that to gain intimacy as a couple, it needs to begin with self-intimacy. Furthermore, partners need to practice distress tolerance and be present with the uncomfortable emotionality that is an inevitable outcome of a partner's natural state manifesting from the betrayal. That is no easy feat!

He states that it is only by having a mind focused on the utilization of "constructively compassionate" interventions that the partner will then be able to gain the ability to remain present. "Constructive compassion" is defined as allowing oneself to be fully present with the experience of oneself while fostering a mutual acceptance of suffering in an effort to bring a kinder presence to distressing emotionality. This is intimacy with the self. That intimacy ripples out into every other aspect of the partner's life. This allows the betrayal trauma response to calm as you gain the ability to be present with the natural, normal distress resulting from the discovery that the unfaithful partner has betrayed you. Your reactivity decreases, and your distress acceptance takes the charge out of the fear equation. The secondary gain is that you begin to apply this constructively compassionate mindset to others as well.

The Early Recovery Couples Empathy Model incorporates these skills to help you become less reactive to your environment and the reality of the betrayal. You replace the fear with a constructive compassion that is cultivated using the *Ford Isomorphic Path to Self-Intimacy*. I know that you want to be less fearful of the unknown, and yet, you are afraid to stop looking for clues that the BT is acting out because you do not want to be betrayed again. It is an auto-exacerbating cycle.

THE AUTO-EXACERBATING CYCLE OF PARTNER BETRAYAL

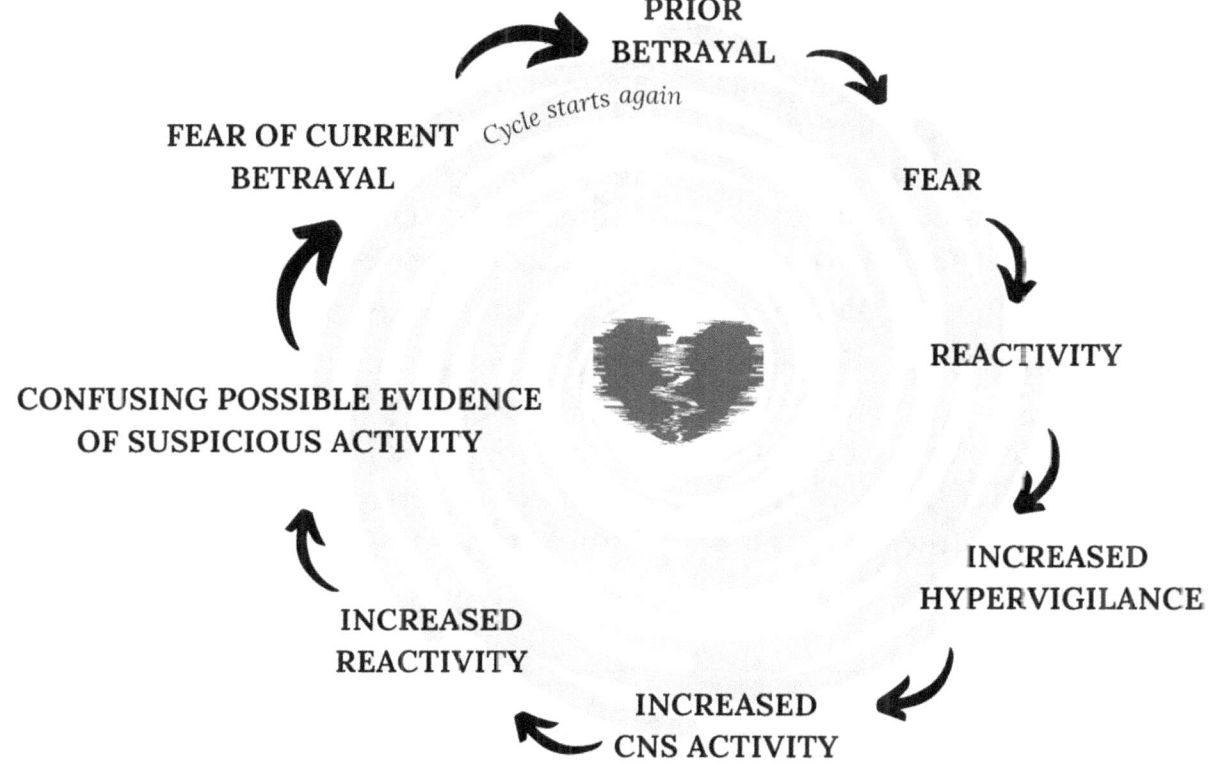

Unless others have lived with your uncertainty, they cannot know how exhausting this cycle is. You likely create a reactive mind state with mind stories that sound like *I will never be able to trust. What my partner did was inexcusable. I do not know this person I married, and I fear I will never be able to recover. How can I ever trust again, and worse than that, how will I ever be able to trust myself?*

In trying to protect yourself, you create "destructive compassion," which Ford explains is when you attempt to reduce the reactivity of the mind at the expense of your long-term healing. You do this by thinking that if you find the potential activity, you may be able to detour it and keep yourself safe. Instead, it does exactly the opposite! It keeps you from being able to be in the moment, enjoy life and trust that if a potential betrayal would occur again, your intuition would take over and you would have a plan that will keep yourself safe. It is a normal protective reaction to want to search for evidence that you will not be deceived again, but that hypervigilant cycle that makes you look for things ten times a day can become addictive, too. It robs you from having your own life.

A more constructively compassionate response might be, *I am going to keep my searches to twice a day, and I am going to spend more focus on the in-between moments. I am going to concentrate on my breathing. I am going to read more spiritual material so I can create more serenity in my life. I am going to call an old friend and attempt to find other things in my life to talk to her about to remind myself that I do have "other things" to focus on.*

The antidote to The Auto-Exacerbating Cycle is "constructive compassion" because working together in ERCEM allows you to repair the damage caused by the infidelity. You get to focus on the new changes that are occurring in the relationship while you trust in yourself and practice a new form of self-compassion that frees you from that auto-exacerbating cycle.

Here is the path we want you to focus on:

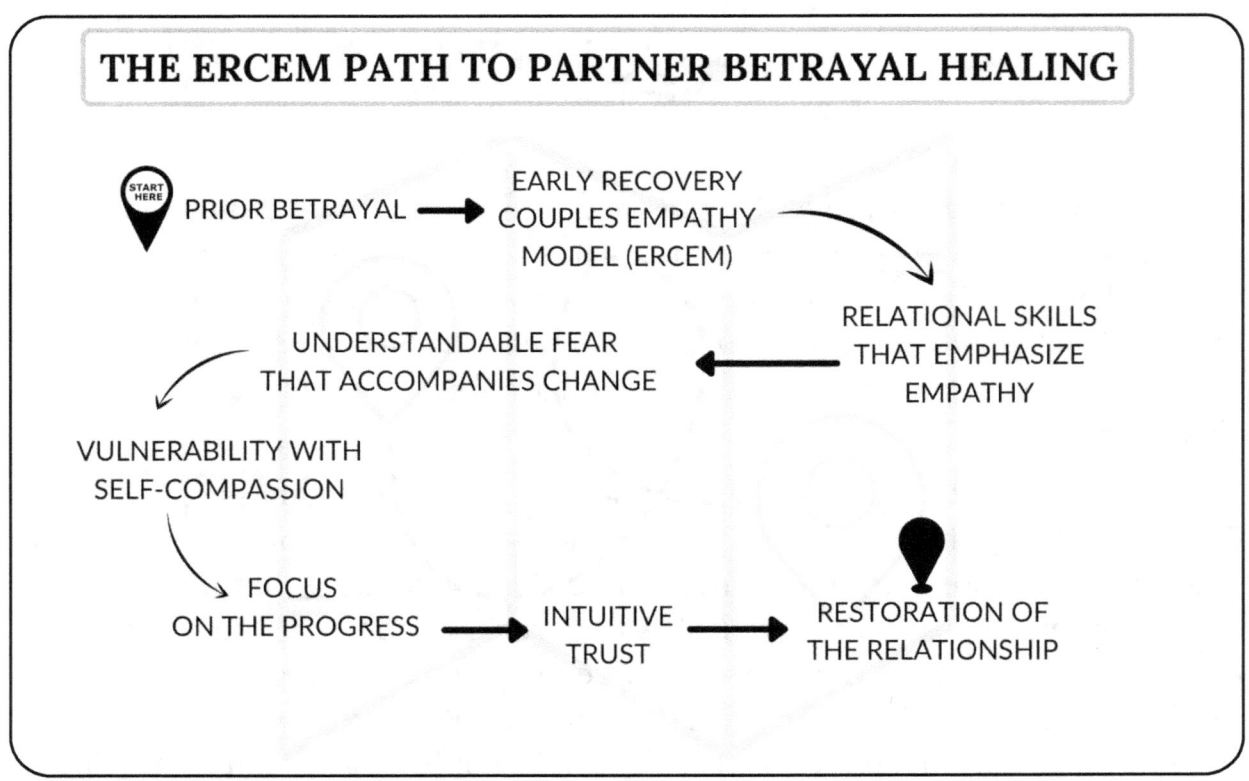

THE ERCEM PATH TO PARTNER BETRAYAL HEALING

START HERE → PRIOR BETRAYAL → EARLY RECOVERY COUPLES EMPATHY MODEL (ERCEM) → RELATIONAL SKILLS THAT EMPHASIZE EMPATHY → UNDERSTANDABLE FEAR THAT ACCOMPANIES CHANGE → VULNERABILITY WITH SELF-COMPASSION → FOCUS ON THE PROGRESS → INTUITIVE TRUST → RESTORATION OF THE RELATIONSHIP

This process results in what Ford calls "equanimity," which refers to you being able to develop a state of psychological and physiological stability and even serenity or calm. Equanimity is considered neither a thought nor an emotion. It is a steady conscious realization of your new reality, congruent with a knowing of oneself and the calm that accompanies the new sense of self. As a partner, it is where you want to live so that you can enjoy life again.

Mindfulness is an excellent way to explore your feelings as an observer and gently remind you that "you are not your mind." All the thoughts, feelings, and beliefs whirling inside of you right now are the result of trauma brain, and you can begin to calm them and take back your life.

It starts by identifying your mind state. "A mind state is a foundational unit that the mind uses to develop a story," and it develops out of the experiences in the environment in conjunction with our biology. According to the Mindfulness Academy for Addiction and Trauma Treatment, there are five mind states that contribute to both Sexual Acting Out and Partner Betrayal Trauma. As you both read the five basic mind states, decide which ones are predominant in the process of sexual infidelity and partner betrayal.

THE FIVE UNSKILLFUL MIND STATES

1. **AVERSIVE**: *When the mind sees and understands reality but pushes away from it.* Some examples of this would be:

   ○ When betrayers are acting out, they may recognize these behaviors are harmful to themselves and to their partners, like my client who frequented prostitutes. He left every encounter disgusted, promising himself that he would never participate in this type of behavior again. He hated himself and wondered what was wrong with him, but later in the day or that week, he would be compelled to call another prostitute and set up yet another meeting.

   ○ When a partner sees that her husband is working on his sobriety and relational recovery but pushes away from it for fear that it is not real and she will get hurt again.

2. **DENIAL**: *Characterized by some awareness of reality but refusing to accept it.* Some examples of this would be:

   ○ A betrayer in denial would be the person who understands the damage this would do to the partner and to the brain. The BT knows that one cannot flirt with other people at work because it will start a cascade of emotional connection. Then, as the BT is in the break room at work, he tells a coworker that they look nice and starts the process of emotional connection based on flattery. Denial is a chronic state for anyone who has difficulty with urges, cravings, and the need for a dopamine hit. As ERCEM specialists, we always work with betrayers to examine their own thinking and keep them out of denial.

   ○ Partners go into denial when they *know* they should take better care of themselves and are actively working toward that, but then they stop their healthy behaviors and forget the importance of intentional self-care. They forget about constructive compassion!

3. **JUDGMENTAL**: *When you have critical thoughts of yourself and others that keep you from self-acceptance.* Some examples of this would be:

   ○ A betrayer goes into a lot of self-loathing when thinking about the past. The BT ends up hating him or herself, which starts a cycle that encourages acting out as a form of medication. Now, the medication (acting out) creates more self-loathing, which feeds the self-judgment. And that starts an auto-exacerbating spiral that keeps the BT unable to untether from negative behaviors.

   ○ A partner will believe that they are not "good enough." A partner in a judgmental mind state frequently believes that the unfaithful partner acted out because there was something wrong with the partner, e.g., not attractive enough or their sex was not adventurous enough.

4. **CLINGY**: *Characterized by the desire to hold onto someone or something because it represents safety or security (even if it doesn't)*. Some examples of this would be:

    o   When betrayers are in clingy mind states, they might cling to the perceived relief that stepping out of sexual integrity will relieve the trauma. It might be seen as a medication when, ultimately, it complicates things and creates more chaos.

    o   A partner may watch the betrayer struggle with being sober and cling to the belief that the BT will eventually gain good recovery. The BP clings to the hope that integrity will occur despite the BT not participating in recovery. The BP is unwilling to set healthy boundaries despite the reality of the real-life condition. Clinging to fantasy keeps the BP unable to set healthy boundaries with consequences for irresponsible recovery attempts.

5. **DELUSIONAL**: *Characterized by a disconnect from reality*. Some examples of this would be:

    o   **For the Betrayer:** This might have looked like believing that the infidelity could continue with minimal or no consequences. "What they don't know won't hurt them."

    o   **For the Partner:** Partners may take full responsibility for the issue, thinking that if they had been more sexual or dressed more provocatively, the BT would not have turned to the affair partner.

Do any of the unskillful mind states resonate with each of you? Which one seems to fit the best? _____

Here is a great diagram to help you understand the process as you read more about how these mind states work for both the betrayer and betrayed partner.

UNSKILLFUL MIND STATES

DENIAL MIND STATE

Characterized by some awareness of reality, but refusing to accept it.

Examples:
- Shopping on a credit card
  - "It's going to be okay."
- Having a sugary snack or dessert EVERY night
  - It's just this one time!"

AVERSIVE MIND STATE

When the mind sees & understands reality but pushes away from it. Exemplified by *hate, worry, misperception, paranoia*

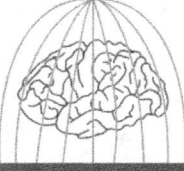

DELUSIONAL MIND STATE

Characterized by a disconnect from reality. Belief one could continue addictive behaviors with minimal/no consequences.

Continually making deals or rules with yourself that cannot be met.

"I can control it this time!"

CLINGING MIND STATE

Characterized by the desire to hold onto; when the mind holds onto things as if they are permanent.

AKA Greed

"The only constant in the universe is change." -Heraclitus

JUDGMENTAL MIND STATE

Characterized by critical thoughts about oneself or others that keep one from self acceptance or attunement.

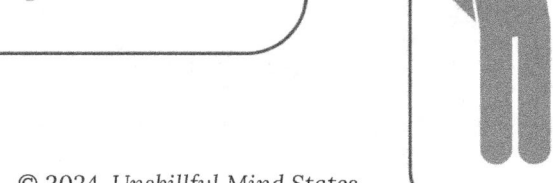

Perhaps you both utilize several of these mind states. Spend some time reflecting on how they may have served you in the past. _____

_____

_____

_____

Why are they no longer helpful in creating a healthier you or relationship?

_____

_____

_____

Spend some time in dialogue with each other. How do you both see your old mind states compensating for the poor choices and trauma that occurred in your life? Once you have identified your mind state, you can understand how you created a mind story to support it. The mind story "is a conscious or unconscious narrative created in relationship to your emotions, thoughts, and beliefs." In both infidelity and betrayal, you tell yourself stories about why this has happened to you that correlate with the mind states. You do your best to understand all that has happened to you in your life, and the things you tell yourself usually have a negative connotation as to the person that you have become.

Part of the grieving process for both of you is refocusing on creating new mind states and mind stories that support your new sense of self, and they co-occur with intentional self-care and compassion. Constructive compassion is crucial for healing.

THE FIVE SKILLFUL MIND STATES

Now, the good news is that you may possess positive mind states. Take a look at this diagram of the five most regularly used positive mind states and decide if you had them, have them in present time, or want to learn how to develop them so you can have more serenity and, as Darrin says, "equanimity in your life."

FIVE SKILLFUL MIND STATES

CURIOSITY MIND STATE

Also known as the beginner's mind. When the mind is focused on perception in an open, spacious manner. Absent of judgment, much like when a child is discovering things for the first time.

COMPASSIONATE MIND STATE

This facilitates open and empathetic mind stories. This fosters mind stories of support, understanding and validation of one's or another's experience, without sacrificing one's right to have healthy boundaries.

GRATITUDE MIND STATE

This is a mind state which facilitates focused gratitude. It supports the creation of mind stories that are calm, integrated and thankful.

GENEROSITY MIND STATE

This mind state gently invites a focus on abundance while decreasing scarcity. It facilitates mind stories that meet discomfort with increased abundance, insight, and determination.

EMPATHETIC MIND STATE

This mind states supports a focusing of the mind on empathy and kindness. It facilitates mind stories characterized by acceptance, connection and openness to personal responsibility.

Which positive mind states would you like to adopt to cope with the uncertainty that occurs when you are both recovering from infidelity?

_____

_____

_____

_____

Why might those skillful mind states be helpful?

_____

_____

_____

_____

I am going to list some common mind stories that women express when sharing their grief about the betrayal.

- Might you be saying to yourself that you must not have been good enough to keep the BT faithful?

- Are you reminding yourself that you were not a good enough sexual partner to keep your relationship satisfied?

- Maybe you believe that something you did in your past caused this action against you, and you wonder if God might be punishing you for your promiscuity, abortion, or pre-marital sex.

- As you think about the mind stories, you may feel your body tensing up further and wonder if the trauma cycle is in full force. This is where you can take control and practice deep breathing with visualization or do a somatic experiencing exercise to refocus the mind onto another body experience. By practicing gentle compassion and changing your focus, you will be better able to regulate those distressing feelings.

- You can tell yourself other compassionate thoughts to remind yourself that you are good enough just the way you are and that your uniqueness has a special quality only you can harness. Whatever compassionate thought you choose to use, make sure to say it gently to yourself.

- When you practice constructive compassion, you begin to become aware of "a calming," which feels very different from your typical reactivity and activation.

- You recognize that your relationship with self has shifted, and there is no judgment in the response to yourself. It allows you to appreciate a new sense of self-intimacy that no longer requires another person to reinforce who you are.

- You begin to develop other, more skillful mind states that feed into that compassion you feel for yourself and others.

The betrayal still hurts, but it is not who you are. You can separate yourself from the intensity of the feelings caused by the infidelity.

When you focus on skillful mind states, you both become healthier, happier, and more appreciative of each other and of life.

COMPASSIONATE MIND STATE

People need to work on having more self-compassion and compassion for others. This can be hard for the unfaithful because they don't believe they deserve to practice constructive compassion and self-care; however, it is a prerequisite for healthy affair recovery! It is equally important for partners because it is necessary to detach from infidelity and take care of oneself. It empowers the partner to take control and assess what would help calm the trauma to find joy again.

GRATITUDE MIND STATE

If you both attend to what is working instead of the struggle, it will neutralize the stress of infidelity with all of its uncertainties. This will result in feeling more positive about life, self, and the relationship.

GENEROSITY MIND STATE

When you as a couple use the generosity mind state, you will be more likely to naturally fear the uncertainty in your life. There is no doubt that partners are afraid to trust for fear of being hurt again, but if the BT is working hard to make you a priority while working diligently on affair recovery, it behooves you to notice the changes which will feed the Generosity Mind State. Your lives will feel fuller because you are looking at the relationship through the eyes of abundance.

THE CURIOUS MIND STATE

When things occur that are confusing or fearful, it benefits you to be curious and open to what each other is thinking. When you practice being non-judgmental, it decreases defensiveness and increases connection. So, instead of saying, "Why did you speak to me like that?" you would say, "I am wondering what is going on for you right now and would love to hear your thoughts about what I said."

THE EMPATHY MIND STATE

Practicing empathy means that you are practicing putting yourself in the other person's shoes. Darrin Ford says that it promotes kindness and an openness to connection, acceptance, and personal responsibility.

To the Betrayer: The pressure of participating in good recovery can feel overwhelming, and it might seem that you cannot get the relational piece down. You believe that you have come so far, and yet your partner seems to get so easily triggered. It leaves you wondering if there is ever going to be connection again. You question whether you are traumatizing the BP at every juncture.

Mindfulness can help you to put into perspective what is happening in your environment. I am not talking about yoga or meditation, although those are two great processes. I want you to go through a self-intimacy process that starts out by identifying your feelings.

1. An MBATT therapist suggests that when you begin to feel the emotional flooding that accompanies your partner's trauma, you reframe it as an awakening to what is occurring inside of you.

2. As you awaken to an awareness, identify the emotions to better understand their gifts.

3. What mind states naturally occur when your partner is discouraged by you? Do you step right into denial and pretend that nothing is wrong, hoping that your choice will keep the environment more neutral? Or are you more likely to take on an aversive mind state where you can see the conflict, but you push it away? You may be exhibiting more of a delusional mind state and searching for a fantasy that will cover up the conflict and please you more.

4. Mind states are an invitation to explore what mind stories you might be telling yourself. What maladaptive thoughts are co-created out of the rejection that you are understandably feeling right now? Might you be saying to yourself that you are a perpetrator of pain, and there is nothing that can change that? Or are you reminding yourself that you will never be a good enough partner to please the BP so you might as well go back to acting out to numb the ongoing trauma that keeps occurring?

5.   As you think about the mind stories, you may feel your body tensing up further. This is where you can take control and practice deep breathing with visualization or do a somatic experiencing exercise to refocus the mind onto another body experience. By practicing gentle compassion and changing your focus, you will be better able to regulate those distressing feelings. Your urges and cravings will be regulated in conjunction with the painful emotions you are feeling.

6.   You can tell yourself other compassionate thoughts to remind yourself that you are a work-in-progress and that your self-acceptance will help you love yourself more so you can love others.

7.   When you practice constructive compassion, you begin to become aware of your "calm," which feels very different from your typical reactivity and activation.

8.   You recognize that your relationship to self has shifted, and there is no judgment in the response to the mind. Your mind is a sense organ that you can calibrate to work for you. It allows you to appreciate a new sense of self-intimacy that no longer requires another person to reinforce who you are.

This mindfulness-based process allows you to shift your thoughts because you are no longer attached to them!

I would like each of you to practice your skillful mind states daily. I tell my clients to focus on one per day so you can really practice them with regularity! You will be surprised at how much better you feel.

I know that this chapter was new information for both of you. Many of my couples have difficulty with it initially, but when used in therapy and coaching, it becomes easy to use. Just in case you don't have an MBATT or

ERCEM specialist, I have created a video for you to watch. Go to: https://sexhelpwithcarolthecoach.com/healing-from-infidelity

The good news is that when you delve into your commonly used mind states and mind stories, you can consciously reconstruct healthier ones that release you from your own trauma. And when you learn to use self-intimacy and compassion, you repair the traumas that have occurred in your past.

Please don't underestimate how important it is to learn how to be constructively compassionate with yourself and with your partner.

Note: Using a tool or resource like the *Calm* app for sleep, meditation, or relaxation can interrupt both mind states and mind stories. It is free and only requires three to five minutes to interrupt your mind stories.

Chapter 13

Relational Skills 101
to Rebuild Trust in the Relationship

Rebuilding the relationship will take time, and I am going to ask both of you to communicate differently when you are working together to reinforce the connection. Although this is a slow process, if you use the following guidelines, you will be more likely to expedite the work and make greater gains.

As I taught these basic skills, I encouraged the betrayer to start very slowly so the skills could be an anchor to building trust. People who were motivated stuck with the process and built a foundation that provided safety and stabilization. As their individual affair recovery strengthened, their relational skills also grew stronger. However, a smaller percentage of men either got complacent and stopped practicing them as instructed or did not realize the magnitude behind the recommendations. When I brought the partner in to do the work, the couple was much better at utilizing the directions that were given.

So even though I thought my directions were a stand-alone intervention and could be implemented by the betrayer, **I found that encouraging the couple to learn them together in conjunction with a trained specialist who is familiar with the work expedited the process and reinforced the connection.** When you work with a specialist who understands this work, you will have the added advantage of having a professional guide to support both of you as you gain these skills.

You have already learned the most important empathy skill, knees-to-knees reflective listening. I hope that you are practicing that with regularity. You have also learned the trigger-busting technique, which should help the partner with triggers.

Lastly, you should be acknowledging the past pain your infidelity has caused and validating the partner's feelings. This is paramount to healing.

Check-ins are crucial to building trust. They help partners feel safe and keep them in the loop about your struggles and challenges—whether you have run into the affair partner, been contacted by the AP, or encountered any other issue that comes up because of your infidelity. Checking in at a regular time decreases anxiety about what the partner doesn't know.

THE CONNECTION-SHARE: A TIME TO CONNECT AND SHARE

Checking in with each other is crucial in developing safety and promoting the teamwork that it takes to rebuild your relationship. Check-ins allow both of you to hear about the progress each of you is making, and it is the building block to committing to a time for ongoing communication. Once infidelity has been discovered, it is natural to want to hide what you are feeling and thinking because it feels too vulnerable for both of you to bring up additional conflict. Check-ins provide that safe place and accountability to talk about the hard subjects.

It is a formal process to access information to develop more empathy. For the betrayer, developing empathy requires that you know how to put yourself in your partner's shoes. BTs do not necessarily know how to do this naturally. For many BTs, they need to practice developing the art of empathy. Even if they were able to guess what was on the BP's mind, it would be dangerous to do so because they might get it wrong and miss the opportunity of truly knowing what your partner thinks or feels.

As a couple, you need more opportunities to check in with each other to find out what is going on in the head and heart of each other. Your relationship requires a lot of repair, and check-ins are another way to reassure your partner of your daily progress. When you both develop and create the daily ritual of spending 5 to 15 minutes sharing your highlights and struggles with each other for that day, you are investing in the connection necessary to develop trust.

Check-ins have been used for decades by the addiction community to hold the addict accountable with his sponsor or fellowship. There are various check-ins that you can follow, but I advocate for a check-in I call the "Connection-Share."

The format for the Connection-Share is simple. It is important for you to customize it for your comfort level as a couple. Most partners want to know what their unfaithful spouse is struggling with so that they will stay aware of their issues. However, if the partner feels this is too activating, the BP may ask the BT to share this daily work with a sponsor, and the partner may choose some alternative "connection statements" that are equally disclosing and connecting. It is important to create a structure that enhances good communication. Whenever you are communicating, it is important to sit and watch each other to pick up non-verbal signs and cues that will enhance communication. Many couples tend to wait till the end of the day and end up shortchanging the Connection-Share or experiencing conflict because you are both tired and ready for bed.

The proper protocol should be that you both sit down face-to-face and check in with these five points:

- Your primary feeling that you experienced today

- A struggle/concern that you encountered

- An appreciation for your recovery

- An appreciation for your relationship

- What you would like to work on for tomorrow's recovery

This format would entail the BT facing the partner and looking eye to eye as the BT shares the process of a check-in.

MY PRIMARY FEELING THAT I EXPERIENCED TODAY:

- "Overall, I feel glad that my recovery and our relationship recovery is a stabilizing factor in my life. I feel happy that you have stayed with me and that we are working on our marriage together."

A STRUGGLE/CONCERN THAT I ENCOUNTERED:

- "Even though I felt happy, I struggled with feeling edgy today and was not able to pinpoint why I was emotionally out of sorts. I realize that once my recovery is rock solid, I will need to focus on how I can give back and pay it forward."

AN APPRECIATION FOR MY RECOVERY:

- "I could not wait to get to my meeting today as I could sense that I was edgy, and I just knew that if I had a chance to listen to others and check in, I would feel better. My fellowship allows me to know that we are all struggling, and it gives me hope that we can get through this together. I wish that we had a way to grow together in a recovery program. I mentioned that to my sponsor, and he talked to me about a group called Recovering Couples Anonymous. The group is for couples who want to work on themselves to improve the recovery for the coupleship. I would love to explore that with you to see if that is something that you might want to do, too."

AN APPRECIATION FOR OUR RELATIONSHIP:

- "I know this is going to sound silly, but it felt deceiving that I didn't let you know that I was having an off day. I didn't want to worry you because I worried that it might trigger you, and I sometimes avoid a conflictual interaction because I hurt so badly when I watch you struggle. And yet something kept saying that Tami would want to know. I guess I was hoping that you would see that something was wrong and would ask, and then I would share and be able to get some reassurance from you. But I avoided that because I did not want to trigger you, even though my therapist has told me to start sharing my emotional self with you. I guess what I am saying here is that I appreciate that we are still together, that I thought about texting you, and that I am sharing it now."

WHAT WOULD I LIKE TO WORK ON FOR TOMORROW'S RECOVERY?

- "I am going to spend more time journaling about what is going on with me internally so that I can connect to you more fully and be more vulnerable. I will re-read *Help.Her.Heal* to gain more empathy and remind myself that I need to be more vulnerable. Guess I need to read more Brené Brown, huh?"

HERE IS AN EXCERPT FROM A PARTNER'S CONNECTION-SHARE

MY PRIMARY FEELING THAT I EXPERIENCED TODAY:

- "I felt anxious today. In two weeks, it will be a year since discovery of your affair, and even though I know we are doing well, it feels scary. I don't know if I can trust it."

A STRUGGLE/CONCERN THAT I ENCOUNTERED:

- "I had to meet with my boss, and since I have not been on my game for months since our disclosure, I wondered if she sensed that I am not running on all cylinders. I hate that my mental state has been compromised. I end up feeling resentful because I think to myself, 'I didn't do anything to deserve this, but it feels like I am the one who is most affected.' And then I get mad, and I want to pull away from you. I feel so conflicted because I can tell that you are working a strong recovery program, but I wonder why I must suffer so much. I am an innocent bystander, and I am the most impacted!"

AN APPRECIATION FOR YOUR RECOVERY:

- "I can tell that I am slowly getting better. Sometimes, I feel like I am going crazy because I want to be close and share my real feelings, but I fear that if I do, you might get lazy and stop doing all the hard work that you have been doing. I also have mixed feelings, and I hesitate to tell you this because I do not want you to think that you are off the hook. But I am forcing myself to be honest so that we can get better quicker, and I know that means that I must be vulnerable and trust you again. I am glad that I am taking that risk. Please do not let me down."

AN APPRECIATION FOR OUR RELATIONSHIP:

- "I appreciate that we are talking more than we ever have for years. For so long, I felt shut out of your life and could not figure out why, but now I can tell that you are working hard to make things right."

WHAT WOULD I LIKE TO WORK ON FOR TOMORROW'S RECOVERY?

- "I would like to learn how to reach out for help. I hate that I need to call my mentor when I feel triggered because I want to try to handle it myself, which invariably adds to the anger I feel toward you for causing the trigger in the first place. I think there's a part of me that doesn't want to let you off the hook. There is a part of me that wants you to suffer like I have to because sometimes the pain is unbearable."

CHECK-INS REQUIRE THAT YOU BE VULNERABLE, OPEN, AND NON-DEFENSIVE

It is important to do check-ins with an open heart. You must be able to hear what each other says and stay open to the feelings and thoughts of your spouse without going into the natural byproduct of the trauma.

To the Betrayer: Your tendency is to move into a shame spiral. Remind yourself that when you hear the concerns, fears, and progress, you must be able to contain the BP's pain. That will assist you in being better able to move forward, put yourself in your partner's shoes, and even anticipate what your partner may be feeling. Over time, this will build on itself, and your empathy will be a natural byproduct of who you are! Of course, it is always good to check in with the BP's emotions and thoughts to see if you are on target. Do these exercises daily so you are available to connect and share. At first, it might feel like you are inviting conflict into your life because it may feel like another opportunity for your partner to vent about the horrendous pain. Remind yourself that conflict is normal and natural, and as you get healthier, you will move through it and may even feel closer as a result.

To the Partner: Your job is to stay as open as you can to the changes and take in the improvements slowly because you need to protect yourself until the BT has proven safety to you. You will know when you can begin to let your guard down. Your intuition will tell you when it is time to enjoy the changes. And when it does, you will recognize that you deserve to be able to trust again!

DARLENE & JASON: *"HE MUST BE ACTING OUT AGAIN"*

Darlene has this gut feeling that something is not right between she and her husband. Jason takes an especially long shower and then reminds her, right as he leaves for work, that he may be late due to a 4 pm meeting. He wants to give her a "heads up" so she won't worry, but she thinks to herself, *I am not buying the "I-may-need-to-stay-at-work-longer-due-to-a-meeting" excuse.*

She remains worked up all day, and when he calls her to check in, she is short with him. Her heart is pounding, and she is thinking about all sorts of scenarios. She cannot get her work done, and she is miserable, questioning why she is staying in a marriage that causes her so much angst. He gets home 25 minutes early. He explains that the meeting was shortened because the VP was ill. She is cold and distant with him. He asks her what is wrong, and she clams up and refuses to share her concerns. She tells herself, *I am not going to be vulnerable and share my fears with him ever again.*

He is confused, and his tendency is to avoid the conflict altogether. He leaves the room and considers going for a run to escape the tension, but he remembers last week's session where Carol had encouraged them to practice AVR in times of conflict. He takes a deep breath, goes back into the room, and moves two chairs together facing each other. Jason says, "Darlene, would you come over here so we can talk?" She says, "I am not in the mood."

He says, "I promise this won't take long. I need to find out what is bothering you, and I suspect I've done something that has caused you pain." She looks up and reluctantly sits down in the chair. He asks her, "Can I practice some AVR with you like Carol encouraged us to do?" She stares at him blankly, but he can see that behind the blank stare is a world of hurt.

He says, "Can we do a knees-to-knees?" She does not respond, so he moves closer to her and touches her knees with his.

He takes a deep breath and says, "I can see that I have done something today that has brought back the pain of my acting out." [He is acknowledging the pain.]

"It seems to have caused you to be angry with me." [He picked anger as the primary feeling that he was witnessing.]

"And I want to reassure you that although I am not sure what happened today, I really do want to understand it because I don't ever want to cause you more pain. Will you please tell me what happened?" [He is providing reassurance.]

She scooted her chair back, broke the knees-to-knees contact, and said, "I suspected that you had something going on today. You took an extra-long shower and then talked about being late due to a 4 o'clock meeting. You *never* have 4 o'clock meetings, and it felt very much like a flashback from your acting-out days. I know you came home early, but I am wondering if you were even at work this afternoon...I just do not feel good about this at all!"

Jason knows that this is the time to practice empathy, although "the old Jason" would have tried to argue or talk her out of her feelings. He takes another deep breath, focuses on her eyes, and says, "It makes sense to me that you would worry that I was acting out, and I would only assume you felt scared and alone. Yet I want to reassure you that I never want to go back to being that guy again, and I like who I am now." (Later, he told me that he wished he had focused more on her feelings when he reassured her.)

AVR looks like a simple formula, but during the conflict, it can feel overwhelming. The BTs that use it admit that it feels foreign at first, but eventually, it gets easier with practice.

WILL & JOANNE: THE WORST DAY OF HER LIFE BECOMES THE BEST

Will and Joanne have been in early-recovery couples work for 1.5 years. Will acted out overseas with prostitutes, and he had created an entire action plan to make Joanne feel safe. After the formal therapeutic disclosure when she found out the entire truth, Joanne would feel nauseous and terrified when he was given overseas assignments. Will encouraged her to come with him, and since the kids were grown, she agreed because she wanted a safeguard that he would not act out. There was still much trepidation about him being away from her, but she felt more assured when she accompanied him on his trips.

Then COVID-19 hit, and it prevented Will from traveling at all. Joanne was thrilled because she got a rest from the nagging fear that he would someday have to walk into the "devil's den" without her. The COVID-19 pandemic gave her extra time to work on her trauma and see a brain spotting and EMDR therapist to work on the target behind the triggers. Then, the inevitable happened when Will was told he would need to resume traveling. Joanne had found out the night before and had not slept at all. She came in anxious and extremely triggered. I had the couple sit down to discuss their fears.

Joanne said that she knew it was going to happen, and she feared that Will would not have enough support overseas to fortify his recovery. She stated somewhat angrily, "You won't have access to your sponsor, meetings, or fellowship. And those guys from Reimagine Love have been a strong team for you. You have been doing so well, and now I am afraid that it will all be for nothing." Then she started to cry.

Will looked at his activated wife and said, "I see that you are in so much turmoil about me going back to my old behaviors. That has to make you feel so scared, reminding you of those gut-wrenching days after discovery, but I want to reassure you that I have already put a plan into place to use the app WhatsApp to have free international calls. I have four guys lined up who work second shift so that I can have around-the-clock support if I need it, and I am willing to take a poly to help you feel safe...We are going to get through this together."

Joanne looked up at him with a tear-stained face and said, "You've already developed a fire drill with your buddies in preparation for this day? Are you afraid of your own impulses, urges, and cravings?"

He looked at her, shook his head, and said, "Well, it's always good to have a backup plan. I feel strong in my recovery, but I know that I should never take my recovery for granted and that I would need a plan for you. I hurt you terribly, and I want to make sure your brain is protected, so I created a backup plan for when this day would eventually come. I didn't want to wait till I got the call to do the overseas work—I wanted to have an action plan!"

Joanne told both of us that something had lifted that day, and she realized that she would need to trust his wisdom and move away from her fear to see if he could maintain his good recovery. That day was a turning point for them, and she later would say, "How could the worst day of my life turn out to be the turnaround for us?"

That is how ERCEM works—the empathy he used became the glue for rebuilding the relationship!

ASSERTIVENESS—DEVELOP YOUR COMMUNICATION BACKBONE

Will was being authentic and honest and showing Joanne that he took his recovery seriously. He was clear and direct about his feelings and his recovery. Unfortunately, most couples have not been taught how to express themselves, so they relate to conflict by being passive, aggressive, or passive-aggressive.

Let's take a look at the three types of maladaptive but commonly used forms of communication, and then we can talk about assertiveness. As you both read these definitions of communication and relational styles, think about which style you predominantly use.

PASSIVE COMMUNICATION

Are you or your spouse passive? People who are passive are easily overlooked or walked on. This allows others to control them or not understand what is going on in their lives. If you are passive, you probably present with poor self-esteem. Deep down, you feel that your opinion does not count.

If you are the betrayer, you might experience so much shame wrapped up in what you have done, and you do not feel you deserve to stand up for what you feel or believe. John Gottman calls this "stonewalling" and says that when you walk away from conflict, nothing can get resolved, and you are contributing to further problems in the relationship. He also says that 85% of all conflicts do not necessarily get resolved, but it is processed, leaving the relationship feeling intact. If that sounds like you, it can be helpful to take time out to assess your feelings or gather your thoughts, but not to walk out permanently from the conflict or communication.

If you are the partner, you may be so saddened by the betrayal that you have no energy to think through your situation and stand up for yourself. You resign yourself that this is as good as it will get, and you are so afraid of what the future might bring that you do nothing and assume a passive role.

Passivity can be genetic or a learned response from your childhood or other primary relationships. Think back over your lifetime and list three times in your past that you exhibited passive communication and let things happen because it was easier or safer than working it out.

The BT's response:

1. _____

2. _____

3. _____

The BP's response:

1. _____
   _____
   _____
   _____
   _____

2. _____
   _____
   _____
   _____
   _____

3. _____
   _____
   _____
   _____
   _____

AGGRESSIVE COMMUNICATION

People who communicate aggressively are trying to communicate by intimidation. You may have witnessed this in your own family of origin. You watched how one of your parents aggressed against the other to keep them in a "one-down position."

As the BT, you may have become increasingly more aggressive in shutting the BP down and protecting your deception. Many betrayers have confessed that they communicated aggressively to stop their spouse from figuring out about the affair. When the BT uses aggressiveness, there is an element of gaslighting that occurs. The spouse, who is trying to figure out what is really going on, ends up feeling crazy because the BT is attacking the vigilance that the BP is using to try to understand what is happening. It ends up being a double betrayal.

Aggressive personality types attack the character of others and appear very demanding. People who communicate aggressively typically want to control and dominate others. They may try to intimidate a person into doing it "their way." There are no stereotypes for female partners versus male partners. Females, in general, may be less likely to be aggressive than males, but when you throw in partner betrayal and a trauma response, you will likely have a more aggressive partner. Male partners may exhibit aggressive behavior, but it is more common for them to detach and act indifferent.

To the BP: Have you found yourself communicating much more angrily and aggressively with your spouse? Are you lashing out, or are you feeling uncontrollable amounts of rage? Your amygdala may be activated, and you are fighting as a response to trauma. You both are wondering what is happening to you because you have never shown this aggressiveness before. If this sounds like you, know that you do not possess an "aggressive personality." Your aggressive style of communication will subside when your trauma gets better; however, you will need a clinical specialist to help you interrupt your reactivity so that you feel better.

To the Betrayer: List three ways you have related to your partner aggressively or have shown aggressiveness in your past to keep the BP from finding out about your affair.

1. _____

_____

_____

_____

_____

2. _____
   _____
   _____
   _____
   _____

3. _____
   _____
   _____
   _____
   _____

To the Partner: Do you believe that you react aggressively? List the ways you have reacted aggressively in your past. Is it normal for you to react aggressively, or do you believe this is a trauma response?

1. _____
   _____
   _____
   _____
   _____

2. _____
   _____
   _____
   _____
   _____

3. _____

_____

_____

_____

_____

PASSIVE-AGGRESSIVE COMMUNICATION

People who use a passive-aggressive style do not feel comfortable with their own conflict within relationships and choose to retaliate secretly to externalize their anger. They cannot express themselves directly, but their anger is so intense that they make the choice to be angry without owning it. Many partners complained that when their spouse was in active infidelity, they became very passive-aggressive. Sometimes, betrayers would leave for  work and not come home on time. They would not answer their phone for hours. They would use DARVO techniques on the partner.

DARVO

DARVO is a type of communication that betrayers might use when they are being held accountable for their behavior. It was coined by Jennifer Freyd and stands for "Deny, Attack, Reverse Victim, and Offender."

Betrayers, at the height of their acting out, will do anything they can to keep the BP from discovering their infidelity. When the partner intuitively senses that something may be wrong, they might ask inquiring questions to try to understand what is situationally happening. As partners begin the inquiry, the BT might:

The BT **denies** that they have done anything wrong.	The BT **attacks** the BP by becoming defensive and blaming them for their inquisition.	The BT **reverses** roles.	The BT will take on the role of **victim** and try to convince the BP that "they are picking" on the BT.	The BT calls the BP *the* **offender** and wants them to believe that they are being unfair.

This scenario might look like the following:

When BTs don't come home after work because they were acting out, they might deny their actions, attack the BP for confronting them, tell them that they are controlling, and reverse the scenario to make betrayed partners think that they were discouraging, blaming, and angry. They would tell partners that they were accusatory and not capable of being reasonable. They would manipulate the situation so that they would appear to be the victims and the betrayed partners, not the offenders.

Betrayers who are passive-aggressive are angry when asked to be accountable for their time and will get even with people behind their backs. Betrayers who forget appointments they did not want to attend or did not answer questions because they did not want to talk about things may be relating in a passive-aggressive manner. If betrayers are not in good recovery, they will disappear, do what they want, and then act innocent, denying their behavior. Again, people in full deception will do anything to protect their infidelity and will sacrifice their partner's sanity and serenity.

GASLIGHTING

An intentional maneuver to create a situation that is so compelling that the betrayed spouse experiences self-doubt.	This self-doubt is perpetuated and reinforced by the betrayer, making the partner doubt his/her reality and doubt his or herself.	The partner begins to question whether they are losing touch with reality and fears that they are going "crazy."

Gaslighting is a serious, abusive form of manipulation where the addict is intentionally and purposely wanting his partner to question her own reality. It is the most serious form of passive-aggressive behavior because it is an intentional maneuver to create a situation whereby the partner doubts her own reality.

In the field of sexual betrayal, you will hear a term called "gaslighting" used to depict what can happen when betrayers purposely belittle and manipulate partners and intentionally try to make them feel crazy for suspecting something is going on. When using this type of manipulation, it leaves partners questioning their own sanity and reality.

An example of this would be a man who notices it seems like his husband is spending hundreds of dollars a month. He might challenge him by saying, "Rob, there are thousands of dollars that are missing out of our account, and I want us to sit down and compare last year's finances to this year's balance."

Rob knows good and well that his husband Thomas is on to him. He immediately goes into defense mode and not only denies the reality but also puts him down in the process by telling Thomas that he is crazy, making Thomas doubt his financial abilities, and bringing up past situations where he may have made financial mistakes. Thomas will start to doubt himself and his abilities. It seems like Rob is being abusive, but Rob denies it and leaves Thomas feeling like he is going crazy. Thomas will doubt his own perceptions to the degree that he also questions if he could be right. Again, gaslighting is a serious, abusive form of manipulation where the betrayer is intentionally and purposely wanting the BP to question his or her sanity.

To the Betrayers: Can you think of times that you used DARVO?

Can you think of times that you used passive-aggressive behaviors to hide your acting out?

1. _____

_____

_____

2. _____

_____

_____

Betrayed partners have used passive-aggressive behaviors in retaliation for how they were treated. I worked with a woman who was regularly beaten by her husband for not cleaning the house properly. Each week, she would come in with a defeated reaction to her life. Her bruises were visible, and she hung her head in discouragement.

Week after week, I would talk with her about her options. I knew that I had to be careful with my advice because if this woman was too forceful or assertive, her life could be in danger. Then, one afternoon, she walked into my office with a totally liberated look on her face. She sat cross-legged on my couch and was animated. I secretly was cheering because I sensed she had left him. I was already thinking about safety plans to make sure that her separation went smoothly. I asked her how her week had been, and she said it was normal. I repeated her statement and said, "So, you had a normal week?" She nodded her head and said, "Yes."

I told her that she looked different and that I noticed less bruising, and she coyly smiled in response. I asked her what was different, and she told me that she had finally cleaned the house to her husband's satisfaction. My heart sank as I thought she had acquiesced to his brutality. I said that I was surprised that she had walked in so gleefully. None of this was making sense to me. She smiled again and replied, "I am now cleaning the toilets with his toothbrush!"

My client had learned how to passive-aggressively get her husband back without his knowing and seemed to find great satisfaction in her new cleaning venture. I, of course, worried that if or when he discovered her retaliation, he might kill her. I worked with her for many more months, creating a safe exit plan so she could leave him and not fear for her life. My client did not feel safe to assert herself, so she used passive-aggressiveness instead.

ASSERTIVENESS IS THE BACKBONE OF GOOD COMMUNICATION

Assertiveness is standing up for your beliefs. It is being clear about what you think and how you feel. When you are assertive, you let each other know the real you, and you stay true to yourself so that you can achieve your goals and move closer to what you need. Assertiveness is conveying a direct message about your needs. It is proactive, and it empowers you to share your feelings so you can eventually ask for a behavioral change. This means you are being clear and direct about what you need and want. **It does not mean you will get what you want; it means you have stated your feelings and facts clearly.**

When you assert yourself, your loved ones or coworkers will know where you stand. Again, I repeat, it does not mean that you get your way, but it does send a clear message of how you feel, what you believe, and what you may need. It is the first step to creating other forms of healthy behaviors, like increasing your communication, setting up boundaries that would keep you both safe, and developing consequences with others if they violate your boundaries. It enables you to set limits so others will not walk all over you. It creates healthy boundaries and enables you to accomplish goals because it reinforces what is important to you.

As you move toward healthier forms of relating to each other, you will need to practice different types of assertiveness. Most couples do not know what assertiveness is, let alone know how to practice it with each other. Are you one of those couples? Are either of you good at being clear and direct in your communication? If so, maybe you saw an important person in your life use assertiveness on a regular basis.

To the Betrayer: It can be daunting to practice assertiveness because you feel shame and guilt for what you have done. However, when you avoid assertiveness, it can propel you into other negative types of behaviors.

As an example, it may be common for you to get discouraged when the BP does not trust your new recovery, and you may want to lash out (aggressive style). At other times, you may want to say, "Oh, forget it," and walk away (passive or passive-aggressive style), which does not resolve the situation. When you resort to passivity, you miss the chance to be your authentic self and let the BP know what you need or want. The following information will be especially helpful in breaking old maladaptive behaviors that keep you from working on connection and intimacy.

As the Betrayed Partner: You may also have had trouble expressing assertiveness and sharing your feelings and thoughts. If you are a female partner, you're likely a better communicator due to your socialization skills, and yet you still may have kept some of your feelings to yourself to avoid conflict and promote harmony or because you fear that level of vulnerability. Does that sound like you?

Many of my female partners have spent so much time attending to the needs of others that they have robbed themselves of the satisfaction of achieving their own goals. If self-esteem is solely based on doing for others, you will not have had the opportunity to know what you want or need. Learning assertiveness will bring clarity to your own needs.

If you are a male partner, it is likely you are struggling with how to feel or who to talk to because there have been few resources available for betrayed men. *After the Affair* is a wonderful book that addresses betrayal and addresses the nuances of being a male BP. Regardless of your sex, both types of partners need to address their own assessment of assertiveness.

What is your assessment of your ability to be assertive?

Betrayer: _____

_____

Partner: _____

_____

What communication style are you most likely to exhibit?

Betrayer: _____

_____

Partner: _____

_____

What situations have both of you experienced where you could have been assertive?

Betrayer: _____

_____

Partner: _____

_____

As your relationship heals, it is important that you both practice being direct with each other. It does not mean that you get what you need, but it does mean that you are clear and direct about how you feel, what you think, and what you would like in the relationship. If you want to have a connection with each other, you will need to get better about communicating your thoughts in a safe way. I know that it will feel scary, but I would encourage both of you to spend some time talking about how you have communicated in the past. As your relationship gets healthier, you will want to share your thoughts and feelings with each other, which requires vulnerability and trust.

A secondary gain of assertiveness is that it creates better self-esteem and helps you to know yourself better. We call it developing your backbone—the backbone of self-esteem.

I would like each of you to ask yourself which profile fits your style of communication. Which person are you? Please check the boxes that most relate to your interactions with others.

- ☐ Do you assert yourself with others?

- ☐ Do people know how you feel and what you think?

- ☐ Do you speak about what is on your mind in a direct, concise manner?

- ☐ Do people know the real you and what you stand for?

Or:

- ☐ Are you afraid to share feelings for fear of hurting others or retaliation?

- ☐ Do you squelch your opinions because you think they are not important, or you are afraid they will be shot down?

☐ Do you feel like you do not have the right to share your feelings because of what you have done in the past?

☐ Are you afraid to speak your mind because if you do, your needs may not be met, and you will feel that double rejection?

☐ Are you fearful to speak your mind because you fear another's anger or wrath?

So, which person sounds more like you? Maybe you are a mix of both types. It is important to be honest so you can make needed changes. Are you the first one or the second one? It is important for the BP to see your self-assessment.

What characteristics most emulate you? Share it with each other so your spouse knows how you see yourself. Work on finding an example for each box you checked.

1. One of my partners asserted herself and said, "I feel like you have done a great job of attending to my healing and to my needs. But since so much of my life feels tarnished, I personally feel the need for a renewal ceremony to recommit ourselves to each other."

2. Another partner told his husband that he wanted a new ring to acknowledge their healed relationship.

3. A BT told his wife that he was angry because his changes were NEVER acknowledged, and what he feared most was that his wife was punishing him.

4. Another partner told his husband that he needed to move out of their home because the bedroom felt haunted by his cheating in the past.

In all four cases, the spouses had honest dialogue with their significant others and compromised on the requests.

Here were the compromises:

1. The BT asked if they could go to a place the BP had always wanted to go to, and he promised to set up all the arrangements to find a special place to renew their relationship. He asked his wife to write out her feelings about the renewal, and he, too, would share his thoughts. The partner picked Barbados on a cliff in front of an official; the betrayer read how lucky he was to have been given a second chance to love his wife and rebuild their trust. The wife read her observations of how he was different and was even able to share the reasons she was able to offer him grace and give love another try. They both told me they had never felt closer to each other after the ceremony.

2. This couple chose to go together to find his husband a new ring. As they were looking, John told Mark that he decided that he would prefer that they both get ring tattoos that symbolized their renewed commitment. The couple chose a cross intertwined with the words, "Faith and forever." After the tattoos healed, they picked out a simple band that was engraved with the same intertwined cross and words.

3. This couple had an honest dialogue whereby the wife admitted she was punitive because she feared that if she began to acknowledge the changes, he would go back to his old ways. Together, they decided to spend some time doing the Connection-Shares so that his wife could get comfortable sharing appreciations. Mike the BT said, "I had no expectations for change, but I feel like my assertiveness was the shift in our relationship that we needed."

4. The couple decided that, despite the financial stress of buying a new house, they would build a home that would seem fresh and new and would allow them to create an environment that honored their new relationship.

Although assertiveness is not necessarily about "getting your way," it more often results in "behavioral requests," coined by John Gottman. Most people have never received any formal assertiveness training. This workbook will help you to polish your assertiveness skills, which is crucial to improving your communication with each other and forming better connections. Oftentimes, people who do not assert themselves get walked on or find themselves putting their needs on the back burner. Assertiveness keeps you out of the victim role. It lets people know where you stand.

Many life strategists stress that you teach people how to treat you. When you assert yourself, you teach others about your feelings, limits, and boundaries. You no longer can get walked on because you have changed your behavior.

There are two basic formulas you can use to assert yourself. Both involve using "I" messages. Begin by thinking about something you have kept to yourself, and then practice using one of these sentences to share your thoughts.

Take a moment now to fill in the blanks in the following exercise:

USING THE BASIC ASSERTIVENESS FORMULA (WITHOUT CONSEQUENCES)

As an experiment, think of one thing that has to do with your feelings that you have kept inside and not shared with your spouse or others. Using the assertiveness formula, practice filling in the blanks and imagine yourself saying that statement to the other person. Be sure to write the statement down, which will make you more likely to use it in your daily life.

ASSERTIVENESS FORMULA FOR THE PARTNER *WITHOUT* CONSEQUENCE:

_____, when you _____,
          (Name)   (Specific Behavior)

I feel _____
                   (Feeling Word)

because _____
          (The message it sends me, or the message I receive is)

ASSERTIVENESS FORMULA FOR THE PARTNER *WITH* CONSEQUENCE:

_____, when you _____,
          (Name)   (Specific Behavior)

I feel _____
                   (Feeling Word)

because _____
          (The message it sends me, or the message I receive is)

THE SECOND PART OF ASSERTIVENESS IS TO SET A CONSEQUENCE IF YOU FEEL MISTREATED

I do not like _____
                         (The Behavior)

and this is what I'm going to do about it if it occurs again: _____

_____
           (Statement of action you will take)

ASSERTIVENESS FORMULA FOR THE BETRAYER WITHOUT CONSEQUENCE:

_____ , when you _____ ,
        (Name)   *(Specific Behavior)*

I feel _____
                    (Feeling Word)

because _____
        (The message it sends me, or the message I receive is)

ASSERTIVENESS FORMULA FOR THE BETRAYER WITH CONSEQUENCE:

_____ , when you _____ ,
        (Name)   *(Specific Behavior)*

I feel _____
                    (Feeling Word)

because _____
        (The message it sends me, or the message I receive is)

THE SECOND PART OF ASSERTIVENESS IS TO SET A CONSEQUENCE IF YOU FEEL MISTREATED

I do not like _____
                    (The Behavior)

and this is what I'm going to do about it if it occurs again: _____

_____
        (Statement of action you will take)

HERE ARE SOME EXAMPLES OF ASSERTIVENESS:

1. Tom knew that their country club was a place where Tanika would go to sit at their bar and flirt with the men who got off the golf course. Tanika was very beautiful and would sit at the bar and groom the men who already may have been intoxicated from a long day of drinking and playing golf. As Tanika worked an affair recovery program, Tom asserted himself and told Tanika that he wanted to put a pause on their membership for one to three years as Tanika proved her fidelity. Tanika suggested that that would mean that they would need to renew their membership at a higher fee if they put a pause on it. Tom asserted himself and said they either needed to put a pause on the membership or move out of the neighborhood entirely. Tanika agreed to this consequence because she was working hard and did not want to lose their friends or disrupt her children's lives.

2. When Sybil gets triggered, she tends to rage at her husband, calling him names and physically pushing and smacking him. In a check-in, Chris revealed, "Sybil, I know that I caused you all of this pain, but when you get triggered, become physical, and start raging at me, I feel angry because the message it sends me is that you are going to punish me for my past and that I deserve this abuse.

    "We have been working on this in Early Recovering Couples Work (ERCW), and I need to remind you that I really do want to hear why you are angry. But when it becomes abusive, I will be forced to take a time out and come back when you have gotten control of your feelings and can share them."

3. Carrie is dealing with her husband who had, on occasion, received ongoing communication from old affair partners. She knows that she can't control him, but she wants to be clear and direct about her need to know immediately after Mark was contacted. He begged for more time because of his busy work schedule, but Carrie wouldn't budge. Their agreement was that he would tell her immediately when this occurred. On three occasions, she found correspondence from other women and decided that Mark was not practicing integrity, and she went to her attorney and requested a formal separation. The separation gave her the clarity to realize that Mark's need for ongoing attention was not going to give her the safety she required. After three months, she decided a divorce was imminent.

4. Arnold has had a lifetime of being subservient to Jay. He did not feel strong enough to use assertiveness, and he told both of us that he was conflict-avoidant and did not want the ongoing stress of fighting to get his way. I reassured both of them that we would practice assertiveness in the office so Arnold could learn the formula. I reminded him that it did not mean he got his way, but he could relish in the fact that Jay would know how he felt. Jay admitted that he tended to "bully" Arnold to get his way, but now that they were working on a whole new relationship, he would try something different. This couple did a great job of making the commitment to change their relational patterns.

Many couples complain that their assertiveness will not get their spouses to change. That is exactly right—being assertive is simply about letting your spouse know how their behavior affects you. It can also result in a boundary that helps reinforce your bottom line. The exciting part of assertiveness is that once you are clear with others, you feel better about yourself. Consequently, you work on doing things that will move you closer to getting your needs met and respecting yourself. When there are consequences, they are there to provide safety for you.

YOUR ASSERTIVENESS HISTORY

Review your history and describe times when you were assertive.

To the Betrayer: Think of three times you were clear and direct about how you felt or what you wanted:

1. _____
   _____
   _____

2. _____
   _____
   _____

3. _____
   _____
   _____

To the Partner: Think of three times you were clear and direct about how you felt or what you wanted:

1. _____
   _____
   _____

2. _____
   _____
   _____

3. _____

    _____

    _____

To the Betrayer: A relationship cannot heal unless there is honesty between both people. You may need to journal to encourage yourself to decide what the best way to share your thoughts honestly is. It is important to be gentle because your partner is dysregulated and will not know whether trust and genuine honesty will ever be achievable.

I typically teach couples to practice the following formula for assertiveness because it includes an explanation of your own personal perceptions of what you believe is going on.

THE GENTLE ASSERTIVENESS FORMULA

Assertiveness helps you own your perceptions. It may create some conflict, but know that if you are being honest with each other, you must face the conflict. That way, your spouse can know where you stand and understand your feelings and truth. It will be important to use a gentle tone as you share your thoughts and feelings to decrease the possibility of triggering your spouse.

To the Betrayer: Your infidelity robbed your partner of a safe place to have an honest, authentic connection, so make sure to validate the betrayal before you proceed to assertiveness. The formula below will help you identify situations that you would like to be vulnerable about and share what comes up for you when you see her reactions. It is easy to use and begins with addressing what you have put the BP through and normalizing the behaviors. I have listed in bold font the acknowledgment of the damage you have caused, which makes this a gentle assertiveness statement.

"Pauline, *I spent a lot of time acting out before I came home.* But now that I am in good recovery, when you get frustrated with me for being late, I feel sad because the message it sends me is that you are sure I am still acting out again."

"Ted, **I realize I have caused you many reasons to not trust me,** but when you go through my texts and read what my Celebrate Recovery group says to support me, I feel angry because the message it sends me is that you don't respect the confidentiality I promised to honor with my group."

"Emily, **I want you to know that I absolutely understand why you would question my integrity;** however, when you go through my texts and demand to know who this person is, I feel irritated because the message it sends me is that you still think I am keeping things from you."

"Tiffany, **I have caused you lots of reasons to be angry with me,** and when you talk about our problems in front of the kids, I feel scared because the message it sends me is that I will never be able to redeem myself in their eyes."

The reality of your assertiveness statement is that the BP will confirm that there is fear that you are acting out or being dishonest.

You may want to alter the sentence with, "What I fear most is:_____, or you may want to use the **Gentle Assertiveness Formula:**

_____ (acknowledgement of reasons for their behavior), however when you
(Name)

_____ I feel _____
(Behavior)   (Feeling Word)

because the message it sends me is _____

Or:

_____, I know that my past actions caused you this pain, however,
(Name)

when you _____
(Name the specific behavior)

I feel or felt _____
(Pick a specific feeling)

because what I fear most is _____

"Pauline, when you get frustrated with me for being late, I feel sad **because what I fear most** is that you will never believe that I am in good recovery and not acting out anymore." And then you might add with a question, **"What else can I do to show you that I am taking my recovery seriously?"**

"Ted, when you go through my texts and read what my Celebrate Recovery group says to support me, I feel angry because the message it sends me is that you don't respect the confidentiality that I promised to honor with my group and **what I fear is that your need to have me share our confidential dialogue compromises my need to be rigorously honest.**"

"Emily, when you go through my texts and demand to know who this person is, **I fear that you will not believe that I truly do not know, and you will understandably go to the fear that I am acting out.**" Then, you might add a question, **"What can we do together to find out who the person behind this unknown text is?"**

"Tiffany, when you talk about our problems in front of the kids, I feel scared **because what I fear most is that the kids will be confused and not be able to process our adult conversation.**" And then you might add with a question, **"Can we figure out where we can talk in privacy?"**

Assertiveness will take both of you some time to learn. It takes practice, but the more you both practice, the easier it will be to create and use assertiveness statements. When you concentrate on changing yourself and not others, you speed up the process of getting what you want and need.

BOUNDARIES AS A COUPLE

There is no doubt that you both have boundaries that will need to be respected. As you begin to do your early recovery couples work, it will be important to remind each other of your boundaries. Most betrayers in early recovery are willing to forego their boundaries to allow their partner a sense of safety and certainty. This is advisable because when he puts you and your needs first, it helps to recalibrate your sense of stability.

Occasionally, there can be understandable pushback, especially if the addiction novice gets "traditional" advice from his support group or sponsor. It is not uncommon for a partner to ask for recovery details as the BP attempts to decide how safety is needed. A partner will ask for the BT to share recovery goals or to change one. The old recovery might look like the following.

SUSAN & TOM: *PARTNERS DESERVE TO KNOW RECOVERY GOALS TO FEEL SAFE*

Susan asks Tom, "What are your current recovery goals, and have you set up time with your sponsor to regularly review them?"

Tom declares a boundary and says, "Susan, in all due respect, I share that stuff with my SAA group, and I am not privy to giving you that information."

Susan becomes disgusted and says, "I'm not sure what you are saying. What do you mean that you can't share where you are in your recovery plan? Tom, this is important for my safety!"

Tom reiterated that his recovery is between him and his fellowship. The fellowship has warned him that too much information is triggering, and it is best that he maintains his boundaries "for her protection."

He says, "This information would only keep you activated. I am not going to share that with you as that is a recovery boundary I will not violate."

That is the "old school" way. Tom does not know that he has been advised from the old model of support. There are still groups out there that do not understand that infidelity is a relational problem in addition to being a sobriety and recovery problem. He has clearly set a boundary based on the advice of his fellowship, but he needs to review his early recovery couples work because the premise of ERCEM is total honesty and transparency with massive amounts of empathy. He has spent so long deceiving her that now it is time to step up and share anything for which she has questions.

Besides, why would he not share his recovery goals with his partner? He should be proud of the work he is doing, and his first goal, in conjunction with his own recovery, is to help her feel safe. Tom got bad advice, and he did not know what he did not know, just like his support group. The good news is that more and more sponsors *are* becoming partner-sensitive, and men like Tom are going back to their Twelve-Step meetings and sharing the partner-sensitive perspective. Other men in the fellowship want the same thing, too, because they know how distraught their wives are from the infidelity. This field is changing quickly, and you both can help further the change by sharing ERCEM and partner sensitivity.

Tom practiced boundaries that he hoped would keep Susan safe, but he was trumping what Susan needed and putting the advice of his support group first. Boundaries create safety, and Susan needed to know that her husband was using his accountability partner—his sponsor—to maximize his recovery team. Since Susan is also on his team, she had the right to make a recovery request.

Sometimes boundaries can feel like punishment, and although they should never be used for punishment, it is true that there will be times when a BP's requests limit your choices and freedoms.

TINA & CHRIS: A HEALTHY COMPROMISE WITH BOUNDARIES

Chris and Tina came into my office with a look of closeness as they sat down to talk. Chris was proud of the progress they were making, and Tina reported that Chris was a better husband than he had ever been. I was pleased that this couple had made so much progress in the two and half years they had worked with me. Chris had several years of recovery, and he had wanted to go back to concerts to get back to a more normal routine. Chris had shared that he really had been craving music, and he knew that music was a healthy behavior that could produce dopamine in a legitimate way (as opposed to acting out).

Tina expressed in the session that something did not feel right to her. She thought long and hard about it for several days. She figured out that she was not opposed to him going to concerts, but she was concerned that he might drink too much when he went to the shows and that drinking was a contributor to his acting out.

Chris had abstained from drinking for the first two years of his sexual integrity and had slowly added it to social events, like a couple of glasses of wine at a fine restaurant or a couple of beers at a party. He had been successful for over a year with his controlled drinking, but going to a concert might be too much for him. Tina decided to use reflective listening and share her concerns, so she asked him if they could talk after dinner. Of course, he agreed. He sat down on the couch and asked her to join him, but she grabbed two kitchen chairs, moved them facing each other, and asked him to join her instead.

She started by asking him to stay open to a fear she had and not to get defensive with her. He looked dumbfounded and said he would not. She said, "Chris, I don't want you to think I am being irrational, but I have a lot of fears about some things you were talking about the other day. I have been thinking about how much you want to return to the concert scene, and I know I will be with you at most of them. But you love hanging out with your buddies, and my fear is that it will prompt you to drink too much and get inebriated, which might cause you to go back to your old ways and look at porn. Then the whole cycle will begin again."

Chris was shocked. He did not see this coming! He immediately felt a pang of anger because he was working a solid recovery program, and he felt it was time to resume some old activities that he loved. He thought, "I can't believe she is going to try to restrict me after all the hard work I have done! It's like she is punishing me for good behavior!" He tried to breathe through it, and he reminded himself that he needed to use his 4-7-8 breathing technique to manage the increased adrenaline he was feeling. He took four deep breaths in through his nose, held it in his belly for seven seconds, and released it for eight seconds straight. He felt better and was ready to rationally discuss her concerns.

He used some reflective listening and repeated back exactly what he heard. He said, "I heard you say that you don't want me to think that you are being irrational, but you have a lot of fears about me going to concerts because you think I might drink too much, especially if I am spending time together with my buddies. Your fear is that it will trigger me to drink too much and get inebriated, which may start me thinking about acting out. And because I have been drinking, I will have less inhibitions, won't work my recovery tools, and will be more likely to act out."

Tina looked at him and said, "Well, I didn't say all that, but you definitely got my point." She started to defend herself, but Chris interrupted her and said, "Can I AVR you?" She shook her head in agreement, and he said, "I can really see why you have concerns, and that must make you feel scared as hell. But I want you to know that I am willing to be alcohol-free at these concerts. I am missing the music, and I know why you would worry about that combination because, to be truthful, I had not even thought about it. But I think it would be a deadly combination, too!"

We talked about what a good job both had done. Tina had listened to her intuition and spent some time processing it before coming to Chris. She set them up psychologically to do good communication. She started off by sharing her fears that he might think she was irrational. (Sharing a fear will usually bring down defensiveness.) Chris felt angry but did some breathing exercises to resource and ground himself. He used reflective listening and then followed it up with AVR so that she felt heard and understood.

Now, that is good relational recovery! I told them that I wanted to do cartwheels, and they both laughed. We talked about all the healthy choices and changes they were making. (I also asked them if they would write up to the best of their ability the events that occurred at home so I could include it in my book.) I often ask clients to be videotaped so I can teach ERCEM specialists how to do this work. I am amazed at how generous they are with their lives.

Now that you have heard Chris and Tina's story, I would like for you to talk about behaviors you may have paused because they didn't feel safe to your relationship.

HOW MUCH INVOLVEMENT SHOULD A BETRAYED PARTNER HAVE IN THE RECOVERY PLAN?

There are all sorts of thoughts on this, but ERCEM believes that when the couple works on safety for the partner, it also entails working together in co-creation. It is important for the BT to know what is potentially unsafe in day-to-day life. The BT must learn to share their life experiences, struggles, and challenges to help the BP know about potential triggers or problem areas so that they can operate as a team and get stronger together.

The partner may want more clarification as to why something is, or is not, a struggle. The BP might want to add something into the plan that will keep the BT out of harm's way. The BT may not have thought about some of these things, but the BP is 10 feet ahead of the BT because that is how a BP thinks. This "hyperalert" state can protect them both, although the goal is to give the BP a break, calm the parasympathetic system down, and let the BT take the lead. Partners may want to contribute to the healthy behaviors plan and make suggestions that the couple might enjoy together.

This is the BT's recovery plan, and it should be done initially by the betrayer. You would not want to do it for the BT and take away the opportunity to evaluate boundaries, but as a partner-sensitive ERCEM specialist, I believe that working on expectations together allows both of you to design a recovery program that is relationally smart and benefits both of you. Knowing the structure of the recovery plan allows for safety in reviewing movies, finding the safest places that promote good choices, or researching vacation spots that are less triggering in the early stages of recovery. Other partners do not want to be involved at all. They explain that this is their spouse's journey to navigate, and they want to steer as far away as possible.

Do You Want Input in the BT's Recovery Plan?

To the Partner: Which partner profile most resonates with you?

List five reasons you feel that way.

1. _____

_____

_____

2. _____

_____

_____

3. _____

_____

_____

4. _____

_____

_____

5. _____

_____

_____

WHAT DO YOU THINK YOUR SPOUSE MIGHT NEED FROM YOU MOST?

Practice doing a knees-to-knees and encourage the BT to share with you what thoughts and feelings might be occurring regarding co-creation. Use reflective listening and repeat back what you heard. After you are finished, ask if you got it right. Listen for the response and then repeat it again.

BOUNDARY STRENGTHENING FOR THE PARTNER

Again, my colleague Dorit Reichental shared how she does boundary work with couples, and I thought it had a lot of value, so I included it here.

Reichental works from the premise that:

1. Infidelity is a violation of a partner's rights in all the multidimensional spheres, and there needs to be discussion about the previous violations in terms of the traumatic impact on the partner.

2.   There are several areas that need to be explored to restore safety and trust. Learning to respect a partner's boundaries is the foundation of a betrayer's recovery. It shows a real understanding of empathy. When that foundation is clear, other safety-building areas can be developed or redesigned, such as empathy building, intimacy, and sexual healing.

3.   Therefore, the boundary must be relational, written by the partner, and then jointly completed by the couple.

The BP goes through all the usual boundary categories using this format and illuminates assertiveness, which we will discuss in this chapter. The boundary always begins with these words: "In order to keep the relationship safe..."

BOUNDARY ASSERTIVENESS

The assertiveness statement starts like this:

"In order to keep the relationship safe...

when you say/do:_____, it makes me feel _____."

i.e.: *"When you forget to call me to inform me that you will be late, it makes me feel:*

- *"Scared that you are acting out again," or*

- *"It impacts me and makes me feel like you do not prioritize me," or*

- *"It impacts me and my sense of security and confidence in our relationship."*

Until you can demonstrate an understanding of the impact on me, I will:

_____

(This should be something that protects you or increases your intentional self-care)

On the following page is a written contract completed by a couple after they had both weighed in on how things could go smoother in the future.

THE COUPLESHIP CONTRACT

FOR THE BT

1. We have agreed that I will make consistent and predictable changes in my words/ actions by:_____

_____

(i.e. *"Setting a regular alarm on my phone five minutes before my target time to leave so that I no longer forget how important it is to hold true to my commitments."*)

2. By when: _____

(i.e. *"I will do this right now as we are sitting here."*)

3. I recognize that it has violated your sense of safety when I _____

_____

(i.e. *"Forget how much you need consistency from me."*)

FOR THE BP

4. Partner then shares with you that it will help them to feel _____

_____

(i.e. *loved, cared for, respected, valued, etc.*)

when you change the offending words/behaviors _____

_____

(i.e. *being late*)

5. As a result of the changes you make, I (the partner) will _____

_____

(*words/actions*)

in order to demonstrate to you that I now feel heard, safer, more trusting, and willing to _____

(*actions*)

For the Partner:

"As a result of the changes you make, I will be vulnerable enough to recognize those changes and lean into them to demonstrate to you that I now feel heard, safer, more trusting, and willing to look for ways to be closer."

To show appreciation because of your _____,

(loving, thoughtful, empathetic, healing)

I will _____

_____.

(actions, plans)

DORIT EXPLAINS:

1. The boundary is now a coupleship contract, signed and agreed to by both. It is an instrument used to change offending behavior into respectful, empathic behaviors over time, consistently and predictably, to heal a damaged relationship.

2. This is very different from a punishing spouse overseeing and controlling (willing or not) the betrayer's recovery.

3. The consequence is not meant to be punitive; it is meant to take whatever actions or words are necessary to create relational safety. It allows for a living amend for violating and offending their partner when breaking an agreed boundary.

4. The BT is accountable and takes full responsibility for the unfaithful actions by making physical, emotional, sexual, relational, spiritual, or relational restitution. When this process is done with intention and integrity, the responsibility for keeping the relationship safe becomes a shared responsibility.

5. This can also be used in a constructive way to safely allow a partner to express anger, minimize the betrayer's overwhelm, and help heal the wounds. When a boundary around anger, rage, and fear is negotiated and established ahead of time, the couple knows exactly what to do and can safely express negative emotions in the hopes of avoiding a triggering cycle.

Note: Now, a partner may have very distinct boundaries to begin to feel that life is back in control. As the relationship strengthens and gets healthier, your new relationship will no longer need as many boundaries for safety because the BP will feel safer and find some room in the relationship for trust. This happens approximately one to two years after discovery.

Chapter 14

Moving Into the Conflict—Using the Seven Principles to Stay Out of Shame

All couples experience conflict. In fact, conflict is normal, natural, and necessary. Conflict in healthy relationships breeds intimacy, and yet the two of you have faced what may seem like insurmountable conflict. Your fear of conflict and shame will take real focus, patience, and perseverance to overcome.

I have seen many couples overcome the anger, sadness, and fear that betrayal trauma has caused, but both people in the coupleship must want to heal from the broken relationship.

To the Partner: The process of working through the anger you feel toward the infidelity requires that you work through the feelings while simultaneously feeling vulnerable. To do this kind of work, you must have a clear vision in sight, and you must fully express yourself so that you can release the negativity and leave space to accept the sexual integrity that occurs as you both work on the ERCEM journey.

As a betrayed partner, are you able to move in and out of the pain, vulnerability, sadness, and anger? Can you let your guard down and be vulnerable again? It is important to know what you need to feel the anger, express it, and then surrender to it so you can release it to rebuild the relationship stronger. You will learn more about this in Chapter 16.

LEARNING NOT TO TAKE THINGS PERSONALLY

In *The Four Agreements: A Practical Guide to Personal Freedom*, Don Miguel Ruiz says that 95% of the beliefs we store in our mind are nothing more than lies, and we suffer because we believe our lies. One of his guidelines is to not take things personally. It is so important for you, the BP, to remember that the infidelity had nothing to do with who you are, what you looked like, how you related as a couple, or how good you were sexually. We know that it greatly affected you, but the betrayer had other choices other than to go outside of the marriage.

When Don Miguel Ruiz says, "Do not take anything personally," he is suggesting that when others do things to us that are abusive, conflictual, or injurious, we should never internalize the message and believe we are at fault. What others think and do is a projection of their own reality. When you own your responsibility but are able to put the shame in perspective, you are better able to hear the opinions and actions of others, and yet you will not be the victim of needless suffering.

Unfortunately, many partners feel responsible and wonder what they could have done to prevent it! As a partner, you have wondered what might have been wrong with you that could have spurred or contributed to the infidelity.

Conflict in marriage is normal, and when the two of you committed to each other, there was a sacred vow you both took that said that you would honor each other, and going outside of the marriage did not honor your relationship. When you have that thought, you are less likely to personalize it. Now that your spouse is in recovery, they have very different views of how things should have been handled concerning the unmet needs that can occur in any marriage.

To the Betrayer: As a person in good sexual recovery, you have come out of the fog and are learning the relational skills to manage your life. This means that you are also recognizing that you cannot change your past, although I am sure you wish that you could.

I created the "Seven Principles of Dealing with Conflict and Shame" to assist you in staying out of shame now that you are diligently working on being a person of integrity. I would like for you to read each one of them within the context of your relationship and answer two questions.

Which principle of the seven most replicates the "Don't take things personally" message that Ruiz wants you to remember from *The Four Agreements*? And which principle provides the most comfort to you?

THE SEVEN PRINCIPLES OF DEALING WITH CONFLICT WITHOUT GOING INTO SHAME

1. When you experience conflict, ask yourself, "How has my past contributed to the present-day conflict?" Recognize that 90% of the conflict is about your past and not who you are today.

2. Hold yourself accountable for causing the pain while not going into shame mode.

3. Know that although your partner's pain is a direct response to your past actions, it is not in response to who you are today.

4. Recognize that you are strong enough to be a container for the pain. You can help your partner work through the trauma and move beyond it while working on your own solid affair recovery.

5. Tell yourself the issue is not about you but about a trauma response from your acting out in the past.

6. Practice saying, "This is not who I am today. This is about the consequences of my past actions." Know that your infidelity was your kryptonite, and your recovery is your superpower!

7. Tell yourself, "I won't give my past guilt and shame the power to make me feel _____."
    (Sad, shameful, inadequate, unworthy, angry)

The principle that most encourages me to persevere and stay in good sexual integrity is: _____

_____."

I know I should recognize that I need to acknowledge the partner's pain and stay out of the cycle of shame. I do this by practicing the principle that helps me to realize that "this is not who I am today," which is Principle # _____ .

The 7 Principles of Dealing with Conflict Without Going into Shame (for Infidelity Recovery)

1 When you experience conflict ask yourself, "How has my past contributed to the present-day conflict?" Recognize that 90% of the conflict is about your past & not who you are today.

2 Hold yourself accountable for causing the pain while not going into shame mode.

3 Know that although the partner's pain is a direct response to your past actions, it is not in response to who you are today.

4 Recognize that you are strong enough to be a container for the parter's pain. You can help them work through their own trauma and move beyond it, while working on your own solid infidelity recovery.

5 Tell yourself the issue is not about you, but about a trauma response from your acting out in the past.

6 Practice saying, "This is not who I am today. This is about the consequences of my past actions." Know that your infidelity was your kryptonite, and your recovery is your superpower.

7 Tell yourself, "I won't give my past guilt and shame the power to make me feel... _____
(Sad, shameful, inadequate, unworthy, angry)

AS A COUPLE, WHICH PRINCIPLE APPLIES TO YOUR RELATIONSHIP?

If you were to apply these seven principles to the relationship, they might look like this:

1. When you experience conflict with each other, ask yourselves:

   - A) How is it directly related to the past?

   - B) How has my past contributed to my present-day conflict?

   - If there have been significant changes in safety and stability, each of you should recognize that the other 90% is about your past pain as a couple and not about what is going on today.

   - **For the Partner:** This will keep you from going into your pain from the past cycle and will help you stay in the present.

   - **For the Betrayer:** This will keep you from spiraling into the shame cycle when your partner is triggered about the past, and it will help you to stay strong. When you stay out of the shame cycle, you avoid "making it all about you" when it should remain "all about the partner."

2. Each of you should hold yourself accountable for staying in the present. (This is a major goal for partners and will help bring safety.)

3. Each of you should know that although the pain is a direct response to past actions, it is not in response to how you are developing as a couple today. Both of you are working hard to get "past your past." It takes constant focus to stay cognizant of all the work both of you have done.

4. Recognize that you are both becoming stronger and that together, you can acknowledge each other's pain. As a couple, you can work together to see the growth in each of you

separately and as a couple. You can move beyond it together if you are both willing to acknowledge the changes.

5. Practice saying, "This is not who we are today. Our work is creating a new relationship that is honest, transparent, and real."

6. When either of us is feeling unworthy, **we will take the risk to share it with each other** so that the other person can see and know the understandable vulnerability that accompanies doing this work.

7. Each one of us can use a mantra that fits the trauma response or shame.

    o   The partner can say, "I won't give my past pain the power to make me feel _____."
        (Sad, shameful, inadequate, unworthy, angry)

    o   The betrayer in recovery can say, "I won't give my past pain the power to make me feel _____."
        (Sad, shameful, inadequate, unworthy, angry)

    o   And the couple can discuss their mutual mantra, "We won't give our past pain the power to make us feel _____."

        (Sad, scared, anxious, inadequate, unworthy, angry)

As a couple, review them again together and decide which principle you think will keep you, in the here and now, investing everything you have in the relationship.

We would choose Principle # _____ because it would benefit our coupleship by _____

_____

_____

_____

When you experience conflict with each other and it is directly related to the past, ask yourself, "How has my past contributed to my present-day conflict?" If there have been significant changes in safety and stability, each of you should recognize that the other 90% is about your past pain and not about what is going on today.

And the BT can say, "I won't give my past behaviors the power to make me feel:

_____

(Shameful, hopeless, unworthy)

Each of you should hold yourself accountable for staying in the present. (This is a major goal for betrayed spouses & will help to bring safety).

The Seven Principles of Dealing with Conflict & Shame Applied to the Relationship

1
2
3
4
5
6
7

Each of you should know that although the pain is a direct response to past actions, it is not in response to how you are developing as a couple today. Both of you are working hard to get "past your past." It takes constant focus to stay cognizant of all the work both of you have done.*

When either of us is feeling unworthy, we will take the risk to share it with each other so that the other person can see and know the understandable vulnerability that accompanies doing this work. Each one of us can use a mantra that fits the trauma response. The partner can say, "I won't give my past pain the power to make me feel:

_____

(Sad, shameful, inadequate, unworthy, angry)

Recognize that you are both becoming stronger and that together you can acknowledge each other's pain. As a couple, you can work together to see the growth in each of you separately and as a couple. You can move beyond it together if you are both willing to acknowledge the changes.

Practice saying, "This is not who we are today. Our work is creating a new relationship which is honest, transparent, and real."

To the Unfaithful: If you are not working a strong recovery program and are practicing "slippery slope" behaviors, i.e. taking calls from APs, looking at pornography, or engaging in any provocative behaviors that could lead you into unhealthy deception or behaviors, you can not use these principles. Instead, be honest with your partner and increase your recovery tools.

These principles will help you both cope with the natural feelings that come up as you both heal. When you use these statements, you will be, as Brené Brown says, "armoring up" to keep you in the present, stay protected, hold yourselves accountable, and put things in perspective. Make sure to make a conscious effort to practice these principles once a week and then check in with each other to report how it improved your functioning. You will be amazed at how it changes your perspective, and you no longer take conflict so personally. (It might be something to report in your check-ins.) Once you have learned these important principles, you will be able to practice the following technique that will catapult you into a forward movement, which is indicative of post-traumatic growth.

"ACTING AS IF" CAN MOVE YOU FORWARD

To the Partner: There is no doubt that there is going to be a natural resistance to being this proactive about your relationship. You are reading this book to create a "new" marriage that will stand the test of time. I don't want you defined by the adultery; I want you to recognize all those other parts of you that have nothing to do with partner betrayal! I am not asking you to be all in, but I am suggesting that you begin to practice the art of "Acting as If."

"Acting as If" originated from the recovery movement. When alcohol or drug addicts did not believe they were capable of sobriety, getting a job, finding a relationship, or changing immature behaviors, the sponsor would validate the fears and then encourage them to practice the behaviors and "act as if" they could do it anyway. The premise was that if someone practices something long enough, it becomes a habit, and over time, they found that they did indeed acquire the skill.

As your spouse repairs the relationship, empathizes with you about the pain caused, and shows willingness to rebuild your trust, there comes a time when you must trust your gut to continue to do the hard work and lean into the premise that change is occurring. You will know if the betrayer is worthy of your trust, although it is normal to second guess yourself. When you act as if you can trust the new relationship you are building, you will be more likely to enjoy and lean into it.

As the BT repairs the relationship, empathizes with you about the pain that was caused, and shows willingness to rebuild your trust, there comes a time when you must trust your gut to continue to do the hard work and lean into the premise that change is occurring.

"Acting as If" will move you forward! We will talk more about the concept in Chapter 18 as you move into post-traumatic growth.

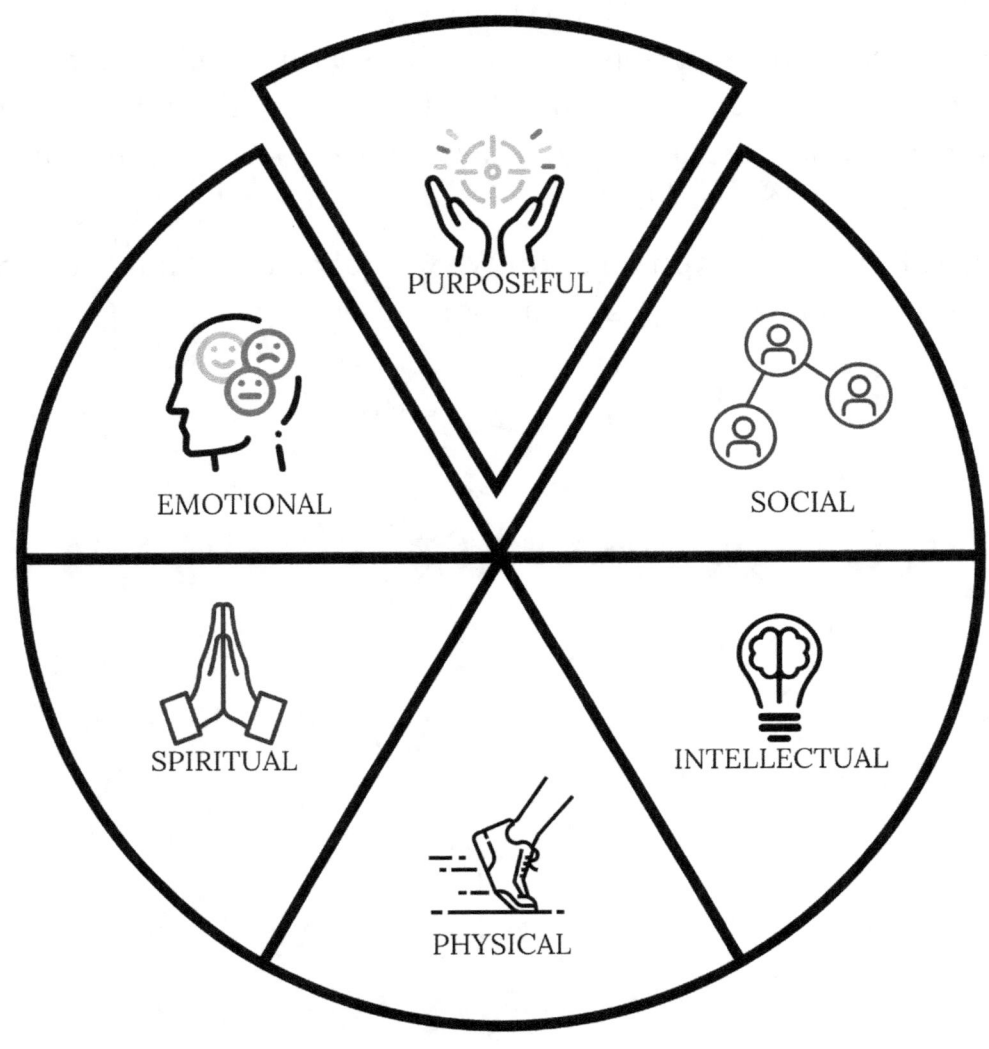

Chapter 15

Your Needs Individually and as a Couple

(The Pie Theory)

THE SIX TYPES OF NEEDS

It is important for couples to know what they need personally and in the relationship. I typically have the couples I work with break down their needs into six segments. Imagine a pie-shaped diagram with the pieces of that pie, including physical, intellectual, social, emotional, spiritual, and purposeful needs. When you think about your life as a couple, how might you deepen the all-important need quotient in the relationship?

PHYSICAL NEEDS

What do you need physically from each other? That might look like, "I would like my spouse to work out with me," "I need more non-sexual touch," "I need more sex," "I need my partner to rub my feet," "I need more hand-holding," or "I need my partner to stop expecting sex." You get the drift. It is so important to think about your physical needs and know there are many ways to deepen or enrich them.

In most cases, betrayers are afraid to talk about needs because the betrayers do not believe they deserve to express them. You said to yourself, 'I have ruined my life with my adultery and self-absorbed behavior, and I want my partner to know that I have changed. So, I will not express my needs, and maybe the BP will know that I have changed."

To the Partner: Partners in the safety and stabilization stage are not ready to trust that the BT will attend to their needs. All partners relate differently and may challenge the BT to meet needs individually. You fall somewhere on that continuum because you want to see where you stand.

Are there some physical needs you might be willing to express and test the waters for some level of comfort? Could you tolerate sitting next to the BT on the couch, sleeping in the same bed, or having your feet rubbed? If the BT is maintaining recovery and is working a solid program, I would encourage you to stretch out of your comfort zone and scan your body for what you might need physically. When partners have triggers, they often want to have the back of their head or neck rubbed to feel the natural self-soothing that can occur from that.

It does require that you stretch yourself to allow your spouse to give to you again, so you may need to look for other forms of connection first before you tackle your physical needs. The most important thing is to really check in with yourself to determine what you might let back into the relationship. This may mean that you specifically journal your thoughts and your feelings because quiet contemplation is the precursor to your own need for connection.

EMOTIONAL NEEDS

What do you need emotionally? We have talked about the first stage of partner betrayal, which is needing safety and stabilization so you can move forward in the relationship. What might you need to get you through the anger, mourning, grief, and loss that you have experienced from this whole ordeal? What do you need to validate your feelings? If you are having trouble really separating yourself from what you have been through, you might want to take an intensive course with other couples to work through any emotional residue that is left from the betrayal.

On the flip side, what would you like to gain emotionally from your relationship? If you could envision your relationship five years from now, what would you like it to look like? Would you like to buy that lake home where you could invite friends over, swim, paddleboard, and enjoy the serenity that the water can bring? Would you like to move to a new location where you could emotionally get a new start, perhaps changing your lifestyle, raising goats, planting gardens, or becoming missionaries and helping people in other countries? When you are looking at your emotional needs, I want you to start small, but I also would like for you to dream big. **You can accomplish anything as a couple if you work on processing your emotions and are vulnerable enough to begin to reinvest in what you need from each other emotionally.** John Gottman, author of *The Seven Principles of Making a Marriage Work*, says that every couple needs a vision, and I know that you would love to be in a place where you could dream about that again. I know one couple who has made it their mission to experience the United States, so they bought an RV and traveled from destination to destination in it. What they have found is that they are making new memories and having fun again, and it has moved them through the agony of the past.

INTELLECTUAL NEEDS

When you think about intellectual needs as a couple, you may decide that you would like to take a cooking course together or want to buy a new computer and work on learning the techniques you need to master using that computer. Many people choose to go back to school, but they do not necessarily choose to do that together. Are there classes, book clubs, or Bible studies that you could participate in that would stimulate you intellectually? As the BT moves toward developing new neuropathways, the BT can build substituting behaviors. After partner betrayal occurs, a partner needs to be thinking about ways of enriching life that are separate from partner betrayal.

There is no doubt that partners are walking encyclopedias on sexual betrayal. You have read everything there is to read, and you have looked up YouTube videos and podcasts to understand what has happened to you and your spouse. This kind of intellectual stimulation helps you feel safe and provides some form of stabilization.

> *But as a couple who are investing in their relationship, it is important to renew the relationship by finding stimuli that take you both away from the pain of betrayal and create a new sense of connection for you both.*

This assessment of your needs is a good place to start the connection process. As you survey your life together, can you imagine taking on a new hobby that requires you to learn it together? Would it feel safe for you both to try something new like golf, tango lessons, woodworking, or skydiving?

SOCIAL NEEDS

As you look at your social needs, there is a good chance you both have made fellowship connections, and you now have a group of people who understand what you have been through and do not judge you. Yet, it is important for both of you to find opportunities to create social relationships that no longer define you as an adulterer or as a partner.

As the Betrayer: When you think about your life, you more than likely have put your social relationships on the back burner because you were not sure who you could trust to share what you had been through. You did not want to engage in what would seem like superficial connections with people who did not understand your relational crisis.

Now, as you look at your life and are assessing your needs, how might you add social diversity back into your routine? Would you like to combine the physical and social needs together and take a tennis class? Would you be up for learning pickleball with a group of people together? Are you able to imagine taking a dance course or joining a meet-up for people who like to hike? You have always enjoyed cards but never pursued joining a card club and meeting new people. Think about branching out socially and ask yourself, if you had all the time in the world, what would you like to learn as a couple that would increase your skills and your social network? Redefining yourself as a couple means developing some new relationships in addition to the old so that you can create a new life together, separate from your past.

As the partner, I can forecast that you may be afraid to seek out new ventures because you do not trust the BT to *not* have a wandering eye. Yet, your spouse has been learning skills that should be practiced in new situations. It is also important to assess how it is progressing. I always tell my partners that if they cannot trust their spouse to be respectful and exclusive, they obviously need to increase emotional safety in ERCEM.

SPIRITUAL NEEDS

As betrayers make ongoing progress and begin to like themselves again, they want to find ways to deepen their faith and give back. As they work on their empathy, they know that this can take three to five years, and they patiently wait for the cues. Their program tells them to give it to God, and that also means to surrender control.

Partners are typically questioning where God was when the BT was acting out. How could a loving God have allowed the spouse to inflict so much pain? Have you wondered where God was as your partner was engaging in the affair? How can you deepen your spiritual connection when you have so many questions and doubts? Have you been able to reckon with the injustice of having to hurt this much? Have you questioned why God had seemed to forsake you?

CAN YOU EVER TRUST GOD AGAIN?

It is likely that as you look at your spiritual needs, you will have to do the hard work of processing why this happened to you. Many people wonder how God could have allowed infidelity to have occurred in their lives.

For the Betrayer: You must reckon with the fact that you continually tried to do it yourself and did not ask for help. Many of the infidelity support programs and the Twelve-Step movements suggest that you must surrender the need to control the acting-out behaviors to your higher power. It is only after you surrender spiritually and rely on your higher power that you can find the recovery you deserve.

For the Partner: It is a bit different. Frequently, I hear partners wonder how God could have let this happen to them. They ask themselves what they did to deserve the sexual betrayal, and if there are things in their life that they feel ashamed or guilty of, they wonder if it is God's retribution upon them to have allowed infidelity to fracture their lives.

Strengthening your spirituality may be necessary for finding yourself again. I know that I do not have the answers, but I frequently tell people that God gave all of us predetermination. That means that bad things can happen to good people, and it is your ability to lean on your belief in good and in your higher power that will carry you through the worst of life's circumstances.

What can you do as a couple to strengthen your spiritual knowing? Would you benefit from attending a new church, temple, or mosque, participating in a Bible study, or reading that new book on spirituality together? Would you like to increase your sense of the spiritual world by studying Buddhism, Taoism, or some other form of spiritual teaching? Would renewing your faith comfort you?

I would encourage you to identify what your primary feeling is regarding your partner betrayal and your relationship with *your* higher power. What I believe to be true is that God understands your anger, sadness, and despair you feel with your spouse and with God himself. You might need to write out your conversations with God to get clearer on how you have been affected by His inability to have protected you. And more importantly, you may want to ask Him how He might use you to help others who are hurting.

Exercise: Individually, but together as a couple, commit to spending 10 minutes a day every day for one month sharing your innermost feelings with God. Each day after you write about it, read it to each other so that you can become more connected as a couple.

To the Betrayer: Have some deep conversations, asking Him why you had the childhood that led up to the many resentments that you felt toward life. If there was any form of trauma in your childhood, make sure to ask Him how He could have left you in your darkest hour.

Undoubtedly, there were hundreds of times when you asked Him to help you stop this affair, and yet He never seemed to answer any of your prayers. And now you have watched your spouse become a shell of a person. You have begged God to take your partner's pain, and again, He has ignored your pleas for help.

Each day, spend 10 minutes asking God:

1. What can I do to feel better?

2.   What can I do to help my partner heal and restore safety in the relationship?

3.   What do I need to get closer to you and renew my spiritual connection?

Write down what He tells you.

CONVERSATION WITH GOD (OR HIGHER POWER) FOR THE BT

To the Partner: Share your real feelings with your higher power. Do not hold back. Get angry, cry, and share your feelings of abandonment. God can handle your genuine feelings. You need to confront them so you can learn from them. God is there to hold your anger and grief.

Ask God:

1.   What would you like me to know?

Be open and receptive to what you need to learn. I am sure He will reassure you that you never deserved this, and you may need to strengthen the bond with Him to move forward in your life.

CONVERSATION WITH GOD (OR HIGHER POWER) FOR THE PARTNER

If you are a couple who does not believe in a spiritual practice, I would encourage you to spend time out in nature observing the miracles of life. A blooming flower, a plane overhead, a mountain urging you both to climb it together. The couples that I work with that are atheist or agnostic report a sense of awe and wonder, noticing how nature reminds them of something bigger than themselves. They don't necessarily believe that there is a higher power, but they are reminded that life is not all about them.

If you are agnostic or atheist, it is likely that you don't have the issue that someone or something was not there for you, although you may walk around feeling a sense of doom and gloom, wondering why "life" is so hard and why have your circumstances been so difficult. You may question why other people have it so easy and why your destiny is plagued with destruction and devastation. If this sounds like you, I encourage you to consider changing how you view yourself and the world around you. My experience is that "like attracts like," and if you walk around seeing the world as bad—you will likely experience more bad than good. In Chapter 17, I talk about the concept of "What You Appreciate—Appreciates." Take special note of that exercise and see if you experience anything different when you notice "what is working in your life."

PURPOSEFUL NEEDS

This may feel premature or unimaginable, but after you have worked through the trauma, you make a conscious choice to find some purpose out of the chaos. You either make the decision to contribute to the lives of others and focus on giving of yourself to improve the lives of others, or you ask yourself what you can do from all that you have learned to make a difference in life.

For many people, this involves being there for others. You may choose to watch your grandkids twice a week, volunteer at the local elementary school, help seniors with their taxes, or become a Boy Scout leader. Or you may decide to become a sponsor in Recovery Couples Anonymous. You may decide to become a mentor to other hurting couples.

The ultimate goal is to do something together that has meaning and purpose. It doesn't have to be a huge goal, but together, ask yourselves, "How can we find more purpose in our lives together?" I have an 83-year-old couple who both sponsor in their infidelity groups, watch their grand-dog together, and allow me to videotape them for the trainings I do to help professionals to learn ERCEM. They inspire me in everything they do!

What might you do as a couple to find more purpose in your life? We will explore this in the post-traumatic growth section in Stage 3.

Chapter 16

Your Sexual Relationship

Authored by Allan J. Katz, Co-authored by Carol Juergensen Sheets

There is no doubt that your relationship has been affected by the sexual infidelity(s) of your partner. Yet, many couples restore their sexuality at different times in their relationship. Some couples immediately have sex after the discovery because that is the number one thing that felt most jeopardized, and therefore, they go right to working on that.

Partner-sensitive therapists do not necessarily recommend that because it can be what we call a "trauma response" to the intense reaction of feeling rejected. Partners may desperately need to feel affirmed, so they immediately seek affirmation and approval by initiating sex to see if they are still desired. Did that sound like you? Did you immediately question whether you were loved and desired, so you initiated sex to see if your spouse was still desirous of you?

Other couples have had sexually barren lives for one to three years after discovery because it feels too vulnerable and scary to reconnect after the sanctity of their marriage was violated. What started as confusion about your sexual life after betrayal developed into a "No Sexual Intimacy Zone" because it just did not feel safe. It is something that easily got put on the back burner to deal with another day, and then it got ignored for days, weeks, months, and years after discovery. The BT is walking on fragile territory because of the pain that was caused. For many couples, when sex is discussed, it has caused so much distress that it was not worth the fight. Understandably, it has created lots of fears about the relationship. The BP thinks, "What happens if we do not rekindle this part of our lives?" and the unfaithful partner fears, "What happens if we never have sex again?"

On rare occasions, I have seen partners who are so devastated and angry they have decided that they will never have sex again. For some partners, it can just feel too overwhelming or hard, but for others, it can be a way of punishing the acting-out partner. Have those thoughts crossed your mind?

In the beginning, after discovery, we often recommend that couples do not have sex for 30 to 90 days so they do not have to deal with their sex lives while they are attempting to get through the crisis. Many couples say that this is a relief as they want to realign themselves emotionally before they resume a physical relationship.

Sex can be challenging for many relationships, and you as a couple are especially vulnerable after sexual betrayal. It is important for couples to know that the biggest sex organ is the brain, and communication is the key to working through sexual issues. It can feel overwhelming to initiate conversations about sex. I also want to encourage you to work on developing other types of closeness, connection, and intimacy, especially if sex must be put on hold.

In many couples, there can be sexual anorexia as life gets busy or as couples get older and lose the hormones that feed sexuality. Couples can also forget to put their relationship first. For a variety of reasons, it is imperative that you get with a good therapist who deals with sexual issues that were there before infidelity and, of course, after the betrayal. You go to a therapist who has been trained in sexual or intimacy anorexia, find a counselor who works directly with sexual issues (AASECT), or work with an ERCEM therapist who can help you work through these issues by building relational and communication skills and begin to restore the physical and emotional sense of safety that needs to occur when restoring sexual intimacy.

Couples who are working toward post-traumatic growth want to restore their sexual relationship but are unsure how to go about doing that because they fear it will be too vulnerable for their partner. It is important to talk about the fears for both of you so you can negotiate what does feel safe.

Oftentimes, they will be experimenting with simple touching experiences that involve non-sexual body parts and positions. My colleagues Dr. Bill and Dr. Ginger Bercaw have a wonderful sexual reintegration program for couples after sexual betrayal. Their books help guide you through the process, even if you are not sure that you are ready to take the leap to physical intimacy.

Talking about sex requires a lot of emotional maturity, and this means that it is important for each of you to spend some time sharing your fears, concerns, and hopes. Sometimes, partners can talk about what would need to happen before sexual activity could be resumed. What do you both need to feel safe? What would you like in your relationship with each other? Has there been irreparable damage done, and therefore, sex is not discussed?

Sex is not necessarily part of the relationship after deception. This may be hard to hear, but a couple can live a healthy and happy life without sexual activity, and yet it can be such a physical and spiritual aspect of the relationship that ignoring or denying it would mean you would have to really increase your other types of connection as a coupleship.

SEXUAL INTIMACY

In most cases, sexual intimacy is something that you learn as you navigate through life with your partner. Many people are uncomfortable with talking about sex, and therefore, sexual intimacy is learned without communication and is based on trial and error. There is no doubt that when infidelity occurred, that intimacy was fractured, and your fear as a couple is that it may never be rebuilt again.

If you are a person who is in good recovery and is seeking to develop a closer relationship with your partner, it can feel intrusive to want to work on your sexual intimacy because of the damage that you have caused. Sexual intimacy requires that you look for ways to be close and develop trust in many different areas. It will be necessary for you to check the temperature of your partner's sexual comfort level. This means that you will need to check in frequently to find out what your partner is doing and thinking and what is needed to feel safe.

When you nurture your relationship inside and outside of the bedroom, you are more likely to build trust, dependability, and empathy in your sexual relationship. Most people have heard the adage "foreplay begins outside of the bedroom," and it is about your ability to care for the kids, do your fair share of household chores and duties, and seek closeness without sexuality. Since this relationship has been so damaged, it can be especially helpful to find ways of restoring trust by asking what your partner would like most in your relationship.

THE FIVE LOVE LANGUAGES

The 5 Love Languages by Dr. Gary Chapman is a simple read based on the concept that we all have a primary love language that increases marital satisfaction, compatibility, and security. You may have already gone to Dr. Chapman's site to assess both your love languages and what your spouse desires most.

Now, as the betrayed, you may be fearful of entering this arena. It may feel too soon, too scary, too hopeful, too positive, and too vulnerable after such a violation of your relationship. That is why we are leaving sexuality last—we know that you must build on the communication and your basic needs for safety first. I understand why you need to go through safety and stabilization and the grief and mourning stages to feel like you are ready to take your coupleship to the next level.

Many couples had poor sexual relations from the beginning of their relationship. You may not have talked about sexual pleasure; therefore, neither of you knew what to do to please each other. Sexual needs could be compromised because you both have different sexual preferences, which results in a stalemate in the bedroom. To complicate things further, sexual acting out interfered with your sexual functioning and skewed how you both felt about your own needs and arousal template.

The arousal template is the part of the brain that signals when you are turned on or aroused. It tells you what you like sexually, whether that is being cuddled and caressed while being pleasured or having the lights on high as you view your partner's body and expressions. Sometimes, it is a certain act or position that is especially appealing.

Everyone has an arousal template that started early in childhood and was a co-creation of your own chemicals and hormones. It also includes the teachings that occurred from your parents, church, and important people in your childhood. Lastly, it is based on experiences that occurred in your lifetime that were both good and bad, including trauma like sexual molestation and exploitation and pleasurable sexual activity that solidified your desires and needs.

It is important to talk with each other about how you are feeling about yourself sexually and what you need from each other since infidelity has made itself known. Talking about sex can often be a vulnerable experience for any couple, let alone for the couple who has experienced betrayal. You may want to get some specialized help by going to a professional who understands sexual betrayal and the collateral damage acting out has caused. It is my experience that a normal counselor does not possess the sensitivity to help a couple that has experienced this type of trauma. As I indicated earlier, make sure you research your professional for sensitivity to this topic.

Let's take this slow and get some understanding of where you are today if you are ready to go back to the basics and examine how you might redevelop your love life and your sex life. I recommend that you both go to Dr. Gary Chapman's website, www.the5lovelanguages.com, and I would like you both to see where your style for love is now that betrayal has occurred. This also applies to couples who have done the Love Language Assessment in the past.

I would like you to talk about the Love Language Assessment during your next check-in and for both of you to share what is most important to you. As you reconsider rebuilding your relationship, allow this book to guide you to the safe ways you can show each other love. It will absolutely take courage on both of your parts to be vulnerable and share how you might work on loving each other again.

THE LOVE LANGUAGE CHECK-IN

Bring your assessment to the check-in and share the ranking of the five languages of love.

1. Sit knees-to-knees and explain why you feel the assessment was valid or did not apply to your relationship.

2. Share any surprises that came from taking the test.

3. Share one "safe" way you might be able to get your needs met, make a behavioral request, and share why you are afraid to ask for what you would like or need.

4. Get your spouse's feedback about the request.

5. Tom and Nancy took the test. Tom was sure that when he and Nancy had done this previously, his love language had been physical touch, but today, it had changed to words of affirmation.

When he sat down with Nancy, they had the following dialogue:

"Nancy, my scores showed that I ranked a nine for words of affirmation, a seven for physical touch, gifts and acts of service were both a four, and quality time was a three.

"I was not surprised by the shift because I found that on the test, I could not even acknowledge my physical needs. I felt so much shame about what I had done to you and to us. I think there is something wrong with me because I have lost my sex drive, and I believe it is because I have so much guilt and shame.

"I know that I am starving to be the man that you can trust again, and when you smile at me or say something nice, I melt inside."

As you can see, sexual intimacy starts with good communication. If you can start with sharing your vulnerabilities and the basics with your partner, you can establish more intimacy, which is a precursor for better sex.

EMOTIONAL INTIMACY

Laura Dawn Lewis coined the concept of the Eight Stages of Intimacy (copyright 2004, The Couples Company). One of the eight stages is emotional intimacy, which covers feelings, trust, security, and safety in a relationship.

Many couples never achieve emotional intimacy because you must accept your partner for whom they are without reservation. At this level of intimacy, the couple feels comfortable sharing anger, happiness, secrets, and sensual and sexual feelings. Each of you knows that you are loved, and you deeply love your partner, no matter how either of you feel or act.

That is the goal for this book and your life. In post-traumatic growth, you have a rock-solid relationship whereby you can trust that your spouse has learned the emotional skills to love and support you. Your partner has full understanding of the collateral damage that was caused and has done everything possible to build in safety, reassurance, and love.

My colleague and co-author of the "Intimacy" chapter in *Help.Her.Heal.*, Allan J. Katz LPC, CSAT, believes that in sexual acting out, there is so much wounding that the emotional intimacy is diminished, and it becomes difficult for the wounded partner to feel comfortable enough to share anger, happiness, and erotic feelings. They don't feel safe enough to engage in sexual activity until they can trust their partner once again.

To build intimacy and empathy, the wounded partner needs to know that the betrayer understands the pain is due to poor choices and is not the wounded partner's fault. Again, there may have been lots of marital problems; however, those problems were never a reason to go outside of the marriage. Emotional intimacy is achieved when trust is established again and the couple can speak about sensitive topics without constantly bringing up past indiscretions.

We have asked some sensitive questions about intimacy that really involve vulnerability. Please look at the following continuum and see where you land so that you can look for ways to strengthen your intimacy quotient. This will likely require you to go to an ERCEM specialist who can help you develop more intimacy.

As a couple, I would like you to sit together and rate each area from 1 to 10. One represents that you are not currently able to achieve the goal, and ten represents that you master it regularly.

THE INTIMACY ASSESSMENT

1. In a state of fear, uncertainty, or danger, your partner is the person you turn to for comfort.

1	2	3	4	5	6	7	8	9	10
NOT GOOD				WORKING ON IT				CLOSE TO MASTERY	

2. Crying, showing frustration, sadness, or anger in front of your partner is healthy. You know he/she will not see you as weak, psychotic, crazy, or out of control.

1	2	3	4	5	6	7	8	9	10
NOT GOOD				WORKING ON IT				CLOSE TO MASTERY	

3. You can speak about sex, secrets, and your feelings without a fear of being betrayed, ridiculed, or compromised.

1	2	3	4	5	6	7	8	9	10
NOT GOOD				WORKING ON IT				CLOSE TO MASTERY	

4. No matter what happens, you know your partner loves you and will not abandon you during a state of crisis, ill health, or financial difficulty.

1	2	3	4	5	6	7	8	9	10
NOT GOOD				WORKING ON IT				CLOSE TO MASTERY	

5. You often show or tell each other, through words and actions, that you love and respect each other.

1	2	3	4	5	6	7	8	9	10
NOT GOOD				WORKING ON IT				CLOSE TO MASTERY	

6. Past wrongs are not dredged up in arguments to get even with each other. The past is discussed, forgiven, and left there. This may take some time recovering from sexual betrayal, but when both partners work on healing themselves, the chances of recapturing the intimacy can be achieved through empathy for each other.

1	2	3	4	5	6	7	8	9	10
NOT GOOD				WORKING ON IT				CLOSE TO MASTERY	

7. Passive-aggressive behavior and name calling does not exist in your relationship.

1	2	3	4	5	6	7	8	9	10
NOT GOOD				WORKING ON IT				CLOSE TO MASTERY	

Use this to identify areas you want to work on as a couple and discuss them with your partner.

QUESTIONS TO DETERMINE EMOTIONAL INTIMACY FOR BOTH THE UNFAITHFUL AND PARTNER:

1.   What will it take for you to feel safe in this relationship?

_____

_____

_____

_____

_____

2. What will it take for you to want to build trust within this relationship?

_____

_____

_____

_____

_____

3. It is likely that you can show empathy when your partner respects and admires you, but how do you build intimacy amidst conflict?

_____

_____

_____

_____

_____

4. Have you shown vulnerable feelings like sadness or even tears in front of your spouse?

_____

_____

_____

If not, what is your fear about being this vulnerable?

_____

_____

_____

What's the worst that can happen?

_____

_____

_____

Has that ever happened?

_____

_____

_____

If yes, did your partner react with empathy or with scorn?

_____

_____

_____

This assessment was created to help both of you begin to think about the many forms of intimacy that you can strengthen in your marriage. I want you to go back to the "Pie Diagram" and refer to those six needs to determine what would enhance both of your intimacy quotients and to check on the temperature of each other's comfort level sexually.

You need safety in the relationship to build intimacy. You both are doing a good job of making that a priority by learning all the relational skills in this book. Couples who are practicing the skills of good recovery and are seeking to develop a closer relationship with each other will automatically feel closer and more connected, but they need to assess whether they want to work harder on the sexual intimacy part of their relationship.

We know it can feel intrusive to want to work on your sexual intimacy because of the damage that has been caused. Be sure to share that vulnerability so your partner knows that this is not easy for either one of you.

There are two simple but not easy-to-use "pieces of advice" that you can begin immediately as you reintegrate into the bedroom together.

1. *Practice "open eyes sex" or "open eyes physical contact."* As uncomfortable as it may be for both of you to open your eyes during sex or physical contact, it is the number one key to restoring safety in a physical or sexual relationship. Dr. David Schnarch runs webinars all over the world to improve sexual performance. He found after surveying thousands of people that 7.5% of couples never have sex, 32% never make eye contact during sex, 42% sometimes make eye contact during sex, and 18.5% have orgasms while looking into each other's eyes. When the BT's eyes are open, you both can admire the closeness within the relationship. It is a testament to the fact that you, the partner, are allowing an opportunity to connect so intimately. It is a real gift for both, and it certainly reaffirms that the relationship is sacred and special. It also keeps both of you focused on the present and reassures you that there is less likely a chance for the BT to be using fantasy.

2. *Practice being verbally vulnerable with each other.* Despite the tendency to want to stay in your own heads while making love or physically connecting, you both can enhance the connection by commenting on how the experience feels and how grateful you both are that you are relearning how to share this with each other. Talking while touching each other can be a roadmap for what you both need. If it feels inconceivable that you would talk during sex or after touching each other, make sure to spend some time after you finish holding each other to talk about what you liked or didn't like.

Again, my colleagues Drs. Bill and Ginger Bercaw have devoted their lives to improving the sexual lives of couples who have experienced partner betrayal. Their books are guides that will walk you through the steps. I highly recommend *The Couples Guide to Intimacy: How Sexual Reintegration Can Help Your Relationship Heal*, as it is respectful of the small changes you will need to make to build more trust and intimacy.

LIVING WITHOUT SEX

The truth of the matter is that you can both live without sex and increase other forms of connection. That being said, I don't advise living a sexless marriage unless you both decide that you are not interested in pursuing sexual contact. Some couples feel that they are hormone deficient and have no desire to pursue sexuality, but they do want to increase other forms of physical intimacy.

There is no right or wrong way to explore sexuality or physicality. I would recommend that if you want a sex life, you should build it slowly.

I encourage you to look at the six types of intimacy and assess how you can expand your connection with each type of intimacy. As couples get more comfortable sharing communication and emotions, they can work through issues that may be barriers to closeness. It can be intimidating to wonder if you, as the partner, can meet your spouse's sexual needs, especially if you are prone to comparing yourself to the images the BT has seen or to the affair partner.

Your sexuality is most dependent on your ability to communicate with each other and to develop emotional intimacy. This means that you need to be honest, open, and forthright. I know that both of you will have times when there is a pit in your stomach because you do not want to talk about your fears or be honest about your inadequacies, but having a solid sexual relationship involves authenticity, transparency, and honesty. If you remember the intimacy pyramid, it also designated vulnerability as a value to work toward when rebuilding the relationship. Even though this part of your relationship has been so badly ruptured, it requires that you begin finding the building blocks to share yourselves totally with each other.

What are your fears about being more honest about your sexual self and your couple's sexuality?

For male betrayers, that might include worrying about sexual performance or being too sexually assertive or needy. There may have been sexual incompatibility from the start of the relationship, and how in the world can you talk about that now that you have shattered the BP's sense of self?

It may be that you have never really communicated about sex, so this is completely new to you. Anything new feels uncomfortable and unfamiliar, as if it is unchartered territory. Or it might be the exact opposite, and now that you are working on sexual integrity, there is something that stops you from having the sexual desire you had in your 20s or 30s. You know you carry a certain level of shame, and you are doing everything you can to live in the present and recognize your progress, but your sexuality has taken a back seat to all the other things that you are working on.

For the Partner: Your sexuality has been affected by the rejection you feel and general feelings of inadequacy. You may be worried that you are not enough and can no longer give your spouse pleasure because there will be no authentic desire. You may have thought you had a good sexual relationship prior to discovery, or you may have known that something was off. Your spouse may not have been a good lover from the start of your sexual relationship, but you never shared that because you did not know how to be honest. You may have known that you were lacking the skills or the "playfulness" to have spontaneity in your sexual life. There are so many confusing questions you have about your sexual abilities, and now I am asking you to reflect, write, and speak to the person who has caused you such great pain.

I recognize that, but if you want to connect again, you must be honest with yourself. I want you to sit down and write about your fears. Write about what sexuality was like for you before the affair, what it is like currently, and what you would like it to be in the future. Both of you need to be honest with yourselves before you can be honest with each other.

What has happened to you has been so devastating, and you do not know how to navigate the pain. You are afraid that if you don't have sex, you will lose the BT completely, but you don't feel ready. It doesn't feel safe, but the last thing you want to do is appear rejecting. This would leave you fearing that your spouse will physically cheat on you again or resort to pornography. It has left you in a very fragile state, and more than likely, it doesn't feel safe to talk to others about what you should do because sex is a private, sacred experience. Instead, you say nothing, and you certainly don't share your vulnerability because you're not sure that you can do that or if they will be honest.

Sexuality is about being vulnerable! You both need to practice being honest and "up" your transparency. You both deserve to know each other's inner thoughts. I implore you both to take the risk and share your fears. I can assure you that it will increase your intimacy quotient. (There are sexuality specialists who can help you in this process. Not every therapist can work through the nuances of sexual betrayal. Go to www.aasect.org, which stands for the American Association of Sex Educators, Counselors, and Therapists.)

Note: You both have done some amazing work to create a whole new relationship and find safety.

To the Partner: As safety is strengthened, you will observe that you simultaneously want to release the pain while accepting the post-traumatic growth that is occurring as you do this work. It will take some radical acceptance and faith that, as a result of the amazing work you are doing in ERCEM, you will be able to create a new marriage that is stronger than it has ever been.

As we move into Chapter 17, you will notice that I start referencing the "betrayer" more often as the "spouse" because I believe it is *time to recognize that the betraying occurred in the past and the unfaithful spouse has been working hard to build safety, create a whole new relationship, and become the spouse you have always wanted.*

As you do these grief and anger exercises, you will release much of the pain that keeps you tethered to the past, which will allow you to stay in the present. These processes will be the catalyst for you to ceremoniously let go of the betrayal. You will always have your intuition to guide you, and grief and anger work will organically move you into an acceptance state that leaves space to create more of a new life together. These grief and anger exercises promote a surrendering to "what was" with a resignation that you might be stronger because of the trauma, betrayal, and pain. And that is why I felt it was time to shift the "languaging" to promote the work that you are each doing.

(If you are together but not married, "spouse" may not be the right fit, but I did not want to confuse you further by calling you both "partners.")

Chapter 17

Getting Through Phase Two of Infidelity and Partner Betrayal:

Anger, Grief, Loss, and Mourning

Now that you are through the shock of what has happened you are both ready to get angry, grieve, and deal with the ordeal that you have been through. It is still incomprehensible how your spouse had made all these choices that stole the sacredness of your marriage. There has always been a part of you that hoped that you could rebuild the relationship and yet there have been so many doubts that your spouse could bring safety back into the relationship. There remain so many underlying feelings that keep hijacking you both. It is important to identify and honor those horrible feelings because they are the pain that you both carry with you.

This will require you to work through the grief, sadness, anger, and mourning for what has happened to your marriage. Lust and sexual betrayal have damaged your sense of self, and no one can know how that feels. But I promise that your spouse is experiencing anguish over the trauma that has been caused. You were supposed to be able to seek your spouse out for comfort, and instead, your spouse has been the source of your pain.

There is something ironic about the fact that your spouse is the reason for your pain, and yet if your spouse witnesses your grief and mourning and supports you through it, it will expedite your healing. Although you can do this work on your own, using the ERCEM method suggests that both of you, working as a couple, will need to address these feelings so you can externalize and release them in order to move on.

As a partner, it would make sense to me that you are reading this and thinking, *Why in the heck would I need to work through these horrendous feelings? I did not cause this, but I have been devastated by it. I don't want to spend another second on it!*

That is your prerogative. However, at some point, you will need to process the feelings and pain so that they do not sit inside of you and cause bodily damage. I promise you, as Bessel Van der Kolk wrote, "the body keeps the score." If you try to ignore the anger, sadness, and grief of what happened to you, it will show up psychologically and physically. There are many autonomic responses to trauma that manifest as conditions and illnesses, and processing them is the only way to heal from the damage it has caused. It is not fair that you must go through this, but you will grow through it if you do the work.

COMMON SYMPTOMS OF TRAUMA

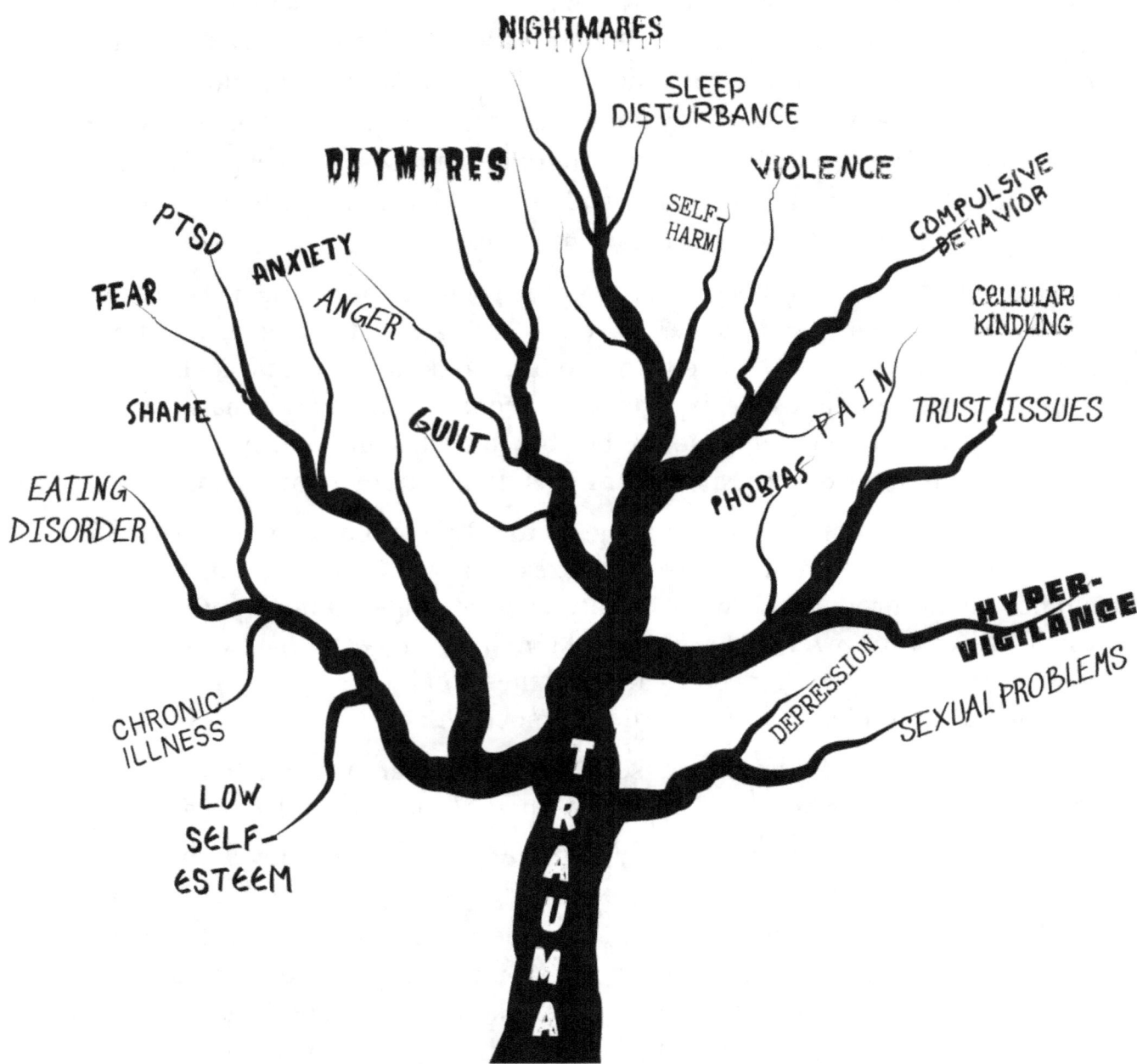

As you look at this illustration, are you able to see how this trauma may be showing up in other areas of your life?

To the Spouse: I want you to help with this work because your partner should not have to do this alone. I know that this will bring out painful feelings for you, too. You are sickened by all the devastation that you have caused both to your partner and your relationship. You might tend to want to avoid doing the hard work, but I assure you that by going through it together, you will help your spouse heal.

To the Partner: Where do you begin? Doing a feeling check-in, as we discussed in Chapter 6, is the place to start. Initially, the best way to recognize feelings and how to deal with them is to write about and verbalize them to others who understand their magnitude in your life.

Do you feel stuck in betrayal? Are you having difficulty detaching from the trauma and moving on? It may be that you have not worked through your feelings. They may have immobilized you and kept you tethered to your pain.

Since your spouse has caused you to feel these feelings, it can accelerate your healing if your spouse is there to help you process them. After many years of working in this field, I discovered that if your spouse could be there and contain your pain while you externalize it, it would assist you in working through it and healing faster.

Initially, assessing how you feel during a daily check-in helps both of you because it allows you to monitor your feelings and helps your spouse know what is going on inside of you. You will want to practice this daily to prepare you for Stage 2. In a couple's check-in, you will be appraising the following questions:

Have you given yourself enough time to be angry and grieve the losses this has caused? Does your spouse know what the losses are and how they have affected you? In your check-in or with your therapist, both of you should write down what losses you have experienced. How did it make you feel? How might you process them?

MY LOSSES—WORKING TOGETHER TO PROCESS THROUGH THE LOSSES AND FEARS

TYPES OF LOSSES	PRIMARY FEELING	PROCESS WORK TO BE DONE
I no longer can count on you for security.	*Angry and Cheated*	*Write an anger letter to the infidelity raging at the injustice that has resulted.*
We are 100K in debt for your treatment.	*Sad and Fearful*	*I will have to keep telling myself that I would have spent any amount of money for treatment for cancer and stand convicted that I (we) did the right thing to get you the help you needed.*
I have lost confidence in myself.	*Scared*	*An ERCEM assignment is to write out 25 examples of my strengths as I have weathered this horrible ordeal.*
I have lost the assurance of your determination.	*Angry and Fearful*	*The spouse should track all daily recovery activities that he is doing as a reassurance reminder.*
I have lost my connection to God.	*Sad*	*Write a letter to God and read it to my spouse so that I can grieve the huge sadness I feel inside.*
I feel the loss of a normal life.	*Anger and Sadness*	*There are several anger exercises to externalize the anger in Carol's book "Unleashing Your Power: Moving Beyond Sexual Betrayal." When I feel this way, I can beat pillows with a racket. I can do a Vesuvius with my spouse hearing all the pain inside. I can write out 50 reasons for feeling angry and read them to my spouse.*
The preoccupation with the infidelity robbed me from quality time with our kids.	*Angry and Sad*	*Write a letter to my children expressing how sorry I am that I lost such precious time with them. This letter should be read to your spouse and not read or given to the kids.*

This chart is a reminder of the ways you can feel, process, and express the pain. If that does not feel safe, I would ask you to find an ERCEM specialist who can walk you through this grief work with your spouse present but as a passive witness to your pain.

Are there areas of your life that have stayed the same despite your desire to change?

WORK TO DO TOGETHER TO WORK THROUGH LOSSES AND FEARS

TYPES OF LOSSES/FEARS	PRIMARY FEELING	PROCESS WORK TO BE DONE <u>TOGETHER</u>
Loss of self-esteem	Sadness	Both BT & BP create reality affirmations to acknowledge the partner's strength.
Loss of security in self	Anger or Sadness	Have the BT write 20 ways that the adultery was wrong and hurtful.
Loss of self-esteem	Anger or Sadness	Have the BT read those to me. "I took away your self-esteem when..."
Loss of relationship	Anger	Do a "Vesuvius" and/or write a "venomous letter to the infidelity" (see format at end of chapter).
Inability to trust	Fear	Write out 25 "What I fear most about my life" statements.
I cannot trust that you will stay faithful	Loneliness	Regular polygraph tests/ The BT sets up quarterly tests.
I fear that you will be tempted to cheat	Fear	BT sets up AVR daily on this issue.
I fear that you will not maintain rigorous honesty.	Fear	Participate in Omar Minwelas' course on "Integrity Abuse."

VESUVIUS: EXTERNALIZATION AND RELEASE OF ANGER

"Vesuvius" is an exercise developed for couples. It has been adapted from "PAIRS." It is a tremendous exercise for partners because it allows you to release your anger and experience the support from your spouse who initially caused you the issues. You can do this by yourself as a couple, but I recommend that you do this with a partner-sensitive therapist due to the strong emotional component in the work.

It helps to have a third person who can sit with both of you to help process your feelings after you are finished. Show this exercise to your therapist and ask them if they would be willing to guide you through this. If they are not comfortable with Gestalt work, contact an ERCEM specialist as they have had training in this exercise.

This exercise encourages you to get in touch with suppressed or repressed anger. Female partners are often taught that they should not have ugly, angry thoughts and feelings. You have been surprised at how angry, rageful, and out of control you have been since discovery, and you likely have thought that you are going crazy because this is not who you are. So much of this is trauma brain, and when you do these cathartic exercises with your spouse in a safe environment, you feel supported and can make a conscious choice to release them to be able to move on.

Doing this work can also clarify boundaries, which is helpful as the two of you continue this journey. Couples who have done this exercise find that the BP's anger creates a sense of empowerment because the partner has been given a sacred place and permission to use their voice. The spouse is there to hold the anger as the partner experiences its externalization, which will create a sense of serenity and calm.

Not only will the partner get to spew feelings, but the BP will also get uninterrupted time to say whatever is locked inside. This exercise gives partners permission to identify their feelings and erupt like the ancient volcano Vesuvius.

PURPOSE OF THE VESUVIUS

This ritual allows for the emotional purging and spewing that needs to occur when your anger has been suppressed and repressed for months, years, or even decades. If you are tired, frustrated, and enraged, you will find this tool a safe way to unload, uncork, explode, and erupt. It is done with permission and for an allotted amount of time. The following steps outline the Vesuvius process.

THE PROCESS

Step 1: You request a certain amount of time to vent your anger, frustration, and rage. In most cases, this exercise requires three to five minutes. (You will likely find that when you have uninterrupted time to say what is really on your mind, you will not need as much time as you would think to find your voice).

Your spouse will silently hold your anger. Your spouse is called the "container" because your spouse metaphorically holds and contains your anger. You share how much time you will need, and your spouse will tell you when your time to vent is up.

Step 2: Your spouse will be learning and practicing how to contain your anger without internalizing it. They will need to visualize a Plexiglas shield, Teflon coating, wall, or any other protective mechanism that prevents them from internalizing the anger that is spewing forth. It may be beneficial to internally speak a mantra such as, "This is not about me."

Step 3: As the partner, you place a chair in front of your spouse and talk into the empty chair. Your spouse cups their hands as if the anger is being contained. (If possible, it would be beneficial if you both had a support person to stand with you, like your therapist, a nonjudgmental friend who knows about the deception, or a loving family member.) You begin by verbalizing your anger regarding a core issue. Here, you emote your dark ugly, and judgmental feelings about the infidelity and all it has done to your marriage. Nothing you say during this period has to be true, fair, or politically correct.

Yelling, screaming, and even cussing (if you are so inclined) are common, expected, and encouraged.

Many times, as you share your anger, your issue will deepen, or your focus will shift to another person who has betrayed you in the past. Many partners have experienced that as they are emoting, their anger shifts from their adulterer to their mother or father because of trauma experienced in childhood. (Please note that this is natural and does not take away from the anger you feel toward your spouse, but it does link together the ongoing trauma that you may have felt your whole life.)

Step 4: Once you have emotionally purged or after time has run out, you thank your spouse for safely containing your anger. Then, it is vital to "de-role," acknowledging that your spouse was there to witness and contain your anger. You were not yelling at your spouse; you were emoting about the pain. Your spouse then uses reflective listening to acknowledge that the spouse's role was to be a support person to help you externalize all the feelings locked inside of you.

Step 5: After you and your spouse debrief, you can do a knees-to-knees and share with each other what it was like to be in this exercise.

Again, I recommend that you have a specialist present for this specific exercise.

EXTERNALIZE YOUR FEELINGS THROUGH LETTER WRITING

If you are a survivor of sexual betrayal, sexual abuse, or other forms of trauma, this exercise can feel frightening yet freeing because you can use it to say whatever you want to the perpetrator(s) in your past, no matter how violent or graphic.

Anger and grieving need to be released. These feelings are on a continuum and require a multitude of ways to be expressed. Many partners report much relief from writing out their feelings because they get to decide how much anger, sadness, and grief they want to emote. It is important for you to write all three letters to begin the process of healing.

To the Spouse: Remember, you will be supporting your partner by sitting as the letters are read. You are not there to console or shut down your partner's feelings. You are there to "contain" the emotions—nothing more and nothing less! You will be helping by being brave enough to see all those strong emotions that have come from the trauma and to support your partner by holding the pain.

THE VENOMOUS LETTERS

LETTER 1A: THE VENOMOUS LETTER IS A LETTER WRITTEN TO THE INFIDELITY

The venomous letter is an opportunity to describe the sexual betrayal that the infidelity has caused and its effects that have permeated every cell of your body.

1. Describe in detail the pain the addiction has caused you. Let the infidelity know what parts of your life have been impacted and the hell you have been through. You are encouraged to let your "shadow side" take over. The important thing for cathartic purposes is to acknowledge all the thoughts and feelings you have had in the past about how this has affected you and how the infidelity has robbed you and the relationship.

2. Next, with a specialist present, read the letter to the empty chair that represents the infidelity while your husband is present and be a witness to your past pain. It is important that you do not share the letter as you are writing it, as you want to deliver the full, completed letter at one time.

3.   The best way to read it is when you are assured total privacy and can stand looking down at the empty chair as your spouse sits on the other side of the chair. You will slowly read to the empty chair. Some people prefer to stand about one to two feet away and read their letters because they say it feels like a different continuation of the Vesuvius.

4.   After you have read the letter, take some deep breaths and debrief from the exercise. Thank your spouse for being there to witness the wreckage. Your spouse may look visibly upset because of how the infidelity has robbed you both of precious time and connection.

5.   You, as the witnessing spouse, are to say nothing unless asked for your observations, feedback, or feelings. As in the Vesuvius, you are witnessing and holding the pain.

6.   Make sure to prep by imagining your forcefield to protect yourself and recognize that you are there to support and help the healing.

Note to the BP: You may find that you want to address past abuse you have experienced as a child. These three letters can be used for sexual abuse, molestation, and sexual assault. You will find them therapeutic in addressing childhood trauma.

LETTER 1B: THE VENOMOUS LETTER IS FOR PAST TRAUMA AND ABUSE

The venomous letter is an opportunity to describe the past trauma and its effects that have impacted your ability to trust.

1.   Describe in detail the pain you have experienced, and do not hold back from writing about the torture you have felt. You may tell the perpetrator that you wished the same thing could happen

to him or her—that there are times that you have thought about doing the same thing so he or she could feel the anguish and despair. You are encouraged to let your "shadow side" take over. The important thing for cathartic purposes is to acknowledge all the thoughts and feelings you have had in the past.

2. Next, find a special time to read the letter to your spouse so your spouse can be a witness to your past pain. It is important that you do not share the letter as you are writing it, as you want to maximize the impact of past trauma and abuse.

3. The best way to read it is when you are assured total privacy and can sit before your spouse, face-to-face but not touching. You will slowly read your feelings about the abuse, looking up at your partner every two or three sentences. Some people prefer to stand about one to two feet away and read their letters as it allows them to feel the strength of their voice and feelings.

4. As the spouse, you are witnessing and holding the pain. Make sure to prep by imagining your forcefield to protect yourself and recognize that you are there to support your partner.

5. After you have read the letter, take some deep breaths and debrief from the exercise. Thank your witnessing spouse for being there to see the wreckage from the abuse, which conveys the possibility of complex post-traumatic stress and the suffering from many layers of trauma. Remind your spouse that you know your spouse is not the perpetrator but there to provide support to you as you share your feelings.

6. As the spouse, say nothing unless asked for observations, feedback, or feelings. You are witnessing childhood or past trauma.

7.   My colleague and I have done this work with thousands of women and couples and have seen the experience as cathartic and extremely beneficial in releasing the suppressed feelings from sexual abuse. We have also witnessed many men's groups that do this experiential work to process the trauma that they experienced as a child. Again, this is a very liberating experience, releasing the pent-up feelings you have been feeling your whole life.

LETTER 2: THE SURVIVOR LETTER

The Survivor Letter is the second letter you read to your spouse, who sits in silence until you are finished. Again, you decide whether you want to sit face-to-face or stand.

The Survivor Letter is a rational, direct, assertive letter telling the perpetrator your feelings and the consequences of the BT's actions. This helps reclaim your strength and move on from the event. You will want to include the boundaries you may be enforcing for your children or grandchildren to keep them safe from the perpetrator or other potential perpetrators.

Finishing with this rational letter helps you reclaim yourself as a strong survivor and provides closure. It further allows you an extra opportunity to regain composure. You can ask your spouse for feedback and observations, or you can share that you would prefer to end in silence. The work will be completed when you finish this activity with the resilience letter below.

To the Spouse: You will sit silently as the letter is read. Your responsibility is to witness and contain the pain and to give feedback if asked.

LETTER 3: THE RESILIENCE LETTER

To the Partner: The third letter highlights what you have learned and what has carried you through as you talk to your past self from the perspective of your present-day self. The truth is that you already have wisdom to share about what has carried you this far in life. This may be a tough letter for you to share with your spouse because you do not want to sanction what the abuser has done in any way, and talking about your resilience may feel like it is "letting the abuser off the hook."

This may be the first time you have contemplated how you have found strength amidst the trauma, and quite frankly, it feels like a foreign concept to wonder how all this wounding as a child might have served you and made you stronger. There can be a tendency not to own your strength because you do not want to legitimize what has been done. We understand your possible hesitance, but an acknowledgment of your resilience is necessary to move forward and set limits that keep you safe from anyone else in your future. It also exemplifies post-traumatic growth, which will free you from much of this bondage.

To the Partner: Devote some time to writing and responding to the following: I am stronger now, and this is what I appreciate about my resiliency...

To the Spouse: I would like for you to write a paragraph about what you noticed as your partner read the resiliency letter. Share how you feel about seeing your spouse finding some strength amidst all this trauma. This might look like: "What I noticed about your declaration of strength was..."

A RATIONAL LETTER TO THE INFIDELITY OR TO THE AFFAIR ITSELF
(LATER TITLED "THE GOODBYE LETTER")

I worked with a couple where the affair partner had been the partner's good friend to both she and her husband as well as to the entire family. They shared meals, went on vacation together, and shared a connection that ended up going much deeper than the family friendship.

Here is how Margaret expressed her feelings and grief toward the affair and the multiple betrayals that ensued.

When she read it to me and her husband, he said that she needed to publish the letter because it was so well done. He said that he knew her expression of pain would help others. I sat quietly as she questioned how that could ever happen. She did not know that I was on my third edit of this book. I continued to listen to their dialogue about her feelings. This letter to the affair was incredibly powerful. At the end of the session, I told her that if she ever decided to publish it, I would be honored if she would allow me to use it in my book. This couple is strong and working on healing. I know you will be awestruck at how she described the pain and her desire to move forward from the betrayal.

LETTER TO THE AFFAIR, OR THE "GOODBYE LETTER"

TO THE AFFAIR:

Opening sentence...why am I writing to you?

I am writing this to unload, I suppose. I am writing to express feelings that spin in unfortunate repeating spirals in my head. I am writing because, for four years, I suppressed feelings and lacked anyone to share them with except for my immediate family. No one knew. I wonder why I didn't find some sympathetic bartender or a stranger to dump my pathetic story upon. Funny, isn't it? *I am writing because my counselor thinks it might help me move past the burdens of resentment, sadness, anger, and general preoccupation with* YOU. YOU have no right to my heart and head.

HOW DID FINDING OUT ABOUT YOU MAKE ME FEEL?

I have been down a spiraling path of feelings that seem to repeat. I pray that, at some point, they will not sting as much as they still do. I still wince when dramas focus on infidelity and casually dismiss the spouse as inconsequential when some great passion takes over. I am struck that YOU get so much play as a "romantic" and desirable experience.

One day, I noticed that the feelings I was coping with often start with "dis-." I have felt dismayed, disgusted, dismissed, disillusioned, disenchanted, deeply discouraged, and, *more than anything*, painfully disappointed. You, AFFAIR, have taken me through every stage of grief. You have killed my faith in myself, my marriage, and even my sense of reality. I am trying to put together the pieces. I am determined, but I am changed.

I have been trying to counter all of those "dis-"es. I try to encourage myself. I have tried to let go of my illusions about the past and my relationships. I have tried to be honest with myself and tried to consider how I must change without destroying myself, believing I can somehow be the "fixer." Truth is, I cannot "fix" what is done. YOU just are my new reality. I cannot erase this thing. I cannot deny or wipe out this reality. Sometimes I just think to myself, "What the hell. It doesn't matter. YOU, AFFAIR, are "over." But so much of life is what we remember. So much is what we are able to comfortably remember. So much is that sense of "well-being" that comes from happy memories and secure relationships.

AFFAIR, you have shaken my security. You have cost me trust and hope and left me feeling small and diminished. I no longer can look back and say, "Well, it wasn't always easy, but our love was strong, and we got through even the toughest times together. And now, in our golden years, we are enjoying our memories together." Oh yes, some days I do manage to see the things we did and talk myself out of the profound disappointment I feel. But here's the thing: There's this little ugly voice that you injected...Now I find myself thinking, "It wasn't me. It was this secret AFFAIR that actually was the foundation for my husband s security. She leaned on him, she made him important, she was excited, and he could always tell her how disappointing I was." Believe me, I fight those thoughts, BUT THEY ARE REAL, AND YOU, AFFAIR, are the reason I think them. I feel like you were the excuse for avoiding reality. YOU were the alternative reality. I am constantly frustrated that the ***convenience of having* YOU, AFFAIR,** robbed our marriage of the intimacy we might have grown and had if my husband hadn't had you as a convenient "fix" for his concerns and for problems *we* should have worked out as a couple. Would he have tried harder when we went to a church "couples' class"? Would he have opened up if there wasn't someone else handy to complain to? Would he have confided in me that he was lonely and that we really needed to work together to change that? Would he have heard me better if he hadn't had the convenient excuse, the CLASSIC EXCUSE, the tragic EXCUSE, that somehow his partner wasn't enough, BUT he just HAD TO have more out of life, never mind the risk. Would he have tried a different path if he hadn't created YOU, that "optional romance" to run to when he needed a more eager and exciting experience? YOU alienated his affection, and I became a "wife-person." I became the one you complain about at the office, or the bar, or in bed with the AFFAIR. That is the worst humiliation. We could have been a lot more, but there you were, AFFAIR. The answer. The fuck fix.

Well, AFFAIR, you have done a lot to shake me to the core. Sometimes I cry, still, when I'm alone and have the need to release some of the crap I am trying to manage internally. Sometimes, I really question whether I am even able to correctly perceive reality. I wonder what new lies might be right in front of me...I wonder what new inadequacy I am displaying.

Bottom line, AFFAIR, I am plain old pissed that I am dealing with this *at this stage of life*. My friends are gloating about grandkids and silver anniversaries. I wince. The divorced ones are even gloating, moving on, and talking about leaving behind their troubled relationships. The younger divorced ones are celebrating second chances after growing a little wiser. I'm 74. I'm still sexually healthy. I'm still otherwise pretty healthy. But I WAS NOT planning on revisiting my decision to have a lifetime marriage. I resent being confronted with the need to even CONSIDER a divorce after pouring myself into a relationship for 35 years. I made a decision to commit to a lifetime partner decades ago. So, now I need to consider abandoning it all? I tried to do my best with all that our shared decisions demanded. I don't find divorce attractive. I never dreamed I would be in a position to consider it, but sometimes, I have wondered if it would be a relief. Crap, here I am considering abandoning my lifetime partner to *escape* **THE AFFAIR. TO ESCAPE YOU, AFFAIR.** To be able to say, "Hey, I have my self-esteem, and I don't have to put up with this deceit. I, too, can just 'check out.'" But that's not me! I don't believe in just checking out and walking away. YOU DO NOT GET TO CHANGE ME LIKE THAT. YOU do not get to make me abandon my faith in relationships and people. YOU STINK, but I am not in your control.

I really hate what you have done to my peace of mind despite all my efforts to stay hopeful. I do NOT want to be a bitter aging woman. I wasn't headed there. But some days, I just feel weary and at a loss to get past your impact. You have shaken my beliefs and wilted my optimism. I really hate you for that.

And I hate you for making me feel like I am somehow weak and cowardly because I haven't walked away. AFFAIR, you probably wonder why I haven't broadcast the news of this momentous experience I am going through. It's like someone close to you has died, but you never tell a soul that you are grieving and weeping alone. I wonder how many other people are walking around with the same invisible sense of loss. I KNOW this is not a healthy way to cope with grief, and yet here I am. WHY? Because I feel it would just make things worse. I don't need to cope with watching others judge or even reject my husband. God knows I'm not interested in spreading the disappointment I feel. I want our marriage to give others hope. I want them to focus on what we HAVE done together and the good of it. I don't want our marriage just written off because of YOU.

What would I gain by sharing the shock I have to cope with? I don't need pity. I don't need to invite casual gossip from those who really don't care one way or the other. I don't want to alienate my partner's friends and our families...So, I continue to walk around carrying a secret that sometimes tears me apart inside. AFFAIR, you have been a burden to two people who say they weren't "comfortable" with their long-held secret. Now, I *have unwillingly joined their secret club*. I didn't ask to carry their secret. I don't want to. But I see no benefit in "going public." It stinks. So, what do I do with it? "My pain has known your secrets..." so goes the poem. AFFAIR, you are a burden.

AFFAIR, I hate your smug presumption that somehow it is "politically correct" to accept people doing selfish, stupid things without FIRST weighing the potential impact on others. But more than that, I resent the *repetitious decision* to go on and on and on. Apparently, once AN AFFAIR is started, honesty just doesn't matter anymore.

THE DECISION, that first choice, set the stage for 25 years of deceit, pretense, and avoidance. One damn decision became hundreds of decisions to cling to YOU to just "keep on" and keep deceiving the poor ignorant spouse who was so naive as to believe she was still "the one." AFFAIR, if you had not started, I would perhaps still have a closer relationship with two people. If you had not started, they could still honestly be friends. If you had not started, three people would not have suffered.

AFFAIR, I hate that you never ended until the truth came out. Until reality was exposed. Until our son threatened to stay away until I was informed. I resent the insecurity that it causes in me every time I re-confront the fact that there was never a decision to separate until my marriage was on the brink of ending. It never ended until the truth came out. So, to this day, I believe that you would be almost as enduring as my marriage. I resent how important you became to two people who claimed to care about me. Indeed, I know that they cared more about themselves and each other than they did about the future of my marriage. I can't make that perception go away. That is the hard truth I now have to accept and live with. AFFAIR, you never ended. The behavior and encounters ended, but YOU sit with us at night in the flickering TV light. YOU are still in our awareness, like a shadow in the room. I fidget and try to change the subject in my head. AFFAIR, YOU HURT ME, and my husband and my children.

AFFAIR, I hate that you hurt my children. I hate the stunning impact you had on us all. I fantasize about a hypnotic trance where you are wiped off my consciousness. Reality is reality. I am a practical person. I deal with you. But I don't have to like you, ever.

AFFAIR, I resent you for making me wonder if my adult children can ever be inspired to have "a marriage like Mom and Dad..." I thought we showed them resilience and strength in a long relationship, even with ups, downs, and plateaus. Now I just feel sad. I just feel I failed at being *all* that I needed to be. So yeah, you got your pound of flesh.

And unlike some Hallmark resolution, I don't have good answers. But I AM done with you, AFFAIR. I am tired of thinking about you. I am sorry you exist, but I am not going to let you control my mind or heart. I still believe in lasting marriage and the ability of people to grow. I still believe in trying to understand. I still believe no one is defined by their worst decision.

So, AFFAIR, get out of my life and my head. I am done with this, so get behind me. Go away!

After Margaret read the letter, she said, "I think this should have been called the Goodbye Letter."

These letters release the venom, the anger, the sadness, and the mourning of what was, what wasn't, and what could have been. I have no doubt that Margaret and her husband will move into post-traumatic growth—despite the current pain. Why do I think that? Because they both want it!

Sometimes, it can be helpful for your spouse to write a letter to the infidelity saying anything that would express—naming all the anger, sadness, grief, guilt, shame, and loss that is deep inside. You then read it to your partner to exemplify your ongoing pain.

When you externalize the feelings together, you can decide how to process them and what to do with the letters. Some couples like to burn them, and some like to rip them to shreds and state the mantra, "I won't give my feelings the power to stop me from making space for the hope and commitment that I feel."

GRIEF WORK THROUGH GRIEF EXERCISES

Do you wonder why you both cannot get over the hurdles and make your life different? It is impossible to move on when you have not grieved as a couple about how the infidelity has robbed you of what you had built together. The grief may be holding you back from becoming the couple you really want to be.

It is important to honor the grief. Betrayal trauma is so complex and overwhelming that it can seem insurmountable to get through it. It comes and goes like waves in the ocean, and that is a natural process. Partner betrayal requires a more structured approach to moving through all the losses that result from it. The format is quite simple and follows below.

To the Spouse: Please be sensitive to all the losses your partner is experiencing. She is having to deal with layers and layers of losses, and this is another loss in her day-to-day functioning.

GRIEF EXERCISE

Let's look at the many losses that have been experienced. I would like you to list 20 types of losses my partner has suffered because of my unfaithfulness.

The immediate losses:

1. My spouse has lost trust in me.

2. My spouse has lost their faith in God.

3. My spouse has lost their sense of self.

4. My spouse has lost ability to trust him or herself.

5. My spouse has lost sense of safety.

6. My spouse has lost _____

7. My spouse has lost _____

8. My partner has lost_____

9.   My partner has lost _____

10.   My spouse has lost _____

11.   My spouse has lost _____

12.   My spouse has lost _____

13.   My spouse has lost _____

14.   My spouse has lost _____

15.   My spouse has lost _____

16.   My spouse has lost _____

17.   My spouse has lost _____

18.   My spouse has lost _____

19.   My spouse has lost _____

20.   My spouse has lost _____

21.   My spouse has lost _____

22.   My spouse has lost _____

23.   My spouse has lost _____

24.   My spouse has lost _____

25.   My spouse has lost _____

LOSSES AND FEARS ABOUT THE FUTURE

Now, think about all the losses experienced for the future. Does your partner believe the two of you can rebuild a future together? Think about growing together as a couple and imagine the feelings your spouse might be having when contemplating what your relationship might look like together. This is a true empathy exercise as you see loss through the BP's eyes!

As a spouse who is rebuilding the relationship, what are 10 additional statements that might describe your partner's fears, concerns, and issues about the future?

1. My spouse fears that life will never be normal again.

2. My partner has lost the ability to see a future for us.

3. My partner has lost faith in my recovery and consistently minimizes the recovery process.

4. My partner is afraid to talk about growing old with me.

5. My spouse does not want to talk about creating a vision with me even though we had previously talked about having a lake place when we retire.

6. My partner _____

7. My partner _____

8. My partner _____

9. My partner _____

10. My partner _____

BETRAYED SPOUSE'S FEEDBACK

Now, as painful as this exercise is, I would like you to ask your spouse if you can review this list together and add five more immediate losses to your list. The Partner adds the losses to your list:

CURRENT AND FUTURE LOSSES FROM THE BP'S POINT OF VIEW

1.   A loss I am experiencing today is _____

\
\

2.   A loss I am experiencing today is _____

\
\

3.   A loss I am experiencing today is _____

\
\

4.   A loss I am experiencing today is _____

\
\

5.   A loss I am experiencing today is _____

\
\

Next, I would like the BP to review your list of losses for the future and then add five more losses of what your spouse fears will never be.

For the Partner:

1. A fear I have for my future is _____

   _____

   _____

2. A fear I have for my future is _____

   _____

   _____

3. A fear I have for my future is _____

   _____

   _____

4. A fear I have for my future is _____

   _____

   _____

5. A fear I have for my future is _____

   _____

   _____

THE LOSSES I HAVE EXPERIENCED BECAUSE OF MY BETRAYAL

Next, I would like you to write five losses you have experienced because of your past.

FOR THE UNFAITHFUL SPOUSE IN RECOVERY:

1. A personal loss I have experienced because of the betrayal that I caused you is: _____

    _____

    _____

2. A personal loss I have experienced because of the betrayal that I caused you is: _____

    _____

    _____

3. A personal loss I have experienced because of the betrayal that I caused you is: _____

    _____

    _____

4. A personal loss I have experienced because of the betrayal that I caused you is: _____

    _____

    _____

5.   A personal loss I have experienced because of the betrayal that I

caused you is: _____

_____

_____

It is a commitment, but you have both already put in so much time and effort that it certainly can help to look toward the future and live the life you both deserve.

Grief is a process, and it needs to be acknowledged and expressed. You can't immerse yourself in the future until you have done your anger, grief, and mourning work. Doing this work decreases the intensity and frequency of the feelings. It does not eliminate the anger and sadness, but it makes feelings more manageable.

If you are a male betrayer, you have likely not been encouraged to express feelings. Historically, men have been seen as weak and vulnerable if feelings were acknowledged. They had it wrong! It is good to externalize feelings and let your partner see your understandable feelings and how you have been impacted by them. There is no shame in sharing your feelings. Expressing vulnerability increases connection.

To the Partner: I know that you are incredibly tired and exhausted by partner betrayal. It can be easy to ignore this second stage because there is a part of you that is undoubtedly depressed, and it is hard to muster up the energy to do this grief and anger work, but you need to mourn what you had or thought you had. You need to grieve what you will never have in your old marriage, and you need to move into a new acceptance of what you can have. This work frees you up to begin to find yourself and find a new coupleship, and you both definitely deserve that!

Chapter 18

What Happens If the Betrayer or If the Couple Is Not Getting Better?

You may be a couple that is really struggling. You just cannot seem to get past the impasse of the acting out. I meet many couples where the betrayer has done a great job of getting into recovery and is doing well and proving the integrity that is so important to regain, but the betrayed spouse has difficulty accepting the concept of the addiction and is struggling with being hurt again.

Understandably, when a couple experiences betrayal, each person goes through many changes. As the partner unravels what has happened, it can feel so incomprehensible that the betrayer could have done this, and despite the desire to understand, it can feel incongruent to want to go on with the marriage.

IT TAKES TIME

The acting out is so unfathomable that it takes months or years of watching the spouse maintain good recovery before trust can become the new reality. This can be frustrating and discouraging for the recovered spouse who is doing well in infidelity recovery. The spouse thinks, *Nothing I'm doing is working*, and wonders if the partner will *ever* get better. The betrayer in recovery questions whether his being in the relationship may be causing more harm.

What I love so much about Pure Desire, The Living Truth, Men of the Battle, and other Twelve-Step groups for men in recovery is that they know that this recovery takes time. They say, "Dude, you acted out for three and a half years, and you think your partner can just 'just get over it' in 18 months? You don't have the right to even think about giving up until you put the same amount of time into the relationship that you did in your cheating!"

It is such a powerful reality call when people can help each other to put the resistance back in perspective. Although I know it is hard to watch your partner be in trauma, I can assure you that the level of anger, disconnection, sadness, and doubt that is experienced is in direct proportion to the trauma experienced in your partner's brain.

As you remember from Chapter 2, women also cheat on their spouses and may need organizations like Sex and Love Addiction or Love Addiction, which offer support groups for women who have experienced infidelity.

To the Spouse in Recovery: If this sounds like your scenario, I urge you to understand that your spouse is more than likely not holding the acting out over your head to punish you. The partner is dealing with so much anger, sadness, grief, and trauma that it is preventing the BP from being able to let the defenses down.

The BP is in survival mode, and although this book is going to help with the uncertainty and work toward healing the brain, it takes time for the brain to heal. The brain is doing whatever it can to find safety in present-day life. Doing these grief exercises together will help process the grief and anguish that the BP feels. Your journey will be to contain your partner's pain as you walk through the grief and mourning together.

It is an interesting phenomenon that sometimes, when there seems to be a real impasse in your relationship, it may be necessary to stop, take a pause, and recalibrate your focus. You both may be concentrating on fear as opposed to growth and change.

JILL & TIM: ARE THERE TIMES WHEN, NO MATTER HOW MUCH WE TRY, THERE IS TOO MUCH DAMAGE TO MAKE IT WORK?

Jill discovered her husband was looking at gay porn. This had left her questioning his sexuality and his desire for her. He adamantly denied any homosexual or bisexual tendencies. He had done a deep dive into his fascination with gay porn, and we had hypothesized that he may have been curious because he was molested by an older neighbor when he was ages eight to ten. He had many mixed feelings about this teenager who showed real interest in him. Their sex play was scary and exciting both at the same time. He felt intense shame and desire for what naturally felt good. He feared that they would be discovered, and the last thing he wanted anyone to think was that he might be gay.

Tim and I talked about "the sex play" that was really molestation due to the age differentiation. Tim said, "It never felt like he was taking advantage of me. He never forced me into anything or coerced or threatened me. He would make suggestions, and I would follow his lead. I know it screwed me up and created a desire to experiment more, but I would never have done anything with anyone else but him. It sounds weird, but it felt safe with him."

He told me, "I don't know when I learned the concept of homosexuality, but I knew that I would be made fun of and ostracized if anyone knew of our experimentation." Regardless of his fears, this behavior continued until his friend found a girlfriend and moved on. Strangely, he felt abandoned, and although he was relieved that he did not have to worry about being discovered, he missed the special attention and the physical attention he received.

About that time, the internet came on the scene, and as a tween, he and his friends would attempt to look at internet porn. It was tough to scout out because there was only one computer in his house, but he still took that "familiar risk" and was able to share sites with his friends. He reported that he looked at typical porn and found it stimulating and curious. He could not wait to share what he had seen with a girl, but he was too shy to ask out any girls. At about 17, he discovered gay porn, which took him back to his younger days. It was like he was addicted to those sites, although he reassured himself that he was not interested in males. His fetish would turn into an addiction in college, and he spent most of his evenings after studying looking at gay porn.

He met Jill at the Union, a hangout for college students. She initiated the conversation and their first date. Jill made it so easy to be together, and he remembered thinking that he needed this type of girl if he was ever going to get on with his life. The truth is that he never dated anyone else. He and Jill were so compatible that when she suggested that they get married, he was "all in." Jill had no idea about his secret life. She did not know that he was looking at gay porn, nor did he talk about his molestation. It was not until a decade into their marriage that she discovered his addiction for gay porn.

One afternoon, when he was at work and she was home sick, her computer crashed, and she decided to use his computer to Google her flu-like symptoms. Although password protected, she opened it up, played around with conceivable passwords, and quickly got past the password protection. "That was easy," she thought as she congratulated herself on knowing him so well that she could guess his password.

But then the unimaginable happened, and it opened to the last site he had been on. She was looking at gay pornography. At first, she thought it was a mistake. She was horrified to see what he had been viewing! She did a browsing history and saw hundreds of gay sites. She was in a state of shock as she opened each site under his browsing history. She thought she was going to throw up on the spot. Her husband was gay. What did this mean?

Her thoughts started to race. Was she married to a latent homosexual? What was going on? She called him immediately, told him what she had found, and insisted that he come home.

As she waited for his arrival, she wondered who this man was that she had married. She was in shock. She kept asking herself, "What does this mean?" repeatedly. When he got home, he looked as shell-shocked as she felt. He kept trying to reassure her that he was not gay, but he could not explain his fixation with gay men. If he was telling her the truth, then what did that mean for their marriage?

For days, she questioned her reality and whether he was ever really attracted to her. Could they ever find that attraction to each other? Could she be attracted to him now that she had discovered his secret?

As they consulted with me, they both felt defeated. She admitted that she did not know whether their marriage could be repaired. Every time she looked at him, she questioned his sexuality. He consistently stated that he loved her and was attracted to her, but that never really convinced her because she had all those images in her head of gay men having sex, which absolutely repulsed her.

She cried in her session, "That is not my life, and I can't make the images stop. I love the husband that I knew, but I can't find it in my heart to love this man I suspect is hiding from himself."

Much of our work together was educating both as to how a fixation can move into a compulsion. Although she understood about trauma reenactment and how he could have developed this compulsion, she was not able to reinvest in the relationship. Her brain had seen images that she would never have allowed into her world. They synced to who he was, and she could never uncouple them.

For months, she told herself that if he had cancer, she would stay with him because she would *never* leave him because of an illness. She tried to apply the same rationale to his sex addiction, but there was so much damage done that she could not recover. She did not want a divorce, but staying with him would have meant living a lie. She wanted to honor her true self.

Together, both her husband and I validated her feelings and encouraged her to start a new life. She admitted that this was not what she wanted, but she knew that she could not live with him, even though he had faithfully worked a good recovery program and was willing to do anything that would make her feel safe. He slept in another room, took three polygraph tests to prove he was not gay, and used AVR to acknowledge the pain.

He reported to me that if the roles were reversed, he would have the same trauma, and he loved her so much that all he wanted was for her to be happy again. And that meant with or without him.

They had the hard conversations and decided on a therapeutic formal separation. Jill felt so relieved to have time to herself and quickly knew that she needed to divorce to regain her serenity. During their last session with me, she described to both of us that her decision to leave allowed her to truly accept that he did have an illness, but she could not be with him as he worked on his recovery. They divorced in integrity, and she moved on with her life.

For some couples, there is nothing that can change the impact of the sexual acting out that has devastated their lives.

WHAT IF THE BETRAYER CONTINUES TO HAVE AFFAIRS?

Unfortunately, there are some betrayers that cannot remain faithful. They want the relationship, but they are not willing to fully invest in the programs that support recovery. Some partners get so healthy that they detach themselves and focus on connecting with others in healthy ways.

Others choose not to tolerate the infidelity and decide to move forward in divorce.

If you decide to leave, I encourage you to get a partner-sensitive specialist, as they know all the hard work you have put into healing this relationship, and they will be able to coach you through the transformation that needs to take place as you continue to rebuild your own life apart from the betrayer. It is important for you to get the support you deserve as you decide how to proceed with your life.

Many women have put into place a post-disclosure or postnuptial agreement to acquire 75% of the assets or sell the house and receive 80% of the equity, etc., if the betrayer cannot stay faithful. There are no right or wrong choices. You decide what you need for your own emotional health and sanity.

IF THE BETRAYER IS WORKING DILIGENTLY, CAN WE MOVE FORWARD?

If your spouse is working good recovery, and you are not ready to walk, I would ask you to participate in the next phase of partner betrayal.

Stage 3 can help you to move into a space where you decide to try on the possibility of a new life together. You both have worked hard on accepting the past, and you both feel better about yourselves. You have more energy now that you are in that state of acceptance, and you are no longer fighting the past.

You have *surrendered* to what you had, what you thought you had, and what you will never have under the old relationship. It can open doors to making the decision to create a new marriage if you are so inclined.

Suddenly, the Serenity Prayer has new meaning to you, and you recognize its true significance.

> *God, grant me the serenity to accept the things I cannot change, the courage to change the things I can, and the wisdom to know the difference.*
> *~ Reinhold Niebuhr*

WHAT IF I CAN'T GET PAST THE IMPACT OF INFIDELITY—YOU ALWAYS HAVE CHOICE

Side Note: If you have done all this grief and anger work and you absolutely are still reeling in the pain of what has been taken from you, consider it may be time to choose a different direction.

If you have done this hard work and still cannot get to post-traumatic growth, I would encourage you to check in with your intuition. Trauma interrupts and interferes with your ability to make decisions Consider taking the pressure off yourself and to "sit with the confusion and the pain, and trust that as you become still...the answer will come."

No matter what you decide, you always have a choice. I am confident that you will make the right one for you. Some partners require a network of people who understand infidelity, partner betrayal, and the many facets of feelings and emotions that accompany it. They find it essential to process their feelings with the supportive community, such as their support group, therapy group, or partner-sensitive specialist. Your community will be able to walk you through this process so you can work through the trauma of partner betrayal, feel your feelings, grieve the deception, find a sense of restoration for yourself, and decide how you want to proceed with your life.

If you do not have this kind of team, I would encourage you to build it so that your experience can be validated by the people in your support group and the professionals in your network. It can expedite your healing on this arduous journey.

Other partners prefer to work things out by themselves using podcasts, books, and workshops to assist them in the education they need to make difficult decisions.

If you feel things are not getting better, a therapeutic separation may give you the space to decide what is in your best interest. It also gives your brain some time to rest and heal. There is no shame in your choices.

Of course, I lean toward support and connection in validating your confusion and doubt. But everyone is diverse and has unique needs.

One woman came in after many months of agonizing and said, "Carol, I am paralyzed in fear! Part of me wants to stay and settle into what we can potentially be as a couple. But my gut says that despite his changes, I will never be able to trust him again. There has been too much damage, and I need to move on. The other part says that I have invested too much energy in repairing this relationship, and he is showing me he is in good recovery. Why can't I get past the impasse? When will I ever be able to make a decision?"

I recommended a therapeutic separation so she could have quiet time to come to her own decision. After eight months, she knew what she needed to do. This infidelity had taken too much of her serenity, and she needed to create a new environment that allowed her a life free from those memories. There is no shame in needing that new life because she left knowing she had tried everything, and she left honoring her emotions. She was then able to move into post-traumatic growth.

There is no disgrace in you both trying to make things work and then deciding that it is time for you both to take a different path. Not every couple will make it to the other side together, so if you need to separate and divorce, I encourage you to keep using your relational skills with empathy as you move on in your lives. These skills can be used anytime, in any situation with anyone. Even if you can't make the relationship work, you can still work on getting to post-traumatic growth.

Chapter 19

The Third Phase of Partner Betrayal: Post-Traumatic Growth

All the work that you have been doing has been hard. The first stage, Stabilization, was the most difficult because you both had to stay in the relationship even though it had been shattered by infidelity.

The second stage was about processing what had been done to the relationship. It was the death of the relationship as you both knew it. Together as a couple, you had to decide how to support the partner as you both went through the grief, anger, sadness, and excruciating pain. You, the partner, had to go through the pain, and your spouse had to walk with you through it. "The old way" would have involved you both jumping into therapy when your brain was not able to function properly, and the much-needed relationship skills were not developed to create safety. ERCEM is based on developing safety and walking together through the three stages of partner betrayal. You both do the work together. This is tough because your spouse *must* contain your pain that the infidelity caused. Your spouse's active participation helps become the antidote for your restoration of yourself and the relationship.

You have now arrived at the third stage of partner betrayal. It is known as restoration of the self, relationship, and connection to the world. In this stage, you have surrendered to the past, and you recognize that you are no longer going to be held hostage by it. I use the word "surrender" because it is not only an acknowledgment of what happened but also a **decision to recreate a new relationship.** It creates a new space to allow you both as a couple to consciously decide how you can renew your connection and build something different that has purpose. It also requires a belief or faith that you both are going to walk this journey together. No matter what happens, you are strong enough to stand firm in your own self-worth.

This is known as the post-traumatic growth phase because it allows both of you to make a choice to live your life with a new realization that a purpose can come out of this tragedy.

Even if you haven't finished Stage 2, I would like you to read this entire section so you will have something to look forward to in the future. It will give you a taste of what is possible even when it doesn't seem probable.

In my sessions with couples, I will utilize some of these exercises as early as Stage 1 and then thread them in parts of Stage 2 because you both are working so hard at recognizing and facing the pain. The recovering spouse is fervently using skills that you see. There is much growth in both awareness and accountability for the pain in the relationship. Reading this section and finding opportunities to practice Stage 3 work preps you for the gifts in PTG!

This is always a sensitive subject to discuss with couples who have been through the trauma of partner betrayal. No one would ever want a couple to go through this, and yet we know that this ordeal and the experience you have garnered from it has taught you both great things individually and as a couple. You may be curious or even confused as to what I am referencing, but I assure you that as you move forward on this journey, you will be able to ascertain how you are stronger and what you have both learned from it.

First, we need to understand what post-traumatic growth is and what criteria define it.

THE FIVE INDICATORS OF POST-TRAUMATIC GROWTH

Post-traumatic growth (PTG) was developed by psychologists Richard Tedeschi, PhD, and Lawrence Calhoun, PhD, in the mid-1990s. They had done research on people who had experienced great trauma, and as they interviewed them, they found that this group of people also expressed that they had gained a "strength from the trauma." Much to the researchers' surprise, they found out that the traumatized population who had endured so much psychological struggle—from being in combat or torture camps to catastrophic events like tsunamis, hurricanes, or accidents—described that following their adversity, they were often able to see positive growth afterward.

Their research showed that when you have experienced trauma, you can get stronger from the wreckage. They were so intrigued by this phenomenon that they interviewed thousands of trauma survivors. They concluded that many people who have experienced tragedy underwent a positive change because of the struggle. They grew stronger and had a renewed sense of self, which made them feel resilient and more alive. Their relationship with others took on a new meaning, and it seemed to deepen as a result of the trauma. They were also surprised to see that trauma survivors looked at life differently and seemed to search for new possibilities. It helped survivors find, as Victor Frankl coined it, "a search for meaning."

As a result, people increased or strengthened their spiritual growth. Thus, the five domains of post-traumatic growth were born and included:

1. A richer appreciation of life

2. A deepened sense of relating to others

3. A better understanding of one's own personal strength

4. A new sense of possibilities for one's self and/or the world

5. An emotional connection and appreciation for their own spiritual growth

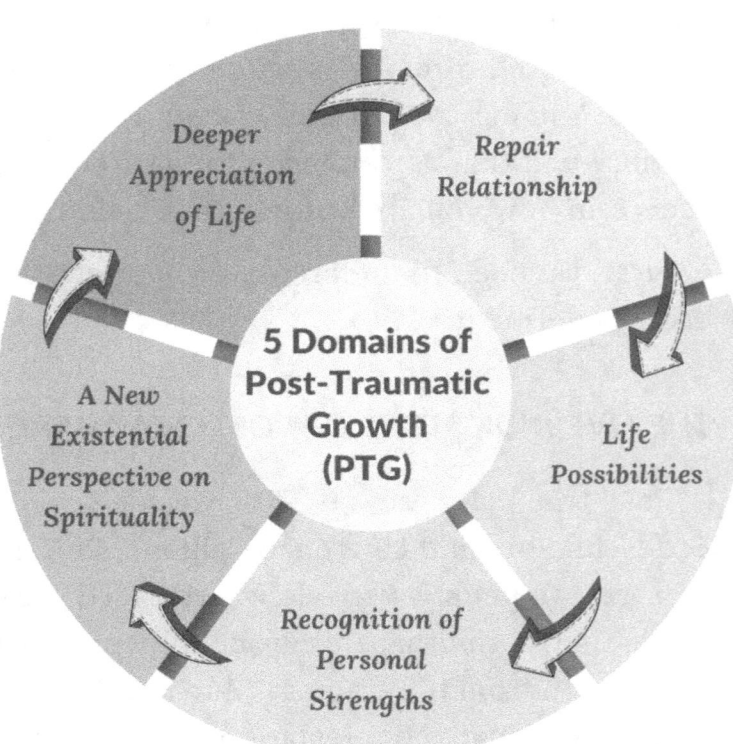

*BASED ON THE PREMISE THAT TRAUMATIC EVENTS CAN BE A CATALYST FOR GROWTH

According to researchers who studied Tedeschi and Calhoun's work, the idea that human beings can be changed by their encounters with life challenges, sometimes in radically positive ways, is not new. The theme is present in ancient spiritual and religious traditions, literature, and philosophy.

What is reasonably new is the systematic study of this phenomenon by professionals and how they work with trauma survivors like you.

The researchers defined post-traumatic growth as an extended period that can last from days to years, in which people develop new ways of thinking, feeling, and behaving because the events they have experienced do not permit a return to baseline functioning. This is a crucial way that PTG is also distinguished from "resilience," which is a return to baseline or resistance to trauma, and "recovery," which has similar connotations. In PTG, a new baseline is created.

As both of you enter this third stage, you may notice that you take on these traits as you move closer together as a couple. Both of you may read these and begin to recognize that understanding the criteria helps you identify your personal strengths individually and as a couple.

Are both of you able to identify how you are stronger? Are you both able to have a new appreciation for life?

When you know your strength and have a new appreciation for what is before you, you might notice that the Universe puts new opportunities before you both. It might be as simple as getting to watch your grandchild on Wednesdays, your pastor asking you to mentor new members at church, or you being compelled to sponsor people in your Twelve-Step group. There may even be a part of you that would like to help other relationships that have experienced infidelity.

The possibilities are endless because you are ready. It may not feel like you are truly in PTG, but when you make the decision to let go of the pain and the fear, you automatically shift to a place of empowerment.

To the Partner: Your brain is back online, and you are aware of increased grace and compassion for your relationship as you practice intentional self-compassion. You are standing strong in your convictions and are exercising your boundaries, even though you are feeling less likely to use them.

To the Recovering Spouse: You may feel more accomplished because you learned how to help with your spouse's triggers. You know what empathy is, and you practice it daily. You are less defensive and reactive. You are practicing skills like mindfulness, and your focus is on healthy things like the family, your church, or your support group.

POST-TRAUMATIC INDICATOR EXERCISE

Which PTG indicator would you currently endorse?

Both of you look at this chart and check each of the five indicators that you believe you are beginning to endorse. Acknowledging the small changes helps to reinforce ownership. As you move into this phase, notice the shift in your perspective.

THE 5 INDICATORS OF PTG	BP BEGINNING TO ENDORSE?	BT BEGINNING TO ENDORSE?
A *richer appreciation of life.*		
A *deepened sense of relating to others.*		
A *better understanding of one's own personal strength*		
A *new sense of possibilities for one's self and/or the world.*		
An *emotional connection & appreciation for their own spiritual growth.*		

You might want to incorporate the five PTG indicators above into your Connection-Shares and let your spouse know that you appreciate the support that you have been receiving. In PTG, you may notice that you have less judgment or are focused on the small things like your son playing with a dandelion. You look for opportunities to start a new program at work, and you are open to the possibility of mentoring employees to actualize their potential.

You might share with your spouse how you have recognized the deeper level of connection you have felt for the integrity changes.

To the Partner: By entering that third stage, you have decided that you cannot live under that cloud of fear and doubt. You are strong and wise, and you know that you are willing to live your best life.

In other words, you both, as a couple, decide what needs to be implemented to be able to enter the new and exciting phase of restoration, which I call PTG.

There are many factors that come into play when you enter this phase because you get to decide how you would like to play out your vision. What would you like your new relationship to look like? What would you like to add into the marriage that would make it more connected, richer in meaning, and focused on the best version of you as a couple?

In the beginning, it may feel like a daunting venture, but there is also great security in creating a life together that brings closeness back into the relationship.

To the Spouse in Good Recovery: I know how exciting this is because your fear was that you would always have to live in a state of purgatory for what you had done. You feared that you would never be forgiven for your betrayals. You have worked hard to get here, and you will never take it for granted again.

Now, you can really see that there is light at the end of the tunnel, but you are scared to believe it because you do not ever want to go through this pain again. You are in solid recovery, and you are so grateful for this second chance. You are scared to believe it because you could not endure the pain it would cause if the rug were pulled out from underneath you. There is still a part of you that fears that your spouse will change their mind.

You cannot believe your partner has offered this grace. You tell yourself that this is a miracle, and it is...It is the miracle of recovery.

POST-TRAUMATIC GROWTH CHART

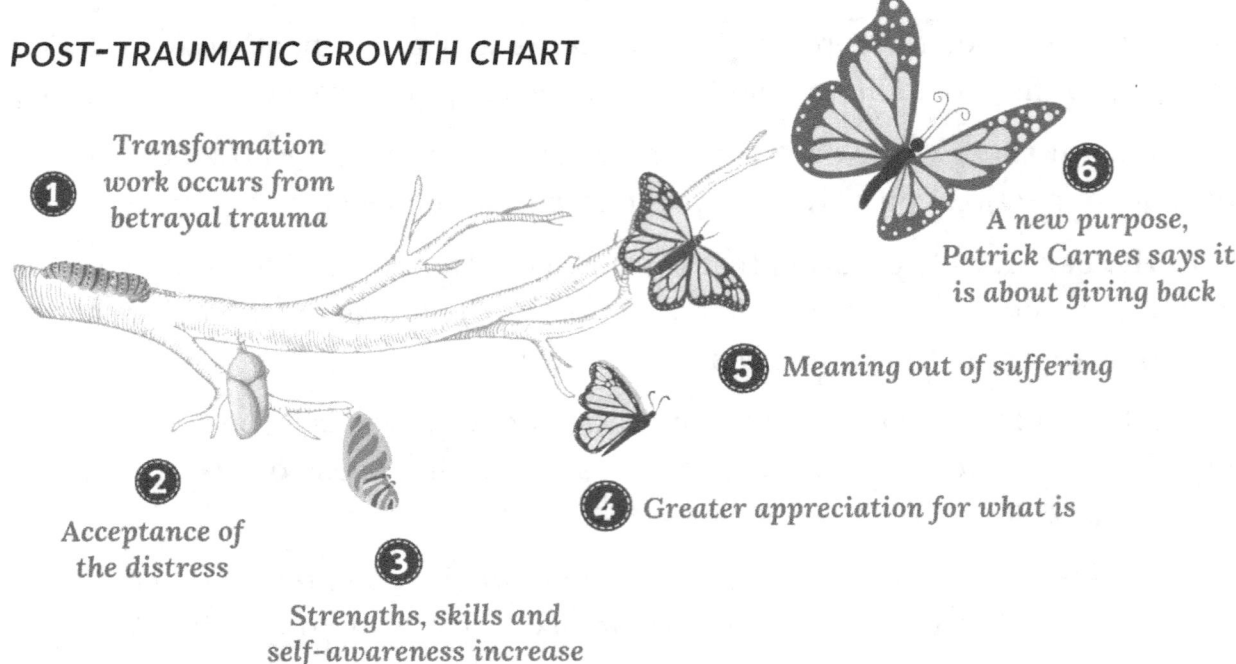

1 Transformation work occurs from betrayal trauma

2 Acceptance of the distress

3 Strengths, skills and self-awareness increase

4 Greater appreciation for what is

5 Meaning out of suffering

6 A new purpose, Patrick Carnes says it is about giving back

CREATING A VISION

As difficult as it sounds, it can be a healthy and helpful exercise to think about what you might want your future to look like now that you both have moved through this crisis and reestablished your own growth.

I know that it might not feel like it is time to begin this process, and your trepidation is normal. But many couples need to start reaching for a new beginning. In her TED Talk on shame and infidelity, Ester Perel said, "Many people will be married two or three times, and some will do that in the same marriage." Well, this is your chance as a couple to devote your time to rebuilding a rock-solid marriage that will be more committed and laced with healthy values. It will be the foundation for the love you feel toward each other for the rest of your lives. When you make the decision to do this, you begin the process of restoration.

You both have really hung in there to support each other. Deciding what you need and want in the future will fortify the changes you have made and the changes you will make in the future.

What is your vision for the future? As you do the exercises in this chapter, I will ask you this question again so you both can declare an intention for how you would like the next chapter of your life to play out. This time, you will make conscious decisions about your relationship that will bring meaning and purpose to your lives as a couple!

MIND STATES AND MIND STORIES THAT WILL TRANSFORM YOU AND THE RELATIONSHIP

A NEW PLAN FOR CONNECTION

It is important for you both to change your focus and spend one day a week reconstructing how you want your life to be.

It can be helpful for couples to place themselves in that imaginary place of seeing the good in each other and reconstructing a belief that they can be on the other side of partner betrayal. To do this, I encourage you both to do what may have seemed in Stage 1 like an insurmountable and overwhelming exercise. But now that you are entering Stage 3, you recognize that much has changed. For some of you, it may feel a bit fake and disingenuous, but I am asking you to do it anyway with as much energy as you can muster.

I created this exercise to help neutralize the fear that accompanies growth and change.

> *You have lived with fear for so long that it feels foreign to walk away from it.*

You are making a conscious choice to shift your focus and live the life you deserve. You can use this exercise when you identify that you are doing better and need a little reminder that you are doing well.

THE CHANGES MY SPOUSE HAS MADE (EVEN IF THERE ARE DOUBTS THAT THE CHANGES WON'T NOT REMAIN PERMANENT)

To the Partner: It will help you to write out ten examples of how your spouse is showing you they are different. As your brain has gotten clearer and your executive functioning has come back online, it will be necessary to remind yourself of the progress and acknowledge it to yourself.

You may say that there is no way you could ever think of 10 positive changes that have been made, but I will tell you that if you stretch yourself and look for small changes, you will be able to acknowledge the small changes that show you your spouse is focused on being a person of integrity and the spouse you have always wanted.

1.   I can tell that you are different because _____

_____

2.   I can tell that you are different because _____

_____

3.   I can tell that you are different because _____

_____

4.   I can tell that you are different because _____

_____

5.   I can tell that you are different because _____

_____

6.   I can tell that you are different because _____

_____

7.   I can tell that you are different because _____

_____

8.   I can tell that you are different because _____

_____

9.   I can tell that you are different because _____

_____

10.   I can tell that you are different because _____

_____

WHAT YOU APPRECIATE, APPRECIATES

The Recovering Spouse: In this third stage, you will need to work on the concept of appreciation for self and the changes you have made in the relationship. Most recovery programs will stress the importance of being humble, and although it is important for you to show humility, it is also important that you appreciate what is working for you personally and in your marriage.

When a spouse in recovery "owns" the things that have been accomplished, it will leave you feeling more secure about the relationship in general. You will likely think, *This is the person that I have always wanted as my partner in life, and I love our common and shared values.*

Your partner needs to know that you believe in yourself and your relational recovery. You have worked hard in this book and on yourself. It is time to acknowledge the changes that you have made.

Write out 10 things that you have changed or are working on that are an investment in the coupleship. How are you showing appreciation for your relational changes?

There is likely a tendency to not want to identify your changes for fear that the changes may be put down or that you do not deserve to have them acknowledged, but it is important for you to stay abreast of your progress.

Although "Openness, Brokenness, and Humility" are signs of good spiritual recovery, it is absolutely essential to know and appreciate the changes you are making.

EXERCISE: WHAT YOU APPRECIATE, APPRECIATES

Write out 10 things that you are doing to appreciate your infidelity recovery changes.

RECOVERY CHANGES	RELATIONAL CHANGES
1. I appreciate my integrity.	1. I appreciate what relational recovery has taught me about myself.
2. I appreciate my fellowship.	2. I appreciate the hard work I have done.
3. I appreciate my readings.	3. I appreciate what I have learned in the book After the Affair.
4. I appreciate...	4. I appreciate...

RECOVERY CHANGES	RELATIONAL CHANGES
5. I appreciate...	5. I appreciate...
6. I appreciate...	6. I appreciate...
7. I appreciate...	7. I appreciate...
8. I appreciate...	8. I appreciate...
9. I appreciate...	9. I appreciate...
10. I appreciate...	10. I appreciate...

For the Partner: Post-traumatic growth does not just happen. You have made a choice to take the next step in your healing. Your spouse is noticeably different, and you have appreciated much growth and effort. The skills may not be perfect, but there has been great improvement. You more than likely have assessed that your spouse sees recovery as a lifeline to continuous sexual integrity.

It is time to consciously appreciate the changes on paper so you can share them with the recovering spouse.

IDENTIFYING THE PROGRESS IN YOUR SPOUSE'S RECOVERY

Write out 10 recovery and relational changes that you have seen your spouse make and consistently maintain.

THE RECOVERY SKILLS AND CHANGES	RELATIONAL CHANGES
1. I appreciate the ongoing discipline to journal.	1. I appreciate that my spouse initiates Connection-Shares.
2. I appreciate that my spouse is mentoring others.	2. I appreciate that my spouse is reading materials on integrity.
3. I appreciate that my spouse is leading Pure Desire Groups.	3. I appreciate that my spouse is communicating honestly with me.
4. I appreciate...	4. I appreciate...

RECOVERY CHANGES	RELATIONAL CHANGES
5. I appreciate...	5. I appreciate...
6. I appreciate...	6. I appreciate...
7. I appreciate...	7. I appreciate...
8. I appreciate...	8. I appreciate...
9. I appreciate...	9. I appreciate...
10. I appreciate...	10. I appreciate...

To the Partner: When you choose to focus on the positive changes, you are in a state of PTG. You have made the conscious choice to stop living the way you were living. You choose PTG for yourself because you want to detach from the anger, fear, and sadness you have felt for so long. You want to take a deep dive into finding yourself again. You no longer want to be defined by partner betrayal. You want to create a new normal, and you have decided to do that together!

> *You no longer want to be defined by partner betrayal.*

Sometimes, spouses in recovery report that they have met more criteria for PTG, but they are afraid to acknowledge it because they don't feel that it is fair to you to feel better than you do, and they tell me that they need to walk beside you in your pain. If your relationship is 75% better, then it is time to reinvest in the relationship. With some trepidation, you can start this journey together and you should claim your changes.

To the Partner: This is when you realistically look at your life and tell yourself, "I am no longer going to be tethered to the past pain. I am going to be fine either way." You want a life with your partner, but you recognize that you are ready to create your own happiness, and it feels good.
In my online course, Partners Find Your Post-Traumatic Growth (on sexhelpwithcarolthecoach.com), I interview eight women partners, one male partner, and a couple who are working together in the field of sexual addiction, trauma, and partner betrayal. They talk about how they made the decision to move into PTG. They discuss what motivated them and the new mind states that occurred that freed them from their fears and anxieties. They also identified what resources they used to help them make the choice to move on. All but one partner in the course stayed in the marriage and worked on personally getting stronger and owning her strength. When they acknowledged their strengths and changes, everything around them changed. This is an incredibly inspirational course for partners, but I would encourage you both to watch it together so that the recovering partner can reinforce the changes that have occurred for you!

There is no doubt that you have extra skin in the game because as you recognize and acknowledge your changes, it validates the hope you have for the relationship.

If You Are a Female Partner: To help women get to the place of PTG, I wrote *Unleashing Your Power Moving Through the Trauma of Partner Betrayal.* It is a book written just for you that goes over many of the concepts that we have talked about in this book, and it gives you empowering exercises to strengthen your sense of self. It can be a helpful resource to do the work you are doing with your spouse because it is all about empowering you as you walk this journey.

You are in a place where you are noticing your own strength and wisdom while simultaneously focusing on changes you have seen in his individual recovery and within your relationship. Your ability to do both simultaneously creates an environment for growth. Recognizing the changes and admitting them aloud validates the change you both are making. Although there are no guarantees that it will change permanently, your new sense of empowerment reinforces that you will be ok no matter what the outcome.

As you do this next exercise, know that I understand how vulnerable you are being because I am asking you to trust me. I know that you may need to recalibrate your energy and focus on what is working or is different in the relationship. You may have a natural resistance to this because you do not want to set yourself up to be hurt again. But I have worked with thousands of partners, and sometimes they must put themselves in that "imaginary place" that allows them to "act" as if these changes are real to move forward and begin to build upon them. And when they do, a natural shift occurs where they feel better and safer. They become ready to move into the journey of restoration of self, the relationship, and the relationship they have with the world.

RECOGNIZING MY OWN CHANGES IN MY HEALING

This exercise will help validate your decision to do all that hard work you did with your spouse in Stage 2. You needed to do the work so that you could move out of fear, anger, and grief and begin to trust both your partner and the relationship again.

Think about all the ways that you have grown in your own healing. Write out 10 ways:

1. _____

2. _____

3. _____

4. _____

5. _____

6. _____

7. _____

8. _____

9. _____

10. _____

ACKNOWLEDGING OUR CHANGES AS A COUPLE

For the Partner: After discovery, you questioned if you would ever have a healthy relationship again. And as with most couples, your spouses' recovery has not been seamless. Every time a poor choice was made, it affected your ability to trust. Poor choices include gazing and objectifying, being late, telling small lies like taking out the trash when it did not happen, hiding information or not sharing it openly with you, etc. But now, you have seen enough growth that you are willing to support the relationship by acknowledging the positive changes in your coupleship.

1. _____

2. _____

3. _____

4. _____

5. _____

6. _____

7. _____

8. _____

9. _____

10. _____

As a Couple: Together, write out 10 indicators that you have increased your skills as a couple. How has your relationship grown? Are you talking more, spending more time walking, going to groups together, practicing check-ins, reading this book together, or praying with each other?

List those changes here to reinforce the concept "what you appreciate *appreciates.*"

1. _____

2. _____

3. _____

4. _____

5. _____

6. _____

7. _____

8. _____

9. _____

10. _____

"ACTING AS IF" TO GET PAST YOUR PAST

It is not uncommon for you or your partner to stay stuck in the cycle of refusing to acknowledge changes because your partner is protective of being hurt again. Even though I said very few partners are punitive, I have known it to happen. Could that be you? Is there any part of you that has wanted to stay in the punishing mode because of all the pain that your spouse has caused?

NORA & SAM: LETTING GO OF THE BETRAYAL HISTORY FOR 24 HOURS

I had a partner tell me that her heart had ached for so long with excruciating pain that she just wanted to hurt him for the rest of his life. It kept her feeling safe and in a one-up position in the relationship, and he seemed comfortable being in that position. She remarked, "I know that it's bad to want him to remain my whipping boy, but I literally cannot fathom letting my defenses down and appreciating the changes he has made without reminding him of what a loser I think he is."

She said, "Carol, what is wrong with me? I know that I love him, but I just cannot stop hating him. I am tired of this merry-go-round, but I can't get off. We have a couple of good days, but then when he does something that irritates or hurts me, I am off to the races with rage again."

I praised her for her insight and desire to change. She did not like how she was showing up in the relationship, but she did not know how to get out of those destructive patterns. There was a part of her that did not want to stop punishing him because her brain was still in the fight mode of partner betrayal.

The second thing I did was AVR her. I said, "Nora, I want to acknowledge that you are going back and forth with two very real feelings that are a part of you. That must make you fearful because it can be exhausting to treat him so differently based on your internal fears. But I want to reassure you that with that kind of awareness, you are on the brink of tempering those feelings. I would like to share a technique that both of you should practice for twenty-four hours. It is like you are trying on a new behavior to see if it makes you feel safer and works toward the goal of becoming closer again. This is all about you, Nora, so I would like you to try it to see if it gives you some relief."

We invited Sam back in the session, and I gave the couple the following assignment:

"Sam and Nora, I would like you to practice some behaviors that will move you forward toward healing. This may be the hardest assignment you have ever done because I am going to ask you to participate in an activity that was developed in the world of alcohol recovery. When recovering alcoholics were struggling with their sobriety, they would complain to their sponsor, 'I have no confidence. I have spent the last twenty-two years screwing up my life. I have two failed marriages, I have lost four jobs, and I cannot even muster up the courage to call my kids, let alone have the self-assurance to find a job!'

"This man was too afraid to put himself in a situation where he would need to show up and face rejection or a hard fall. The sponsor listened to his woes and then gave him the following advice:

"'I realize that you lack the confidence to move forward in your life, but I want you to act as if you are playing the part of someone who does know what they want. This means you act as if you can call the potential employer and ask him where to submit your resume or grab the phone and act as if you not only want to call the kids but also want to hear how their lives are going.

When you act as if, you put one foot in front of the other, just taking one step at a time but all the while walking toward your destination.'

"Nora and Sam, I want you to spend twenty-four hours letting go of the pain and the resentment and acting as if you could really appreciate each other for who you both are today. I recognize that this can feel like a daunting task because, Nora, you are probably fearful that if you 'act as if' he will think that you have forgotten what he did to you in your past. And Sam, you may want to do this, but you fear what Nora's reactions might be, and that fear of the unknown may keep you in the state of uncertainty and fear of rejection.

"However, you both have been working hard, and you deserve to have a respite from your history. You are two people who want to rebuild your relationship, but to do that requires that you move forward in a well-thought-out, measured way. This twenty-four-hour exercise will help you to rekindle or build on a new relationship. It is based on the premise that *you can be happy* again. So why don't you give it a shot and agree to take the next twenty-four hours to be the couple that you really would like to develop into? That includes no talking about betrayal, infidelity, *or* recovery."

YOU DESERVE TO BE HAPPY—ACT AS IF

Now, when I ask couples to do this, they feel shaky because when they go for a walk or drive to the grocery store, they are not sure what to talk about. They say it was as if they needed to retrain their brain to bond without trauma.

But you deserve to be happy! You have done all this hard work, and now it is time to decide how you are going to proceed in your new couple's identity. You have risen from the ashes, and you are stronger. How can you move on with your life and create a new identity that follows those five indicators of PTG?

THE "ACT AS IF" EXERCISE: WRITE OUT SOME ACTIVITIES THAT WOULD MAKE YOU BOTH HAPPY

ACT AS IF YOU ARE FREE FROM FEAR

You might want to use the time to talk about creating an activity that is forward-thinking, like going out on a date, planning a family activity, or working on your next project or vacation. Since you will not be talking about recovery, you might want to share appreciation for each other or things that you are grateful for, like the beautiful clouds in the sky, your exercise program, or the friendships you want to cultivate from church. This may include things you have talked about early in the relationship or the small desires you have had inside of you that have been put on the back burner.

Use your Connection-Share to talk about your vision in the here and now. What can you do in your daily routine that would reinforce your new, healthy, and happy relationship together?

Would you be willing to do the "Act as If" Exercise and spend 24 hours interacting with absolutely no reference to infidelity? This is tougher than you think. If you do fall back to an old conversation or routine, just acknowledge it together and then proceed as if nothing happened to reinforce the concept that you can move on in your lives, feel close, and relate like a couple who did not carry this baggage.

THE POST-TRAUMATIC GROWTH INDICATOR ASSESSMENT

Take another look at the five indicators of PTG and ask yourselves:

- How can we as a couple stay cognizant of our strengths that we listed above?

_____

_____

_____

- What are we appreciating today that we no longer take for granted?

  _____

  _____

  _____

- What opportunities can we find today that open the door to new possibilities for ourselves, our family, our friends, our community, our church, and our work?

  _____

  _____

  _____

- How can we show more empathy and compassion to others?

  _____

  _____

  _____

- And how can we make the world a better place?

  _____

  _____

  _____

As you are doing the hard work to restore the relationship, it is important to stay as balanced as possible regarding what you need to do to focus on yourself. As a couple, you are going to be working diligently on restoring the relationship, but what is truly necessary is that you continue to develop a mindset where you can appreciate the changes you both have made in the coupleship and in yourselves.

One of the things that therapists and coaches know is how important it is to have a healthy mindset. That means that you must remain positive despite your history. You were not aware of how your mind can create your reality and that what you project out in the world will persist. If you stay focused on the chaos, devastation, and trauma that has been caused by this partner betrayal, you will be chained to that history. If you have done your work in Stages 1 and 2, you can choose to unlock the chains and focus on happiness instead.

One of the easiest formulas that we use in coaching is looking at three areas of your life that have to do with happiness. In Marci Shimoff's book *Happiness for No Reason*, she discusses three fundamental principles that create happiness, and these tools are excellent strategies for dealing with addiction and betrayal.

HAPPINESS PRINCIPLES TO RESTORE THE HOMEOSTASIS OF YOUR RELATIONSHIP

STAY IN THE MOMENT

What you have been through as a couple has been very difficult, so it will be necessary for both of you to stay in the moment and celebrate the subtle changes that you both are making. This means that as you think about your past, you shift your perspective and make a concerted effort to train yourself to stay present and focused on one day at a time.

To the Recovering Betrayer: Betrayers who are in good integrity naturally want to stop reliving the past since that keeps them in a state of despair, self-loathing, and shame. You will need to remind yourself that you are no longer a perpetrator—you are in recovery. You are learning skills that will make you healthier and more relational. Your interpersonal skills and relational skills contribute to your success as a person and a loving spouse. You should continue healthy introspection, connection, and relational skills that bring connection to your relationship.

I always ask my clients to ask themselves, "Are my thoughts and behaviors moving me forward toward a healthier relationship or further away?"

Staying in the moment helps you to appreciate what is occurring right before you. As Darrin Ford states, focusing on the moment or the present state "gives you a greater propensity to manifest choices that are more skillfully related to a life of fulfillment." The supports you have accessed have encouraged you to work on yourself "one day at a time."

When you are in PTG, it is important to stay out of that shame cycle. If you keep ruminating and reliving the trauma of the past, you will stay in that cycle of shame, which absolutely does nothing for who you were meant to be. Staying in the moment requires that you ask yourself, "What can I do today to help restore the relationship, and what do I need to do to make things better—one day at a time?"

Staying in the moment and living in the present is tougher for partners due to their innate trauma response. However, a partner in post-traumatic growth will be moving away from frequent or severe trauma reactions.

To the Partner: Your natural inclination is to relive the past or predict the future. When you do that, you ensure that you will not be duped again and that you will remain safe. Your reaction is understandable, yet staying in the past or ruminating about the past will keep you in an activated state of trauma.

Holding yourself accountable for your own mental health and learning how you can rebuild a new life with your spouse (or without) requires that you stay in the moment. When doing so, you look at what is occurring in your life and with your spouse, and you stay focused on what is in your present-day experience.

There is no doubt that you are also worried about the future, which makes staying in the moment difficult. Staying in the moment keeps you in a reality state and is imperative for feeling ongoing safety and stabilization.

STAYING IN THE MOMENT AND ACCOMPANYING EXERCISE

For the Partner:

1. One thing that I fear is that if I let my guard down and stay in the moment, my spouse will hurt me again.

2. I fear that if I stay in the moment, I will not stay one step ahead, and my partner will be more likely to make the wrong choices.

3. If I stay in the moment, my spouse will sense that I have let my guard down and will take advantage of the situation.

NEXT

1. If I stay in the moment, I can enjoy the things that are working in my life.

2. If I stay in the moment, I can stop trying to control things, which depletes me and makes me feel exhausted.

3. If I stay in the moment, I will be better able to take control of my own life and detach from the outcome. I realize that I control my destiny.

4. If I remind myself to stay in the moment, I can appreciate...

   _____

   _____

5. If I work on staying in the moment, I can remind myself that...

   _____

   _____

6.   If I stay in the moment, I will…

_____

_____

FOR THE PARTNER'S SPOUSE:

It will be easier for you to stay in the moment because your program has taught you to live one day at a time. But you also have fears that the PTG you are currently experiencing is too good to be true, and you fear that you will not be able to trust its reliability. But when you stay in the moment, you are more likely to enjoy "what is" and be more present to what your partner needs and your needs simultaneously.

1.   What I fear most about living in the moment is that I will not be able to do it, and I will let myself and my spouse down.

2.   I am afraid to trust staying in the moment because I fear that I will get too comfortable with my recovery.

3.   I am not very good at living in the moment because I constantly fear that lust will hijack my brain.

NEXT

1.   Even though I fear living in the moment, I will be more successful on a day-to-day basis.

2.   Even though I fear staying in the moment, I know it will decrease my urge to put my needs first.

3.   Even though I fear having my brain hijacked, staying in the moment will teach me to appreciate "what is."

Now it is your turn. Write out three of your fears about staying in the moment. After writing about those fears, add a more realistic statement that reinforces why living in the now can help your sense of stability and serenity and move you closer to that mind state of happiness.

1. What I'm afraid of if I stay in the moment is...

   _____

   _____

2. What I fear most about staying in the moment is...

   _____

   _____

3. What I fear most about living in the present is...

   _____

   _____

STAYING IN THE MOMENT

Now, honor the fear but strengthen the thought by making it more realistic and pro-recovery.

1. If I stay in the moment, I will...

   _____

   _____

2. If I stay in the moment, I can...

   _____

   _____

3.   Staying in the moment will benefit me because...

_____

_____

STAYING IN THE MOMENT—PRESENCE—REQUIRES PRACTICE

It is normal for you both to move back and forth as you work on this concept. As a result of the trauma, you have trained yourself to watch the past and be weary of what the future could bring. Of course, living in the moment would feel counterintuitive and unnatural, but the more you practice the "power of now," as Eckhart Tolle would call it, the more you will be able to appreciate what is right before you in your daily living.

To the Partner: What do you do when you are working hard to stay in the moment, but those thoughts get interrupted by your fears?

You are supposed to be in post-traumatic growth, but your brain just got hijacked. You continue to agonize over the fear because you go back to an old thought that seems locked into your mind. The thought reminds you that it is difficult to believe that your spouse could have lived a double life and not thought about the collateral damage that was occurring in the relationship.

What does that mean for your future? Can your spouse really stay in integrity? Can the new behavior be real? Will it really last? And then your mind is off to the races.

You want to live in PTG, but it can feel discouraging when something activates you and sends you back to that old mind state. Just allow the feeling and then use a reality statement that reminds you of what is in the moment.

This is where you have a choice:

You can gently imagine yourself pushing away the old questioning thoughts and breathing in the mantra, "Staying in the moment can restore my life to sanity."

Or, you can be gentle with yourself and tell yourself that of course you would understandably get scared and go back to the past to protect yourself.

However, that thought sends you right back into ruminating about your past and fearing for the future, which creates an auto-exacerbating cycle of agonizing for you.

When you are in PTG, you take back your thoughts, and you utilize your choices. You decide what thoughts you are going to let go of and what thoughts you are choosing to store in that precious space called the mind.

Remember: Mindfulness reminds you that you are not your thoughts and that you can choose the thought that works for you and liberates you from your fears. You are not your mind!

Staying in the moment allows you to free yourself from those thoughts and live today, noticing what is working and feeling content with what is before you.

Remember, where your attention goes, energy flows!

MINDFULNESS—STAYING PRESENT

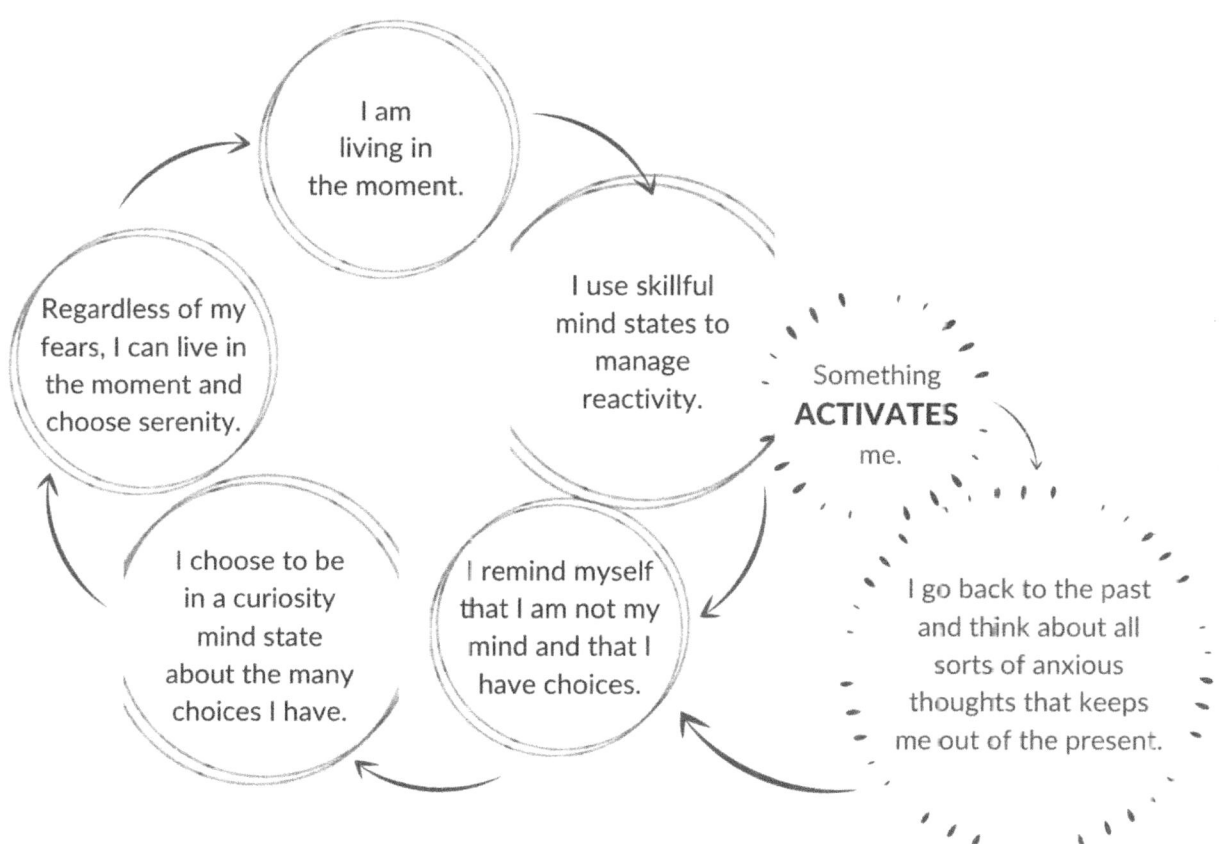

Changing your mind states and stories takes work, but it is worth the time to invest in your serenity. You deserve that, and I so badly want you to have it.

I wish I could develop a "thought coach" who could sit on your shoulder, notice every time you start down the road of fear and uncertainty, and remind you to stay in the moment while noticing the distress and then look at your choices that are built from self-care and constructive compassion!

You both can do this for each other. Practice encouraging each other to acknowledge the fear, move it aside, create a thought to keep you in the present, and enjoy your new sense of awareness!

GRATITUDE: FOCUS ON WHAT IS WORKING IN YOUR LIVES

The second factor that contributes to more happiness in both of your lives is having the attitude of gratitude.

The attitude of gratitude means that you look at "what is working in your life." You take on that mind state and notice everything around you that supports it. That may be that you got up 15 minutes early to read your devotional, and it was a beautiful, warm day with plenty of sunshine. As you walked into work, you felt the cool breeze on your face and felt a sense of serenity. It may be that you are reading this book together and are thankful for the opportunity to rebuild the relationship.

To the Recovering Spouse: You may be grateful that your integrity recovery is strong. You feel a surge of gratitude because you are connecting with your partner better than ever. You feel very in sync with your life because you are operating on all cylinders. Your life has changed now that you have focused on healthy integrity behaviors, and you are supporting your spouse in new and different ways. You couldn't be happier. Not only are you looking at what is working in your life, you are working it!

For the Partner: Perhaps you found that all-important support group and perfect coach to help you get through this difficult time. I had a partner tell me that when she got into a healthy support group for partners, it moved her into PTG because she really started to focus on herself. She became an inspiration to the group, which motivated her to create her own sense of identity.

As you can imagine, it can be tough to be a partner and look at what is working because you're afraid to move away from the fear that feels oddly familiar and predictable.

However, you deserve to let go of the partner betrayal and work toward who you really want to be. There will be times in PTG when you revisit the first stage and find that you need more safety and stabilization, but you will not remain there. You have done so much work, and I will use these skills to move you right back into PTG.

In PTG, you are always aware of the choice to move away from pain and suffering and look for some normalcy in your life. You are capable of noticing the small things, taking them in, and feeling gratitude for them. There are things in your life that remain positive, hopeful, or uplifting, even if it is petting your cat or your dog as you drink your coffee or tea and watch the sunrise. Now, that being said, I do not want to minimize the impact of what you have been through, but I want to emphasize that you want to move out of this traumatized state, whether you are a partner or a recovering spouse. You will also need to accept that this fear can be a normal condition of the betrayal, and you can move through it.

Looking at what is working in your life helps to neutralize the impact of infidelity and deception. It does not alleviate it, but it allows your brain to take a break from the trauma.

10 THINGS THAT WE SEE WORKING IN OUR LIVES

So, as a couple, review the day and list ten things that worked well or that you felt grateful for. Share them with each other.

1. _____

2. _____

3. _____

4. _____

5. _____

6. _____

7. _____

8. _____

9. _____

10. _____

As I review my last 24 hours, I might list the following: I am grateful for my birthday today. The warmth of my puppy, who loves me unconditionally. My delicious cup of coffee. My friends who celebrated with me last night. My family, who reunited for my aunt's funeral. My husband's kindness for cleaning up as I went to bed. The sunrise. The fall foliage. You for reading this book!

Now it is your turn. Get good at sharing it with each other!

REFRAMING

The third indicator of happiness is when you can begin to reframe. Reframing is when you take a picture of your life and decide to put another frame around it. When you put that other frame around your life, you create a different picture. This picture is one of empowerment and personal choice, and there are two ways you can access it. One is by asking yourself, "How am I growing stronger?"

When you ask yourself this question, you take yourself out of the victim state and view life from an empowered state. Now, I know that you would not have ever asked for this horrible ordeal, yet you can take yourself out of the victim state by asking yourself two questions: "How am I stronger?" and "What have I learned from this crisis?"

You both are stronger!

You both have put a lot of time into this book, and I promise you that this work changes lives. I can assure you both that recovering spouses are learning skills they never had before, and if they did seem to have them, the addiction robbed them of those skills early on.

For the Partner: You are learning about your needs, boundaries, and feelings, and you are putting yourself on the front burner. You are no longer willing to take a back seat and let life pass you by.

You have been through a devastating experience, but you are choosing to "grow yourself stronger."

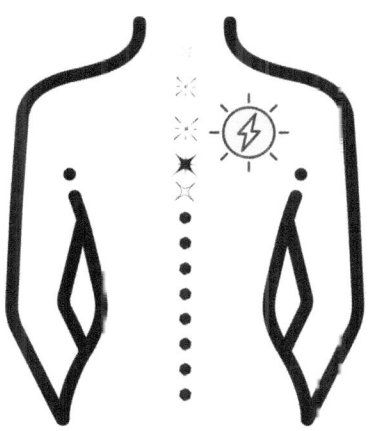

I remember a doctor reassuring me after I broke my back that I would heal even stronger than before. He explained that when bones break, it obviously takes a certain amount of time to allow for the bone to grow back. When it does, the point where it broke is stronger than any other part of the bone.

If you remain in your fear, sadness, and anger, it will stall your personal growth and the development of what you want your relationship to be.

You are making a choice to be stronger for you!

You obviously want to restore the relationship, and their choices were theirs alone to make. It affected you greatly and impacted your life. Initially, you may have been the reason that your spouse worked so hard on integrity, but after recovering spouses have utilized the tools to get healthy, they like who they are in full integrity. I know you may say, "I do not want the responsibility of my spouse doing it for me," but the truth is the desire shifts and it becomes all about doing it for the both of you!

These three happiness fundamentals are easy tools you can use anytime to remind yourself that you do have control of your life. You can shift your energy and find the happiness you deserve to move you both in the desired direction.

It will never erase the damage that has been caused, but it will begin to create a new foundation for both of you and remind you that you did this together.

WHAT ARE FIVE THINGS YOU BELIEVE ARE STRONGER NOW AS A COUPLE?

1. _____

2. _____

3. _____

4. _____

5. _____

WHAT ARE FIVE THINGS YOU HAVE LEARNED ABOUT YOURSELVES AS A COUPLE?

1. _____

2. _____

3. _____

4. _____

5. _____

MINDFULNESS

Mindfulness is single-handedly the best tool to use to recalibrate your brain. It assists partners and their spouses because it teaches them how to get centered and resourced and stay in the present. Everyone benefits from this new paradigm, which always begins with mindfulness.

You also have dedicated yourselves to repairing the relationship by using relational skills that always involve empathy. You are both relating to each other by looking at two views: one that involves your perspective and the other being mindful of how your spouse might see, feel, and experience the relationship.

Even though you are both in PTG, there will be challenging moments. You will need lots of support as you look for ways to find your purpose. The work is slow and laborious. Because you have both been through so much together, it is not uncommon for either or both of you to develop an indifference to the relationship and feel like this experience has "worn you out." This indifference and feeling of emotional exhaustion is called compassion fatigue.

Darrin Ford says this can lead to a diminished ability to empathize or feel compassion for your partner, so it is very important to have LOTS of resources available to offset that fatigue. Mindfulness and other tools help remedy the natural fatigue that you might feel while helping your partner work through the three phases of partner betrayal.

For the Partner: You could be experiencing compassion fatigue due to the exhausting nature of watching and assessing whether you are safe. Many partners describe the phenomena of wanting to believe changes but being afraid to, therefore continuing to be on guard despite the respite you could be feeling. You can offset this natural phenomenon by using mindfulness.

Many mindfulness experts say that five minutes of meditation a day exponentially increases focus and awareness. But mindfulness is more than meditation—it is also self-compassion and intentional self-care. Self-care is the antidote to recovery and partner betrayal, so together, you must find things that feed your soul.

REALISTIC AND AFFIRMING POSITIVE SELF-TALK

It is imperative that both of you practice being gentle with yourselves, which includes how you speak to yourself and the language you use to get you through the day. We have 60,000 thoughts per day, and many of them are negative. They may be as ordinary as "I am going to be late," "I am not going to be able to do it," "Life works against me," or "I can never do anything right." Or they may be more critical and involve your life, situation, and shame. They might look like: "Can I really trust this?" "I just want a normal life," "I am a screw-up," "I am disgusting," "Is my spouse really going to change?" "I am unlovable," or "Will I ever be forgiven?"

Do not let these negative thoughts overwhelm you. It is possible for you to be in post-traumatic growth and have some negative self-talk. Positive self-talk is a practice, and it takes time and effort. Do not get discouraged if you fall back into old patterns of thought and communication.

If you want to invest in yourself and your relationship, you will need to alter the way you talk to yourself to keep it more proactive and realistic. This means that you will have to consciously try to speak more gently and with more self-compassion.

POSITIVE SELF-TALK EXERCISE

I would like each one of you to spend 15 minutes in quiet contemplation in the same room. Ask yourself to think of three fears that continue to show up in your life. Write them out.

FOR THE RECOVERING SPOUSE:

1.   One thing that I fear is that my spouse will never be able to trust me again.

2.   I fear that we will never be able to have fun together.

3.   I fear that I will not be able to do recovery perfectly, and it will interfere with my partner's ability to regain confidence in me.

Now restate your fear and concern with a more realistic, kinder thought:

REALITY AFFIRMATIONS

Reality Affirmations always start with your fears or apprehensions and begin with: "***Even though*** _____." The 2nd part of the affirmation begins with "***what I know to be true***" and gives a more realistic *present time* descriptor of the work.

1. ***Even though*** I fear that she will never be able to trust me again, ***what I know to be true is*** that I can remind myself that when I was late the other night, she commented that she was angry with me but DID tell me she knew I was not acting out.

2. ***Even though*** I fear that we will never have fun together, ***what I know to be true is*** that he did smile at me and laugh about our son's antics during the baseball game.

3. ***Even though*** I am not perfect in my recovery, ***what I know to be true is*** that she does keep assuring me that she is more interested in me being honest about my imperfections.

Now try a reality affirmation that starts with the reality of your fears or doubts about the progress being made. Follow the format of:

> ***Even though*** _____
>
> (*the reality of your fear or challenge*)
>
> ***what I know to be true*** _____
>
> (*noticing the progress that is being made*)

1. ***Even though*** you told me you were struggling with not objectifying women, ***what I know to be true*** is that you promised me you would be honest about your challenges.

2.   **Even though** you ran into your old affair partner, **what I know to be true** is that you came home and told me immediately.

3.   **Even though** I am exhausted by all the work I am doing, **what I know to be true** is that we are experiencing connection more than I ever thought we would.

FOR THE PARTNER:

1.   I fear that these triggers will never go away.

2.   I fear that I will never be able to fully trust.

3.   I fear that I will never stop comparing myself to other women and images.

Now, restate your fear and concern with a more realistic, kinder thought:

1.   **Even though** I continue to struggle with triggers, **what I know to be true is** that they are less frequent and less haunting.

2.   **Even though** I have recurring thoughts about not being able to trust, **what I know to be true is** that I need to keep reminding myself that "this is a process" and that it is normal to be afraid periodically.

3.   **Even though** I find myself comparing myself to other women and images, **what I know to be true is** I keep reminding myself of Tom's statement to me that now that he has his priorities straight and is living by the values that are important to our marriage, he loves me more than he ever thought he could love anyone.

Can you do some reality affirmations?

1. **Even though** _____

   _____

   what I know to be true is _____

2. **Even though** _____

   _____

   what I know to be true is _____

3. **Even though** _____

   _____

   what I know to be true is _____

It is paradoxical that treating yourself with more compassion and kindness requires awareness and a sincere desire to nurture yourself and your relationship. It seems ironic because upon hearing the old negative tapes, you must acknowledge your awareness and then reword the thoughts in your head. This requires discipline to acknowledge the negative thoughts and redirect your thoughts and feelings in a way that recognizes your effort, vulnerability, and progress in this process.

When you create an intention that you will speak to yourself with compassion, you have committed to the self-love and nurturance you deserve. It is a type of self-parenting that you likely never received and, therefore, never learned to give to yourself.

When you are in post-traumatic growth, you know that you must be gentle with yourself and that you do not need to do anything perfectly.

I have decided to help you identify things you can say to yourself to offset the 60,000 negative thoughts you hear daily in your own head. I have compiled two lists of statements that may be applicable to you when you want to diffuse some emotional reactivity.

Read the statements and circle the self-talk that you might use to dim down the negative thinking.

PRACTICAL COPING STATEMENTS

Try using some of these "practical" statements the next time you feel yourself becoming overwhelmed by your feelings. It is important to own your feelings but not let them overtake you. When you are in PTG, you notice the feelings and make the choice to acknowledge them and move on.

Many people have benefitted from these statements as they encourage people to change their focus. As you read the following statements, feel free to create your own.

Can you choose five of these statements that would support you as you walk through life together? Please number your top five, with number one being your favorite practical statement that would reassure you as you walk through life together.

1. Stay calm. Just relax.

2. As long as I remain in good recovery, I am in control.

3. Just roll with the punches, and do not get bent out of shape.

4. Think of what you want to get out of this.

5. You do not need to prove yourself to anyone.

6. There is no point in getting mad.

7. Look for the positives and reframe.

8. I am not going to let this get to me.

9. If my intentions are true, what they think of me is none of my business.

10. He is probably really unhappy if he's acting that irritable.

11. What she says about me does not need to define me.

12. I cannot expect people to act the way I want them to all the time.

13. My muscles feel tight. Time to relax.

14. I will look for a solution that is a win-win opportunity for both of us.

15. Let's work this problem out. Maybe he has a point.

16. I am not going to be pushed around, but I am not going to lose it either.

17. I am under control. I can handle this.

18. I have a right to be annoyed, but let's try to reason this out.

19. Slow down. Take a few deep breaths.

20. I can breathe through this.

These next statements are more philosophical in nature and are coping statements to remind you not to be hijacked by your situation or emotions. Which statements resonate with you? How might you apply them to your relationship so that you take things less personally and trust that the universe has your back? Being in post-traumatic growth does not mean you do not have challenges, but it does mean that you are less affected by the challenges and are more willing to believe and know that you will get through them.

In a check-in, share with your spouse which philosophical statements brought comfort to you as you think about struggles in your life.

PHILOSOPHICAL COPING STATEMENTS

1. It is time to take care of you.

2. Create a family of choice.

3. Spray yourself with Teflon and let go.

4. Fake it until you make it, and act as if.

5. One day at a time.

6. Face your fears head-on.

7. There will only be one of you at all times—fearlessly have the courage to be yourself.

8. You can do it.

9. Keep it simple.

10. Happiness is a choice.

11. You own the power.

12. Trust your head, your heart, and your gut.

13. Nurture yourself.

14. Replenish your energy—slow down.

15. Focus on the positives.

16.   Appreciate your strengths.

17.   Do not be so hard on yourself.

Lastly, I thought I would include some statements that come directly from the recovery world. There is a lot of wisdom in this community, so I thought I would include some slogans here. Hopefully, it will help you both in your coping, and as you strengthen your mental agility in the third phase of post-traumatic growth, you will find these coping skills help you stay focused on the mindset you need to move forward in new possibilities.

RECOVERY SLOGANS

1.   One day at a time.

2.   Let go and let God.

3.   Act as if.

4.   This too shall pass.

5.   Expect miracles.

6.   I cannot; He can. I think I'll let Him.

7.   Sobriety is a journey, not a destination.

8.   Faith without works is dead.

9.   To thine own self be true.

10.   Live in the NOW.

11.   If God seems far away, who moved?

12.   Turn it over.

13. Willingness is the key.

14. More will be revealed.

15. Before you say I can't, say I will try.

16. The price for serenity and sanity is self-sacrifice.

17. E.G.O. = Edging God Out

18. Serenity is not freedom from the storm but peace amid the storm.

19. Remember, nothing is going to happen today that you and God cannot handle.

20. Pain is the touchstone of spiritual growth.

21. Have an attitude of gratitude.

22. You will intuitively know.

23. We have a choice.

24. F.E.A.R. = False Evidence Appearing Real

25. This too shall pass.

THE PROCESS OF FORGIVENESS

As partner-sensitive professionals, we will tell partners that they never *need* to forgive their spouse. And although I endorse that wholeheartedly, I also believe that for you both to heal the relationship, you will need to work on forgiveness as a goal.

For the Partner: You have likely heard that forgiveness is for the person who feels the anger and resentment. Letting go of the resentment that has fueled your anger will set you free.

If you think about all the feelings attached to the betrayal, you will feel hijacked by them, which keeps you locked into a mind state of terror and control. Releasing your feelings will liberate you and allow you to experience a new possibility for your life.

Forgiving does not mean that you condone the behavior, but it is a process that allows you to emotionally detach from the betrayal.

TRAUMA-BASED MODEL OF FORGIVENESS

In this model, forgiveness is an ongoing process that takes time rather than a distinct event. Gordon and Baucom (1998) presented a three-stage forgiveness model that conceptualized recovery from affairs as essentially the same as the process of recovery from any interpersonal trauma.

I have not been able to find any research that talks about forgiveness after infidelity and partner betrayal, but these stages fit the PTG research.

The stages in this model are:

> I. Dealing with the impact

> II. Searching for meaning

> III. Recovery or moving forward

Individuals who are in Stage I report the least amount of forgiveness, and individuals in Stage III report the highest levels of forgiveness. That fits the integration of the three phases of partner betrayal and the research about post-traumatic growth. It also endorses why it can take three to five years to work through Stages 1 and 2—so that you get through your own search for meaning as a couple and then begin to move forward as a couple and give back.

1. Do you have a fear that accompanies the thought of forgiving your spouse for the infidelity?

   _____

   _____

   _____

2. How might "not being able to forgive" keep you protected emotionally?

   _____

   _____

   _____

3. How might it keep you from moving forward?

   _____

   _____

   _____

4. How would your life be different if you could forgive your spouse?

   _____

   _____

   _____

5. They say that forgiveness is for the person who has been wounded—how might it benefit you?

   _____

   _____

   _____

The tough questions involve finding meaning from this ordeal. The toughest questions that I will ask you are:

1.   What has this excruciating pain taught you?

_____

_____

_____

2.   What meaning have you applied to this ordeal?

_____

_____

_____

3.   Has it given you a new sense of purpose?

_____

_____

_____

4.   Are you helping others as a result of it?

_____

_____

_____

In PTG, many couples find that trusting in the following beliefs is crucial to their healing. For agnostics and atheists, what word or words might you use to replace "God?"

- God can bring purpose.
- God can give purpose to your pain.

- Love is a choice.

- Forgiveness is a choice.

- Happiness is a choice.

You can choose to let go of your suffering and allow it to transform you into something that gives YOU purpose as a couple. When you do, you have rounded the corner of post-traumatic growth!

YOUR NEEDS AS A COUPLE

As you strengthen PTG, you will find opportunities to bond and co-create together. This requires that you pay attention to what each of you needs and make a note to brainstorm activities that you implement in your outer circle. This is the fun part of the relationship. You are working hard on making new memories, and you are also furthering your trust.

Start working on your couple's healthy circle behaviors and make plans that you can do together.

Ask yourselves, "What can we change to fine-tune our marriage?"

1. More appreciation?

2. More teamwork?

3. More intentional self-care?

4. More time to myself?

5. More check-ins?

6. More family time?

7. More family meetings?

8. More volunteering?

Working on strengthening and building a solid marriage takes good communication. Do not be afraid of asking the hard questions that will move you both toward a happier life.

EXERCISE: HOW CAN WE MOVE FORWARD AND GIVE BACK

Ask yourselves the following questions:

1. What can we use from this experience?

    _____

    _____

    _____

    _____

    _____

2. How can we give back to our friends, our family, the community, etc.?

    _____

    _____

    _____

    _____

    _____

These are great questions to ask each other and talk about in your check-ins.

Other additional questions for check-ins that increase your satisfaction in the relationship as you move forward are:

1. What do I want most from you?

    _____

    _____

    _____

    _____

2. What can we do to practice mindfulness together?

    _____

    _____

    _____

    _____

3. What can I do to show you how much I want us to be together forever?

    _____

    _____

    _____

    _____

4. What can I do to reinforce my love for you?

    _____

    _____

    _____

    _____

Create new dreams and realities that fortify how you want to live out the rest of your life. Stop being haunted by the infidelity! You can choose to be happy and you will survive and get stronger regardless of what happens to you. Journal about what you might want to focus on to create a more loving relationship and discuss it in your check-ins. This helps you follow my most important coaching rule: "I am one-hundred percent responsible for my behavior, no matter what has happened in my life and who has wronged me." When you ask yourself, "What do I need to do to create a more loving relationship?" you are accepting that you have the power to contribute in an important way to this relationship.

DECLARATION STATEMENTS

It is important for you to be intentional in declaring what you want for this relationship. We talked about the need for you to put into practice the belief system of: "When you conceive it and believe it, you will achieve it!"

The same thing works for the conceptualization of your marriage. What do you want to achieve as a couple? How would you like to feel as you enter into your new marriage? Create some declarations that honor your marriage and your growth.

As a couple, we are *resilient.*

Repeat them to yourself as mantras for what you want in your life. They might be single-word adjectives and might look like:

As a couple, we are NOT *perfect*

As a couple, we want to be *inspirational.*

Or, they might be full sentences:

As a couple, we are living our purpose and want to create the life we deserve.

As a couple, we are NOT going to falter on the skills we learned to be authentic, transparent, and honest.

As a couple, we want to be aware of our quest for meaning in our lives and depend on our higher power to get us through challenges and struggles..

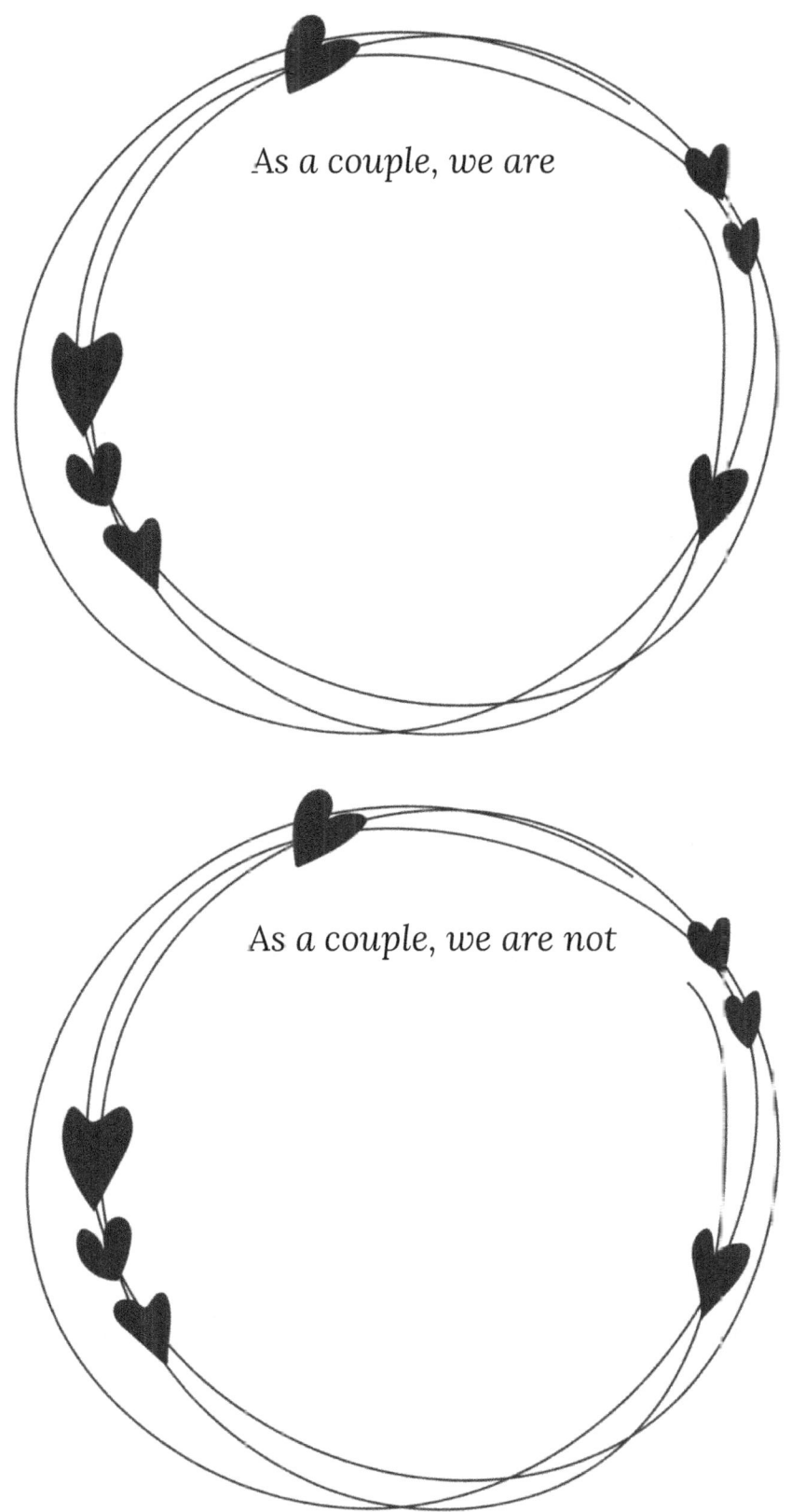

As a couple, we are

As a couple, we are not

As a couple, we want to

PHILOSOPHIES TO LIVE BY

PTG does not just happen—you must embrace it. That means you need to ascribe to the mindset that supports both of you being happy. There are some coaching principles that can reinforce these PTG philosophies. Look and decide which attitudes or mindsets you would like to adopt. Which ones feel like the "best fit" for you?

- What you conceive and believe you will achieve.

- Your energy flows where your focus goes.

- Good things come from change.

- Does this move us toward each other or away from each other?

- I create my own happiness.

- Nothing that is ever meant for me will be missed by me.

- As you change your view, you will change your world.

- When you change the way you look at things, the things around you change.

- The Universe has my back.

- You are never given a dream without also being given the power to make it come true.

It is so important for you to find inspiration from others. Some of you may have abandoned the guidance you acquired growing up. Others may have put inspiration on the back burner as you focused on the survival skills you needed to take the next step through partner betrayal. Now that you are in PTG, it will be important to revisit those tools that brought you comfort and clarity in your past. You may even decide to adopt some new strategies that come from inspirational teachings or guides. Be on the lookout for spirit-filled messages to take you forward on your journey as a new and stronger couple.

Ask yourself the following:

- Are there coaching strategies that I believe have guided me/us through this process?

- Are there spiritual principles that have helped me/us get to the other side?

- Are there biblical scriptures that have comforted me/us on this journey?

- Are there Eastern religious spiritual principles that have supported us as we walked this journey together?

This phase is all about changing your mind state and your mind story. Would you be willing to focus on gratitude so that you can practice feeling grateful for your life, your spouse, and your family? Is there a mind state from Chapter 12 that reinforces the changes that you have both made to strengthen you so that you will contribute to this world in a different way? When I was training to be certified in compulsive sexual behavior, we spent an entire module learning how to reinforce the concept that recovery is the gateway for you to do great things. ERCEM is the model that reinforces the brilliance in you both as a thriving couple.

This community needs more couples who won't hide from their own brilliance. In her book *Return to Love*, Marianne Williamson says, "Your playing small doesn't serve the world." Ask yourself, *Now that we have grown from this ordeal, how might we serve others, our community, and the world?*

I have a special gift for you. On my website, sexhelpwithcarolthecoach.com, under "Resources" is the Marianne Williamson quote. I want you to download it and then put it somewhere special to remind you that:

> *"As we liberate from our own fear, we automatically liberate others."*

Chapter 20

In Review

I wrote this book for both of you! Although I developed the ERCEM model to help couples who struggled with Compulsive Sexual Behavior Disorder and Partner Betrayal, I created it so couples could imagine they were in my office every week doing the hard work of healing together. As I was working with the sexual addiction community, I was getting more couples coming to see me after infidelity. It was then I decided to use ERCEM to help healing couples who had experienced infidelity, and it worked equally well.

I realized that the recovery process was virtually the same. With infidelity comes the three stages of partner betrayal, combined with the couple's version of infidelity betrayal.

Infidelity requires the same couple's sensitivity because of the trauma it has inflicted and ERCEM addresses both spouses needs.

You may have finished the course, but you have not finished the journey. You will have many opportunities to strengthen your relationship, and for that, I am so grateful.

I believe in my heart that couples who have experienced the trauma of infidelity can heal if they work individually and together on developing the relational skills and tools to get through partner betrayal together. Your marriage can be stronger than 85% of the other relationships out there if you continue to build your identity as a couple and find purpose together in your lives.

This book has outlined how to do that together. Although a couple never has to stay together and must assess what is in their best interest, most of my couples choose to stay for a variety of reasons. The mental health therapist and coach in me wants to help you do this because you deserve to learn how to create a new marriage with empathy, vulnerability, and trust.

You have learned what it takes to get through the three stages of partner betrayal, and the beauty of this model is that it uses the betrayer to assist in that healing. You also have my permission to alter the exercises to customize what you both need.

I have developed ERCEM, which is a certification program for clinicians and coaches to assist you in doing this work. They have specialized skills to get you through all three phases of partner betrayal with the use of empathy.

I am also honored and humbled to walk beside you on this journey. It is the hardest thing you have ever done, but it has taught you so many skills you can both use for the rest of your life and pass on to your families, children, and grandchildren.

My wish for you is that you stop talking about the past, stay fully in the present, continue to work on your future, and live your life in happiness. I have seen couples do this and know that you can, too.

Thank you for believing in me enough to practice the principles in this book. Just know that my voice can go with you as you create the life you both deserve.

As I say in every podcast, presentation, and teaching, "There will only be one of you at all times. Fearlessly have the courage to work together to create the happiness that life intended you to have!"

My intention for you both is to grow stronger together every day and make a difference in this world!

Blessings to you both!

~ *Carol Juergensen* **Sheets,** LCSW, CCES-S, CCPS-S, CPC-S, CSAT-S, EMDR Certified

Aka **Carol the Coach**

Founder of *Early Recovery Couples Empathy Model* (ERCEM)

Addendum

THE ERCEM WAY

Professionals who have learned The ERCEM Way can walk you through safety and stabilization, grief, and mourning and take you into post-traumatic growth. ERCEM is the only training format that addresses the three phases of partner betrayal as defined by APSATS.

I created a curriculum, a certification program, and the book *Help.Them. Heal.* to teach you both how to navigate partner betrayal and further explore the work necessary to get through Stages 2 and 3 effectively. This had not been formally developed because this is such a new field.

ERCEM is a structured, organized, systematic approach to teaching you both how to work through infidelity together. I have been honored to take the skills and exercises from The ERCEM Way and give them to you in book format.

However, you may find it more efficient to rely on an ERCEM specialist to get you through this work. You may have spent time and money working with professionals who did not seem to understand the dynamics of partner betrayal, so I want you to get the Gold Standard of Care when it comes to your relationship.

For a complete list of ERCEM-trained or certified specialists, go to my website www.sexhelpwithcarolthecoach.com/findhelp and look for an ERCEM specialist in your area who can guide you through this process. If there is no one in your state who can provide telehealth, look for a professional coach who has the designation of ERCEM specialist, Certified Empathy Coach (CEC). They are able to work anywhere in the world to help you heal.

Intensives for Couples

Heidi Kinsella, LMHC, SUDP, CSAT, CPTT, CMAT, EMDR-trained: She is an equine-assisted mental health practitioner-in-training who is licensed in the states of Washington, Alaska, Hawaii, Idaho, Montana, and Arizona. Office locations are in Issaquah, Washington, Kirkland, Washington, and Maple Valley, Washington. She offers three-to-four-day intensives over long weekends for Sex Addiction and Betrayed Partners, using the partner-sensitive *Help. Her. Heal.* and ERCEM models. She will customize an intensive for infidelity.

Resources

- Training Organization for Certified Partner-Sensitive Specialists: *The Association of Partners of Sex Addicts Trauma Specialists* www.APSATS.org

- Training Organization for Certified Empathy Specialists: *The Early Recovery Couples Empathy Model* www.sexhelpwithcarolthecoach.com

- Training Organization for The International Institute for Trauma and Addiction Professionals: https://iitap.com

- Religious Leader Training: www.drbarbarasteffens.com/

- Free Affair Recovery Training: www.goreimagine.com

- A Twelve-Step Program of Recovery from Lust, Sex, and Pornography Addiction: Sexaholics Anonymous www.sa.org

- Focus on the Family intensive-marriage-counseling: https://www.focusonthefamily.com/

- Affair Recovery: https://www.affairrecovery.com

- Groups for Men Wanting to Heal from Unwanted Sexual Behavior and Betrayal Trauma:

  - Pure Desire Ministries www.puredesire.org

  - Men in the Battle wild@heart.org.

- Living Truth—Freedom. Hope. Healing: www.living-truth.org

References

CHAPTER 1

Brown, B. (2013). *Daring Greatly: How the Courage to Be Vulnerable Transforms the Way We Live, Love, Parent and Lead.* London, England: Penguin.

Juergensen Sheets, C. (2022). *Help. Them. Heal: Teaching You Both How to Heal Your Relationship After Sexual Betrayal.* Claremont, CA: Sano Press.

Juergensen, K., Sheets, C., & Katz, A. J. (2019). *Help. Her. Heal: An Empathy Workbook for Sex Addicts to Help Their Partners Heal.* Long Beach, CA: Sano Press.

CHAPTER 2

Kenneth Paul Rosenburg M.D., *Why Men and Women Cheat.*

CHAPTER 3

Alcoholics Anonymous Big Book. (2002). 4th ed. New York, NY: Alcoholics Anonymous World Services.

CHAPTER 4

Nisenson, A. (2025) *A Man's Guide to Partner Betrayal Overcoming the Pain and Repercussions of a Cheating Partner.* Claremont, CA Sano Press

Weiss, R. (2018) *7 Reasons Why Some Women Cheat. Psychology Today,* August 28, 2018.

CHAPTER 5

Carnes, P. (2001) *Facing the Shadow: Starting Sexual and Relationship Recovery*. Carefree, AZ: Gentle Path Press.

Herman, J. (2015). *Trauma and Recovery*. New York, NY: Basic Books.

Steffens, B. and Means, M. (2009) *Your Sexually Addicted Spouse: How Partners Can Cope and Heal*. Bernards Township, NJ: New Horizon Press Books.

CHAPTER 6

Brown, B. (2021) *Atlas of the Heart: Mapping Meaningful Connection and the Language of Human Experience*. New York, NY: Random House Publishing Group.

Carnes, P. (2009) *Recovery Zone, Vol. 1: Making Changes that Last—The Internal Tasks*. Carefree, AZ: Gentle Path Press.

Corley, M. & Schneider, Jennifer. (2002). *Disclosing Secrets: Guidelines for Therapists Working with Sex Addicts and Co-addicts. Sexual Addiction & Compulsivity*. 9. 43-67. 10.1080/107201602317346638.

Caudill, J. & Drake, D. (2019). *Full Disclosure: How to Share the Truth After Sexual Betrayal, Volume 1*.

Caudill, J. & Drake, D. (2019). *Full Disclosure: Seeking Truth After Sexual Betrayal, Volume 1: How Disclosure Can Help You Heal*.

Caudill, J. & Drake, D. (2019). *Full Disclosure: Seeking Truth After Sexual Betrayal, Volume 2: Preparing for Disclosure on Your Terms*.

CHAPTER 7

Juergensen Sheets, C., & Turo-Shields, C. (2020) *Unleashing Your Power Moving Through the Trauma of Partner Betrayal.* Long Beach, CA: Sano Press.

Knowlton, L. (2022). *Connected Recovery Disclosure Booklet A: The Betrayer's Disclosure Process.* Self-published.

Knowlton, L. (2022). *Connected Recovery Disclosure Booklet B: The Partner's Disclosure Process.* Self published.

Knowlton, L. (2022). Connected Recovery Exercises Booklet. Self-Published.

CHAPTER 8

Brach, Tara-The R.A.I.N. Model (2000)

Brown, B. (2013). *Daring Greatly: How the Courage to Be Vulnerable Transforms the Way We Live, Love, Parent and Lead.* London, England: Penguin.

Caudill, J. & Drake, D. (2019). *Full Disclosure: How to Share the Truth After Sexual Betrayal, Volume 1.*

Caudill, J. & Drake, D. (2019). *Full Disclosure: Seeking Truth After Sexual Betrayal, Volume 1: How Disclosure Can Help You Heal.*

Caudill, J. & Drake, D. (2019). *Full Disclosure: Seeking Truth After Sexual Betrayal, Volume 2: Preparing for Disclosure on Your Terms.*

Fisher, J. (2021). *Transforming the Living Legacy of Trauma: A Workbook for Survivors and Therapists.* Eau Claire, WI: PESI Publishing and Media.

CHAPTER 9

Brown, B. (2013). *Daring Greatly: How the Courage to Be Vulnerable Transforms the Way We Live, Love, Parent and Lead*. London, England: Penguin.

CHAPTER 10

Gottman, J. (2000). *The Seven Principles for Making Marriage Work*. London, England: Orion.

Katie, B. Mitchell, S., Loving What Is, Four Questions That Can Change Your Life, Revised Edition (12/2021). New York, NY: Penguin Random House.

CHAPTER 11

Juergensen Sheets, C., & Katz, A. J. (2019). *Help. Her. Heal: An Empathy Workbook for Sex Addicts to Help Their Partners Heal*. Long Beach, CA: Sano Press.

CHAPTER 12

Carnes, P. (2001) *Facing the Shadows: Starting Sexual and Relationship Recovery*. Carefree, AZ: Gentle Path Press.

Ford, Darrin (2018). *Awakening from the Sexually Addicted Mind: A Guide to Compassionate Recovery*. Claremont, CA: Sano Press.

Gottman, J. (2000). *The Seven Principles for Making Marriage Work*. London, England: Orion.

Neff, K. (2015) *Self Compassion: The Proven Power of Being Kind to Yourself* N.Y. New York: Harper Collins.

CHAPTER 13

Eating, R. (1970) *Your Perfect Right: A Guide to Assertive Behavior.* Hanover, MA: Pinnacle Publishing.

Freyd, J.J. (1997). "Violations of power, adaptive blindness, and betrayal trauma theory." Feminism & Psychology, 7, 22-32.

Henderson, W. (2002). *The Science of Soulmates.* Booksurge LLC Edition. International Service Organization of SAA. (2000). "The Three Circles Redefining Sexual Sobriety in SAA."

Juergensen Sheets, C., & Katz, A. J. (2019). *Help. Her. Heal: An Empathy Workbook for Sex Addicts to Help Their Partners Heal.* Long Beach, CA: Sano Press.

Stern, R. (2018) *The Gaslight Effect How to Spot and Survive the Hidden Manipulation Others Use to Control Your Life.* New York, NY: Harmony Publishers.

CHAPTER 15

Juergensen Sheets, C., & Katz, A. J. (2019). *Help. Her. Heal: An Empathy Workbook for Sex Addicts to Help Their Partners Heal.* Long Beach, CA: Sano Press.

Ruiz, D.M. (2001). *The Four Agreements.* San Rafael, CA: Amber-Allen Publishing.

Wiseman, R. (2014) *The As If Principle: The Radically New Approach to Changing Your Life.* New York, NY: Simon and Schuster.

CHAPTER 16

Bercaw, B., & Bercaw, G. (2010). *The Couple's Guide to Intimacy: How Sexual Reintegration Therapy Can Help Your Relationship.* California Center for Healing, CA.

Chapman, G. D. (2010). *The Five Love Languages*. Farmington Hills, MI: Walker.
Juergensen Sheets, C., & Katz, A. J. (2019). *Help. Her. Heal: An Empathy Workbook for Sex Addicts to Help Their Partners Heal*. Long Beach, CA: Sano Press.

Lewis, L.D. (1998) *The Eight Levels of Intimacy*. Couples Company, Inc.
Schnarch, D. (1991) *Constructing the Sexual Crucible An Integration of Sexual and Marital Therapy*. New York, NY: Norton and Company, Incorporated.

CHAPTER 17

Van der Kolk, B.A. (2014) *The Body Keeps the Score: Brain, Mind, and Body in the Healing of Trauma*. New York, NY: Penguin Books.

CHAPTER 18

Alcoholics Anonymous World Services.

Dyer, W. W. (2007). *Change Your Thoughts-Change Your Life: Living the Wisdom of the Tao*. Carlos Bad, CA: Hayhouse.

Calhoun, L. G., Cann, A., & Tedeschi, R. G. (2010). "The posttraumatic growth model: sociocultural considerations." In T. Weiss & R. Berger (Eds.), *Posttraumatic Growth and Culturally Competent Practice: Lessons Learned From Around the Globe* (pp. 1–14). John Wiley & Sons, Inc.

Ford, Darrin (2018). *Awakening from the Sexually Addicted Mind: A Guide to Compassionate Recovery*. Claremont, CA: Sano Press.

Gordon, K. C., & Baucom, D. H. (1998). "Understanding betrayals in marriage: A synthesized model of forgiveness." *Family Process*, 37(4), 425–449. https://doi.org/ 10.1111/j.1545-5300.1998.00425.x

Juergensen Sheets, C., & Turo-Shields, C. (2020) *Unleashing Your Power Moving Through the Trauma of Partner Betrayal.* Long Beach, CA: Sano Press

Shimoff, M., Kline, C., & Canfield, J. (2009). *Happy For No Reason: 7 Steps to Being Happy From the Inside Out.* New York, NY: Simon and Schuster.

Wiseman, R. (2014) *The As If Principle: The Radically New Approach to Changing Your Life.* New York, NY: Simon and Schuster.

www.ingramcontent.com/pod-product-compliance
Lightning Source LLC
Chambersburg PA
CBHW080944120626
46546CB00010B/2832

* 9 7 8 1 9 5 6 6 2 0 0 8 5 *